D0397908

Praise for *View From the Top*

"This is a seminal and compelling work. Dr. Michael Lindsay, university president and sociologist, gained unprecedented access to hundreds of leaders of America's elite institutions, and reached many unexpected conclusions. For example, it's not a privileged upbringing, but the influence of a caring mentor early in a developing career (as well as grit and opportunity) that launches careers of highly influential leaders. Dr. Lindsay found that the best leaders are not primarily ego-driven, but are able to influence a shared organizational vision and submerge their egos so as to be credible stewards of a greater cause. *View From the Top* reveals the hidden attributes of those blessed with the platform of leadership—and explores what defines a leader's identity beyond the title on their business card."

—Rich McClure
President, UniGroup
(United Van Lines
and Mayflower Transit)

"Michael Lindsay's *View From the Top* recounts the experiences of a wide variety of leaders—in both success and failure—to reveal a deeper understanding of leadership: cause-oriented, people-driven, sacrificial, and reflective. Drawing from a variety of fields, Dr. Lindsay draws out some of the common elements of excellence. Anyone interested in the subject of leadership—or interested in exercising it—would benefit from reading *View From the Top*."

—Michael Gerson
Columnist, the *Washington Post*

"This is an informative and inspiring book for any leader, drawing on unprecedented personal access and a keen sense of the dynamics of leaders' institutions and personal lives. It contains both celebrations of the ways power can be used for good, and warnings of how slippery its effects can be on both leader and led. It is an indispensable catalog of stories and insights for those of us who want our use of power to be both effective and redemptive."

—**Andy Crouch**
Executive editor, *Christianity Today*,
and author, *Playing God:*
Redeeming the Gift of Power

VIEW
FROM THE
TOP

CONCORDIA UNIVERSITY LIBRARY
PORTLAND, OR 97211

VIEW
FROM THE
TOP

AN INSIDE LOOK AT HOW PEOPLE IN POWER
SEE AND SHAPE THE WORLD

D. MICHAEL LINDSAY, Ph.D.
WITH M.G. HAGER

WILEY

Cover image: Elevator Up-and-Down Button © Image Source/Corbis
Cover design: Chris Wallace

Copyright © 2014 by D. Michael Lindsay, Ph.D. All rights reserved.

Published by John Wiley & Sons, Inc., Hoboken, New Jersey.
Published simultaneously in Canada.

No part of this publication may be reproduced, stored in a retrieval system, or transmitted in any
form or by any means, electronic, mechanical, photocopying, recording, scanning, or otherwise,
except as permitted under Section 107 or 108 of the 1976 United States Copyright Act, without
either the prior written permission of the Publisher, or authorization through payment of the
appropriate per-copy fee to the Copyright Clearance Center, 222 Rosewood Drive, Danvers, MA
01923, (978) 750-8400, fax (978) 646-8600, or on the web at www.copyright.com. Requests to the
Publisher for permission should be addressed to the Permissions Department, John Wiley & Sons,
Inc., 111 River Street, Hoboken, NJ 07030, (201) 748-6011, fax (201) 748-6008, or online at
www.wiley.com/go/permissions.

Limit of Liability/Disclaimer of Warranty: While the publisher and author have used their best
efforts in preparing this book, they make no representations or warranties with respect to the
accuracy or completeness of the contents of this book and specifically disclaim any implied
warranties of merchantability or fitness for a particular purpose. No warranty may be created or
extended by sales representatives or written sales materials. The advice and strategies contained
herein may not be suitable for your situation. You should consult with a professional where
appropriate. Neither the publisher nor the author shall be liable for damages arising herefrom.

For general information about our other products and services, please contact our Customer Care
Department within the United States at (800) 762-2974, outside the United States at (317)
572-3993 or fax (317) 572-4002.

Wiley publishes in a variety of print and electronic formats and by print-on-demand. Some
material included with standard print versions of this book may not be included in e-books or in
print-on-demand. If this book refers to media such as a CD or DVD that is not included in the
version you purchased, you may download this material at http://booksupport.wiley.com. For more
information about Wiley products, visit www.wiley.com.

ISBN 978-1-118-90110-6 (cloth); ISBN 978-1-118-90139-7 (ebk);
ISBN 978-1-118-901151 (ebk)

Printed in the United States of America

10 9 8 7 6 5 4 3 2 1

Contents

Introduction

"What? What does that mean, 'I'm *not* the job?'" I could hardly hear Price, the search consultant, on my cell phone over the screeching of the subway car pulling in next to me. I was changing trains at the Park Street T station in downtown Boston, on my way to interview Diana Chapman Walsh, the highly successful president of Wellesley College. I had traveled to Boston from Houston—where I worked as a professor at Rice University—for a dual purpose. Not only was I completing additional interviews for my research project, but I had come to be interviewed myself. I was a candidate for the presidency of a Christian liberal arts college north of Boston, Gordon College.

"You *got* the job!" he repeated. This time I understood. In that moment, surrounded by strangers in that subway station, my life changed forever. I agreed to meet the board chair and the head of the search committee back at the hotel after the Walsh interview, and I hung up in a euphoric daze. I don't know how I managed to find my way to the Cleveland Circle T stop where I met up with Walsh, but I sobered up as soon as we greeted. I had been conducting interviews with leaders like Walsh for years, but now I had an even keener interest in learning from her. What went well for her early on, and what missteps does she wish she could do over? How does she handle her critics, including her inner critic? The lessons about leadership and power that I had been picking up for years were no longer strictly academic but were suddenly, startlingly relevant.

In other words, my social-scientific study had begun to morph into something more. The insights I had been gathering, sorting, and coding from interviews I conducted became a second doctoral education of sorts for me—one where the professors shared not only their achievements but also their failings, where their personal and institutional lives were the curriculum, and where the student's task was to synthesize these insights and then draw his own conclusions. What follows is, in essence, my "dissertation" from this priceless education.

The research took 10 years to complete and formed the largest study ever undertaken based on in-depth interviews with high-profile leaders in the United States. There is great diversity among the leaders I met; they work in different sectors, have different backgrounds, and pursue varied purposes. They include over 250 CEOs (including the leaders of 20 percent of the Fortune 100), former presidents Jimmy Carter and George H. W. Bush, and dozens of cabinet secretaries, members of Congress, and heads of federal bureaus and agencies representing nine White House administrations (from Johnson to Obama). Also included are more than 100 leaders of the world's largest nonprofit organizations, including the American Red Cross, M.D. Anderson Cancer Center, and Harvard and Stanford universities. Working with a team of two dozen research assistants, I collected data on the lives and institutions of all 550 people I interviewed and then applied hundreds of analytic frames to their responses and life stories, searching for patterns as well as inconsistencies in their ascent to the upper reaches of power. The combined response rate of interviews requested was 87 percent.

The leaders in this study account for less than .003 percent of the United States population, but they have a disproportionate impact for such a small group. Their influence varies according to the power inherent in their positions, the dominance of their organizations, and the scope of their industries. While local elites can be found all over the world, leaders with global impact are clustered in major cities and commercial centers. So when I traveled to conduct interviews for this book—from Bar Harbor, Maine, to Pearl Harbor, Hawaii—79 percent of the meetings were in cities with over 1 million people. One-third of the interviews were held in New York City and Washington, D.C., alone. Half of the leaders I interviewed worked in business, a quarter in government, and a quarter in the nonprofit world (which includes higher education). I interviewed not only standing CEOs but also those who had recently retired or recently risen to their positions, allowing me to consider change over time. The average age of my subjects was 59, and they ranged from 27 to 91. Half are politically conservative, 41 percent liberal, and 9 percent do not identify either way. Among those who shared their religious identity with me, around 76 percent identify as Protestant, 9 percent as Catholic, 5 percent as Jewish, 3 percent as followers of another religion, and 8 percent as nonreligious.

People often ask me if I maintain relationships with the people I interviewed. In one way or another, I've stayed in touch with about half of them. Several of them have spoken at my college, and I have sought the advice of many others since assuming my current role. There is a bond that forms between two people when one of them shares her story of success and failure, of early life influences, and deeply personal motivations. And once you have established these relationships, there is a connection that can transcend rank or experience. Over and over again, I've found tight bonds between leaders who would seemingly have little connection.

In fact, without networks, I would have been unable to complete this study, as CEOs are not usually responsive to cold calls from social scientists conducting interviews for research. I had to rely upon my own connections to gain access at first. Then once I had a few interviews under my belt—President Jimmy Carter, Secretary James Baker, and the CEO of Walmart—more doors started opening. After interviews, I would also ask the leaders to recommend others who might be worth including in the study. I often even solicited their help in making the right connections. These recommendations from peers usually gave me the "in" I needed for scheduling my next interview.[1]

I traveled all over the country to conduct the semistructured interviews (of 60 to 90 minutes), with approximately 10 weeks elapsing from the time the interview was granted until it was completed. During that time, my research team conducted background research on the informant. We typically conducted many hours' worth of background research for every hour-long interview. This allowed us to maximize each interview by avoiding questions that could be answered elsewhere. Interviews were digitally recorded and professionally transcribed, and informants had the option of reviewing the transcripts for accuracy (though only 8 percent chose this option).

Each interview was then combed through for qualitative analysis as well as coded for 122 variables that mapped the informant's demographic, social, professional, and network profiles.[2] Most of these data were drawn from the interview transcript, and additional data was drawn from electronic and print sources.

In this book, I do my best to evenhandedly portray top leaders, warts and all. I utilize narratives from the lives of individual leaders to explain general principles, but I acknowledge that this book presents only part of the story for any single individual. I employ an analysis technique called critical empathy, developed by R. Marie Griffith, a historian of American religion at Washington University in St. Louis.[3] The intention of critical empathy is to recognize and share the content and spirit of study participants' perspectives while also acknowledging a broader analytic framework that allows for additional interpretations. The point is neither to poke holes in participants' stories nor buy into every tall tale and justification. Rather, I seek to acknowledge the value of each leader's perspective while also evaluating his narrative account against the public record. After all, a benefit of studying senior leaders is that much has been written by and about them, providing background information for each interview. I also realize that collecting and analyzing interview data can introduce a number of biases, especially when these tasks are conducted by a team, but we followed standard conventions to minimize these potential problems.[4] With all of these caveats, I think one of the greatest benefits of this study is its unique ability to shed light by revealing perspectives previously hidden beneath the surface. Talking directly *to* these leaders provided remarkable insight, and the size and scale of this study allows comparisons among them that previously could not have taken place in a systematic way.

PLATINUM LEADERS

Leader. Today the term is used lightly as both an ideal and a casual superlative. The title is applied liberally across fields and positions. Leadership is the subject of books and lectures, the dream of ambitious men and women, the goal of programs and elections, and both the savior and scapegoat of nations and companies. Much is made of leadership, but relatively little is known about the lives of those who sit atop the world's most powerful organizational pyramids. Who are they? How did they get there? And what do they do with their power?

It was in pursuit of a desire to know how power and leadership really work and can be used for pursuit of the common good that I undertook this research. As the interview transcripts piled up, I further began to identify a subset of leaders who held particular influence *and* skill at wielding it. These individuals are *platinum leaders*. In this book, I specify the three unique attributes of these leaders that distinguish them from their peers: (1) the scale of their organizational influence (they direct the world's most significant institutions); (2) their penchant for maximizing opportunity and catalyzing change; and (3) their talent for garnering trust and goodwill, which opens for them doors of influence beyond the walls of their organizations.[5] In the end, 128 informants (or 23 percent of the study population) are platinum leaders.

You may recall from chemistry class that platinum, the precious metal, is most commonly used as a catalyst in chemical reactions. The automobile industry uses platinum in the production of catalytic converters, and it has proven useful for many different applications. For example, it has a unique ability to assist with the conversion of crude oil into gasoline where it facilitates the joining together of certain molecules. Platinum also has been used for decades in chemotherapy treatments; it is especially effective in fighting aggressive cancers. Jewelers and watchmakers treasure platinum too, because—unlike gold—it neither tarnishes nor wears down.

So platinum is valued because of its rarity, its density, its multiple applications, and its durability. Platinum leaders are similarly special. They are catalytic in shaping the institutions they direct. They often have a transformative effect well before they hold real authority. And these leaders outlast their peers, using their networks, their opportunities, and even their challenges to advance their own visions for the common good. By disposition, platinum leaders are agents of change. And by position, they effect that change both within their organizations and *through* them to a larger world. In essence, platinum leaders outshine their peers and resist corrosion.

This book is for those who aspire to the top. Just as hopeful basketball players study the habits of great NBA stars, so also is it for those who want to be great leaders. We learn from the best. In my role as a college president, I want to apply the insights from my research to prepare our students more effectively and to sharpen the angle of their trajectory as they seek opportunities to make a difference in the world around us.

After spending thousands of hours analyzing the lives and institutions of these 550 leaders, I determined that many of our basic assumptions about power and influence are simply not true. What we think is important in preparing the next generation of world leaders matters very little, but some of the most significant forms of preparation receive scant attention.

At root, *leadership is the exercise of influence in the service of a shared cause*. There is no potential state of leadership; it exists only when action is taken. Power, on the other hand, is often latent. It can be activated by someone in authority, but it also can involve inaction—exerting influence by moving slowly on an issue or by preventing topics from being discussed. Social thinkers such as Michel Foucault and Steven Lukes have persuasively argued that power also involves the shaping of desires and beliefs. Securing the consent of others may be the least visible aspect of power, but it is most potent when it becomes taken for granted. This line of thinking emphasizes the *relational nature of power*. As Foucault writes, "Power has its principle not so much in a person as in a certain concerted distribution of bodies . . . in an arrangement whose internal mechanisms produce the relation in which individuals are caught up."[6]

To best understand this relational nature of power, Chapter 1 explores the *matrix of power*, a nationwide—and ultimately global— crisscross of personal connections concentrated in major cities and at major institutions. We will see that great leaders in the matrix of power act personally, but they think institutionally. There is no dream team of one. Institutions, not individuals, wield the real, world-changing power. Practically every book about power focuses on the traits of individual leaders, but I insist that the most important trait of a leader is her ability to take the helm of a greater vessel that can cast a shadow far broader than her own. Success comes to those who wisely navigate their organizations to direct power to the right places. This is not to say that individuals are helpless slaves to an established system. Most certainly, people can—and do—change their institutions from the inside out.

LEARNING FROM STORIES AS WELL AS STATISTICS

In our data-driven age, we know more about people in power than ever before. It takes only moments to find the salary, biography, scandalous history, or political donations of prominent figures. But data points like these have little value beyond break room chatter. Much more intriguing and important are the aspects of these leaders revealed in this book: the tension between their roles as organizational heads and their identities as regular people with their own quirks, personal habits, and unique histories; the programs and activities that *really* propelled them forward; how they prepare for and survive public failures that would send most people spiraling into despair. They may be positioned to exert great influence over society, but the substance of their influence depends heavily on core personal characteristics. Looking at their lives allows us to understand both their place in the world and how we, ourselves, can make a similarly meaningful difference.

Consider the career of Donna Shalala. The grandchild of Lebanese immigrants, she served in the Peace Corps before moving into a successful career in academia and, finally, national government. Her biographical details can be learned on Wikipedia. But you cannot understand Shalala's impact without understanding the greater context of how she herself views her life. How did she achieve her positions? Approach them? Manage them? Most importantly, what has she learned along the way, and what can that teach those of us with similar vision and ambition?

Shalala, like most young leaders, had an undistinguished childhood. Counter to what many people think, it doesn't really matter what future leaders do before they're 20. Shalala was a mediocre student as an undergraduate (again, typical). After serving as a Peace Corps volunteer, Shalala went into higher education because, as she candidly admits, she could not find a job as a journalist. Shalala followed no obvious path, but, like other leaders profiled in Chapter 2, she knew the areas where she was strongest and built careers around those strengths. She saw no opportunity in journalism, so she built a career as an academic based on her cultural and international experience.

All leaders start out with at least two things: potential and opportunity. Leaders can't control the hands that are dealt them anymore than you or I can. But they inevitably and often ingeniously make the most out of what they're given. They use this skill—the *ability to maximize opportunity*—to leverage their education, connections, and experiences toward success. For young people like Shalala, it starts with maximizing one key relationship (a mentor, a boss, a teacher) or skill; young people able to capitalize on these connections thereafter begin their ascent.

Professional life socializes us into becoming experts of particular domains, but Chapter 3 shows how platinum leaders cultivate what might be called the "generalist mind-set" early in their careers. Wide networks and broad knowledge pay off more than deep specialization when climbing the ladder to the corner office. Executives at engineering firms, for instance, must not only lead with technical fluency; they set strategy, manage budgets, and communicate with internal and external constituents. The aspiring leader who keeps the most options open relationally (staying in touch with many different kinds of people) is most likely to develop the wide network required to move up at a faster pace. This requires a *liberal arts approach to life*. Would-be leaders must be dabblers of sorts, conversant in other kinds of business, knowledgeable about current affairs, and able to connect across divides. I found that this approach to life seems to come naturally only to some, but all platinum leaders figure out a way to develop it. You can discern it in others through simple things—their ability to converse at dinner parties with different kinds of people or the range of topics represented in the books they have stacked on their bedside reading tables.

Taking advantage of opportunities and capitalizing on connections lay the groundwork for success, but future leaders need a final push to enter the pipeline to power. I call this push their *catalyst*. Young people need catalysts rich with opportunity to see firsthand the broad, generalist perspectives required of senior leaders, even before they are ready to take on such roles themselves. Catalysts also distinguish young leaders from their peers, establish for them a strong foundational network, and give them the confidence to take the risks necessary for platinum leadership.

Donna Shalala's network of friends was essential to her ascent. Because of her connections, she ended up landing a position as an assistant secretary in the Department of Housing and Urban Development under President Carter. Connections also helped her get her next position as president of Hunter College (part of the City University of New York). Shalala next became the president of the University of Wisconsin–Madison and so the first woman to lead a Big Ten school. In her seventh year at UW–Madison, she was approached by the Clinton transition team to serve as secretary of Health and Human Services (HHS). Shalala had not been looking to return to politics, but she told me, "You can't turn down a cabinet position." Indeed, ambition is the spur for upward mobility. Shalala was secretary of HHS for a record eight years.

Unlike many leaders who feign humility, Shalala is not shy when it comes to touting her accomplishments. She told me, "Every place I've been, I've made better." She continued, "You will not go to an institution where I was where they won't talk about the golden years of my presidency." She is particularly proud of her work at the University of Miami, where she currently serves as president.

Chapter 4 describes how leaders face and tackle the challenges of their jobs—specifically managing productivity, people, and the cultural environments of their institutions. Surprisingly, the stereotypical executive type isn't necessarily the best leader. More than just delegating and vision casting, leading well requires relational intelligence. Leading others is significantly easier when followers enjoy being around the leader, and interpersonally gifted people are at a significant advantage in power. The challenge is that those in power rarely have time to develop relationships with those beyond their inner circles. Once someone secures a powerful position within an institution, he has access to tremendous resources and opportunities. But getting things done requires connections—both up and down the ladder.

We look at the leadership DNA of successful leaders, which includes not just individual traits but also managerial approaches. For example, when moving to a new role, Donna Shalala does not bring her staff with her, preferring to start anew. She considers herself a "chameleon," able to adapt to any structure and situation. Some might see this as a weakness. To her, adaptability is what allows her to thrive in different contexts and roles. And Shalala's efforts to transform "Suntan U" into an academic contender have been successful—by 2000, the University of Miami had made it onto *U.S. News & World Report*'s top 50 universities list. Under her leadership, the university has grown significantly, but many in the UM community are concerned that it is unsustainable.

Of course, the portrait that Shalala (and any of these leaders) paints of herself is not complete. She has had critics at every stage of her leadership. Indeed, the limelight can cast a long shadow. In Chapter 5, we take an in-depth look into how platinum leaders manage to survive the crucible of both personal and public crisis. In 2010, Nevin Shapiro, a prominent University of Miami football booster, was convicted of orchestrating a $930-million Ponzi scheme. Shapiro implicated UM in his downfall, accusing the university of countless NCAA violations under Shalala's watch. Pundits expected heavy penalties from the NCAA as more and more dirt was uncovered, but they did not count on Shalala's political savvy. She was swift to institute internal sanctions and both accepted responsibility for *some* of Shapiro's claims and criticized the

NCAA for a poor investigation. When judgment was handed down in fall 2013, it was relatively light, thanks in part to Shalala's shrewd management of the investigation.

We all read about scandals like these in the papers, but most of a leader's greatest work never sees the light of day. Platinum leaders spend a significant amount of time keeping bad things from becoming public or working on opportunities that never materialize. Most of their work takes place behind closed doors, and because outsiders don't know the full story, those in power get most of the blame and, actually, little of the credit. We tend to think of crises as testing grounds for leaders, as contexts in which they develop their moral fiber and leadership talent. In reality, crises do not mold character; they simply reveal it. Constituents will not put up with incongruity between a leader's speech, personal choices, and professional actions. In this way, much of leading an institution is like the work of a priest. It is a complete and consuming role.

I have learned I may not be wearing a suit every minute of the day, but there is never a moment when I am not president of Gordon. Like many people, I work long hours, but being Gordon's president requires my involvement in evening and weekend activities that go far beyond a 60-hour workweek. Even when I am on vacation, I think about the college. Indeed, I've learned that I relax more if I can spend an hour every day on vacation keeping up with email; I wonder less about what's going on back at school and have less dread about returning to an overflowing inbox. This is the paradox of leading an institution: you cannot power off, because even when away, you're always on. This is exactly the phenomenon we examine in Chapter 6: How do these leaders keep it all in balance and perspective? (And what happens when they don't?) The people in power, if they succeed for any length of time, lead not through their roles or their authority. Instead, they lead with their lives.

Chapter 7 reveals how, when they are at their noblest pursuit, leaders can influence our country and the world for the common good. Sometimes this happens through large gifts to charitable causes, sometimes, through more personal involvement. For many leaders, the charge to influence the future of their world is *the* compelling motivation they feel.

From Jamie Dimon of JPMorgan Chase to John Seffrin at the American Cancer Society, hundreds of leaders talked to me about how gratifying it is to invest in younger colleagues as they begin their own professional ascents. I assumed they were saying this because it seemed like a nice sentiment. But I always sensed something more meaningful under the surface. I'm now convinced that the most gratifying part of leading a major institution has little to do with achieving organizational goals or redirecting a company culture. Instead, the dividend of power comes from relatively small deeds, the most common example being investing in young people. At the end of my first year as president of Gordon, a friend asked me about the best part of my new job. Almost without thinking, I related the story of helping the Gordon student-body president apply for the Rhodes Scholarship. In the end, he was not selected, but the experience of working with him was incredibly special. It represented, at a micro level, the things that I love about higher education—helping a student reach a significant milestone, investing in something that can be life-changing for another person, and strengthening that which is good for even greater excellence.

ON TOP OF THE WORLD

Crisscrossing the country for this line of research took me to many interesting places, including the top of the world. On the 62nd floor of 30 Rockefeller Plaza, I clicked my recorder on and asked Vernon Jordan if he had ever expected to end up here. In the executive suite at Lazard (the international financing powerhouse with the connections and influence of Goldman Sachs but without the bad press), we enjoyed an unrestricted view of nearly all of Manhattan, from the Statue of Liberty to beyond Central Park. After a long and successful career in law and business, Jordan was a man with few regrets, accustomed to power and privilege. Yet how had he gotten here? What had he done to earn one of these coveted offices in the clouds? Looking back, Jordan said, "It was clear to me from the first grade that I was going to be a leader." And he is. But he is best known as a close friend of President Bill Clinton, a "D.C. power broker," "the Quicker Fixer-Upper," or the "the First Friend."

Of course Jordan was not born with this recognition. He earned it from people with power who liked him. He grew up in Atlanta during the era of segregation and began his career as a civil-rights lawyer in the 1960s. He served as the president of the National Urban League for nearly a decade, a position through which he established a good reputation. He served on President Clinton's transition team in 1992–1993 and has been close to Clinton for decades. Jordan has also served on over a dozen corporate and nonprofit boards, including American Express, Xerox, Revlon, JCPenney, and Dow Jones.

Before I had even met Jordan, one knowledgeable source told me that virtually every Fortune 500 CEO could cite an instance when they had called on Jordan for counsel. Indeed, his name came up many times when I talked to CEOs. But Jordan himself was closemouthed when I asked him about any decisions he had made or counseled others on, saying, "What happens in the boardroom stays in the boardroom."

Jordan expressed pride that he had not applied for a job since he had been a Chicago bus driver in 1957. This kind of career movement would have been impossible without his many cross-industry connections. Senior leaders like Jordan use their superior networks for both their own advancement and the promotion of others. Even when it appears effortless, you can bet they have carefully cultivated their connections, laboring many hours to secure their privileged positions. Jordan said, "Giving is reciprocity. You give, and you ask. Every time you ask, you're committing yourself to give, because the person that you've asked is going to ask you. And if you don't understand that, you ought not to be in the business."

As influential as he is, Jordan is still just one node in our nationwide matrix of power. Together, the institutions and 550 high-level leaders in this study form a complicated and convoluted knot of relationships, associations, and connections.[7] It is, however, this inscrutable knot that holds the nation—and so the world—together. Adding to the complexity is the fact that I myself am only a node, a synapse working to interpret the actions of power being captured, converted, and released by those in positions of influence.

WHY STUDY POWER FROM WITHIN THE HALLS OF FAITH?

My interest in all of this is deeply personal. I saw up close the burden and the blessing of leading institutions through my family. My mom served as head of school of Jackson Prep, a fantastic independent secondary school in my hometown of Jackson, Mississippi. My dad, a career golf pro at Colonial Country Club, became one of the leading authorities on the rules of golf and eventually served as president of the Professional Golfers' Association of America. Living in their home, I experienced the thrill a leader experiences when his team overcomes a big challenge. I witnessed the toll that personnel decisions can take on the person at the top. And I overheard the conversations leaders have with themselves when trying to figure out the best way forward. So when I was a graduate student at Princeton, I was drawn to a research project that involved interviewing other people like my parents.

Some are surprised that I, as a Christian, am interested in power at all. Didn't Jesus eschew the trappings of power and overturn prevailing notions of greatness and influence?

The conviction that Christians should not pursue power is as old as the church itself, one that is still held dearly by many within the Christian family of faith. The Anabaptist tradition has advocated this belief for centuries, and many people I respect hold it. In my own life, I have certainly seen God work mightily through the witness of people far from power—a Burmese woman, a grandmother who never went to college, and a child with Down syndrome. God can and does work through the simple people of this world to shame the learned.

But I am not persuaded that the countercultural claims of Jesus require Christians to disdain power. I have spent years thinking about this and have come to a firm conviction that much good can come from people devoted to their faith sitting in positions of influence. Indeed, much good can come of the faithful leading major institutions, provided their motives are kept in check by a life of prayer and accountability. With these things in mind, I have spent the past 10 years investigating power and leadership, and now I want to pass along what I've learned to others who seek to promote the common good.

That awkward freshman at my next orientation workshop might be tomorrow's next game-changing CEO. And when she is, I hope that she remembers the phrase that I misunderstood at the beginning of my power-leadership journey. For good or ill, I *am* the job.

CHAPTER 1

Act Personally, But Think Institutionally

Develop Your Network Beyond Your Organization

I grew up in a neighborhood that was a sort of lower-middle class, [even a] working-class neighborhood in New York. And we were all the sons and daughters of hardworking people, but people whose network basically extended to family and neighborhood friends. It was not very expansive, nor was it very . . . "vertical." And at the end of the day, from the point of view of making your way in this world, it wasn't very helpful. You had good people like your grandmother, who would give you good advice on a personal level, and love and nurture. But they really couldn't help you navigate the space above the lower-middle class, because they had no relationships there.

Richard Parsons was born into a poor neighborhood in Brooklyn and did not have any "connections." But he went on to become the chairman of Citigroup, the twelfth-ranked company on the Fortune 500 list. This is the so-called American Dream, the ability to come from nothing and work your way to the top of the food chain. There are many ways to "make it," but they all require networks, something Parsons was lacking at the beginning of his career. But all it took was one connection to change his life.

While Parsons attended Albany Law School, he interned with the New York state legislature and drew the attention of the governor's office. They extended him an offer, and Parsons began working for the man who would eventually shape his entire career: Governor Nelson Rockefeller. Parsons and Rockefeller hit it off; Parsons said they had "good chemistry":

> *Falling into the orbit of Nelson gave me three things: One was a role model in terms of how someone of his stature and position navigated the world. Two was an introduction to his world and an introduction, therefore, to his network of people who, if they chose to, were in a position to be enormously helpful to you as you made your way up the vertical ladder. And then three was a sense of confidence in myself. At the end of the day, if you could play in that company, you got comfortable doing so.*

Eventually, Parsons practiced law, and Rockefeller frequently referred clients to him. Parsons recalled that when *Forbes* magazine first published its list of the 400 richest Americans, 5 of the top 10 were his personal clients: "It was all because either they were people that I'd been introduced to by the governor, or who basically said, 'Well, I've heard you're a good lawyer. If you can represent the Rockefellers, you can certainly represent me.'" He later cashed in on these connections to establish his career in business. And for a while, this helped him enormously. But networks cannot do it all; Parsons later became chairman and CEO of Time Warner and oversaw perhaps the most disastrous business deal of all time when Time Warner merged with AOL. His story serves as a reminder that connections can only do so much; to have a lasting legacy, leaders must also have business savvy and a good deal of luck.

While Nelson Rockefeller—the scion of an oil family that used connections and wealth to conquer both business and politics—is the kind of person we usually think of as a powerful leader, leaders like Richard Parsons—an African American from a poor family who moved from law into big business—are certainly more common today than they once were in the highest ranks of the elite network.[1] The network of senior leaders is still exclusive, but it allows for fresh blood. The way to enter is through connections—like Parsons' connection to Rockefeller and (as I describe in the introduction) Donna Shalala's connections that got her into the White House.

If relational networks were essential in my gaining access to these prominent leaders, they are even more so for the people who live and operate in this realm. Those in society's upper reaches use their connections to secure influence and garner status. Many of the offices I went into were lined with photos of the leader playing golf with the president or shaking hands with a foreign head of state. Interview responses were littered with references to other elite leaders, sometimes because they were necessary to convey the story, and sometimes simply (I assume) so that I would be impressed.

While this name-dropping can become excessive, the truth is that an elite network is necessary for leaders to get anything done, and aspiring leaders must recognize this fact. A strong network serves to tighten the bonds of a leader's own ranks and selectively escorts others into the upper echelon. To gain access, rising stars seek out opportunities to interact with respected leaders. They find ways to build connections and use novel touches (like handwritten notes) to differentiate themselves from the pack. This understanding of the connections between relationship building and influence may seem Machiavellian at first blush, and some successful leaders do rely more upon the spur of ambition than the nudge of social graces to get things done. But in the real upper reaches of power, a leader must not be too pushy or self-promoting—the top tiers of society still resist the overbearing aspirants.

That said, leaders cannot be passive, either. If they overlook the value of a wide-ranging network of acquaintances, they will neither find the opportunities nor gain the relational resources to achieve significant goals and make names for themselves. Not only this, but certain individuals serve as entry points into highly selective networks, and these individuals must be, to an extent, pursued.

Nelson Rockefeller (not to mention family members John and David) is an example of a network superstar, a leader whose influence and reach extends across multiple sectors and generations of leaders. These superstars have a unique ability to draw people together—what I call "convening power," in that they are able to use their wide networks to unite disparate people who would otherwise have no point of connection. Other network superstars who were mentioned repeatedly by leaders during the interviews include Jack Welch and Warren Buffett.

Ted Turner's office is a testament to his networking versatility. He has a wall filled with his 44 honorary doctorates, his office showcases five Emmys and an Oscar, and a World Series trophy sits prominently on his coffee table. Indeed, many of the people profiled in this book can claim great accomplishments in multiple areas of society. With each accomplishment comes access to a wider, and so more powerful, network.

At the same time, one does not need to have connections to the White House or a network superstar in order to leverage connections effectively. Sometimes the most helpful contacts are internal to a particular organization. One nonprofit executive told me that when she would hire "smarty-pants McKinsey people," as she put it, she would sit them down and tell them where the power really lies:

> *You're going to run into some older person who you think is slower and dumber, until we get into a really bad situation. And the only way to get out of that situation is that they're going to call somebody that they know and that they have a relationship with, and they're going to solve the problem. And then you're going to realize that all your smarty pants matters not at all, because you didn't learn how to build relationships. And at the end of the day, all organizations are webs of relationships; that's all they are.*

Networks are even more important when leaders have to get things accomplished outside of their own firms or fields. One university president shared with me a conflict he had with a politician who was looking to cut state education funding. The president "was able to unleash enough firepower among major [political] players" in the state to avoid the budget cut. He credited his fire power to the loose set of acquaintances as well as loyal friends that he had established through a variety of formal and informal ties. Networks are powerful forces in the stratosphere of society—not only because of whom they include but also what they can do.

As the networks of people in the upper reaches overlap, they form a complex matrix of power involving individuals, institutions, and organizational fields that ultimately reaches across the country and around the globe. It is through this matrix that decisions of national and international consequence are made, elite newcomers are assimilated, and resources of all kinds—economic, political, social, and cultural—are distributed. In essence, this matrix is how power operates in our society. So how do people get attached to these golden webs?

MENTOR RELATIONSHIPS

One of the main ways that newcomers become integrated into the matrix of power is through *mentoring chains*. These are lineages of relationships, rarely recognized formally, that link emerging or potential leaders with already established ones. For mentors, these networks give them the opportunity to gain leverage over the future by investing in their own legacies through the people who will ultimately interpret them. These chains also help build up leadership capabilities within their own organization. For young leaders, mentoring is one of the best ways to acclimate to a new network of social peers, gaining social capital as they rise. A banking executive told me, "When you have a mentor, you're able to take that risk at a little younger age because [your mentor] is looking out for you. And so it allows you to be . . . more confident before your age." In fact, mentoring was a markedly consistent factor in the early lives of the leaders I interviewed. Fifty-one percent of them mentioned a specific mentor or sponsor who had aided them in their climb to the top. Having a good mentor proved more significant in predicting career success than where one went to college or how wealthy one was as a child.

Emerging leaders learn as much as they can from their predecessors, but they also bring the values and innovations of their own backgrounds into their new social contexts. (This fresh blood keeps the matrix of power from stagnating.) So while the connections that gained Donna Shalala an appointment as a Cabinet secretary are obviously important, her other, nonelite connections (the people she served alongside in the Peace Corps, her family, her colleagues at Teachers College) have also been vital to her development. Kenneth Langone, an executive who serves on the boards of General Electric, Home Depot, Yum! Brands, and New York University, said:

> *There ain't no such thing as a self-made man. There just ain't. I don't care who it is. . . . At a given point in time throughout our lives, a part of the process of where we are, . . . if we look hard and objectively, we'll admit that we got a shove or a push or a pat on the back.*

Langone related these thoughts to me in the context of a story from college. He had scraped through high school and found himself struggling in his freshman year of college. Just before Thanksgiving, his economics professor pulled him aside and said that while Langone's grammar and writing were horrible, he had real talent in economics. Langone shared that he was close to flunking all his classes, and the professor volunteered to speak with his other professors if Langone would commit to giving his schoolwork more effort. Langone took the deal: "I jumped into it with both feet and enthusiastically, really turned it around." Looking back, Langone credits the professor's intervention with his later success.

Networks do not only matter for the powerful. In the same way that great leaders use their connections in their rise to the top, people at all levels of society employ networks regularly to get things accomplished. They provide important linkages to one's fellow climbers down the ladder as well as up. Indeed, much to my surprise, the leaders I interviewed frequently rely on nonelite influences for inspiration, moral direction, and a sense of purpose. Their pastors, best friends from childhood, favorite uncles, and high-school coaches still impact the decisions of some leaders and are especially significant in their thinking when it comes to major life decisions (such as job moves and family transitions). Nearly all the leaders I interviewed were able to identify such a person outside of their immediate family. Elite networks then, are only the tip of the iceberg; under the surface, these leaders have many more mentors, connections, and relationships that impact their lives. Some people only do a good job at maximizing either upward or downward connections. A key characteristic that distinguishes average leaders from those who are truly remarkable is the ability to take advantage of both.

INSTITUTIONS

Networks of senior leaders are constituted in the same way as are networks of ordinary people. What differentiates the points in *these* networks, however, is their access to leading institutions. The people who populate elite networks are working for major government bodies, large corporations, and prestigious cultural institutions. A connection to these people means a connection to the people and resources they influence. Because of this, they provide newcomers access to those places where decisions of national and international consequence are made.

I refer to this process as "institutional tethering," and it is how affiliations with certain institutions can serve as elite "on-ramps" whereby people from humbler backgrounds can rise in status and opportunity. This is why an invitation to dinner at the Four Seasons with a CEO can make a bigger difference in someone's life than dinner with a friend from home. And within these elite networks, organizations are both the means by which leaders *gain* influence and power (such as being invited to serve on the board of a company or a nonprofit organization) and the vehicle through which they *exercise* this influence and power (such as using one's board membership to influence policy).

Today there is a high level of distrust in society's institutions. They are seen as containers of insurmountable bureaucracy, yet in truth, they are fundamental to society's well-being. As one university president put it, "There is no civilization without institutions. I think that society can't organize itself to do the most human things, the most important things, over a long-term basis . . . without institutions."

The conceit of the Internet age is that now anyone with a wireless connection has the capability to influence millions—through a tweet, viral video, or Tumblr feed. But this conceit is as shallow as the media forms themselves. Social media lends itself to sound bites—140 characters and three-minute videos. Though widespread, these ephemeral forms of communication are not nearly as weighty as major institutions such as Harvard University, Procter & Gamble, the *Wall Street Journal*, and the Supreme Court. Events such as the Arab Spring of 2011 demonstrate that social media *can* precipitate revolutions, but they cannot maintain and organize that revolutionary impulse for long-term change. For that, society relies on institutions. Leaders are attracted to organizations; that is how they have a real impact on society. The COO of a billion-dollar nonprofit told me, "I really am attracted to scale, which is the reason I'm not interested in being the CEO of a much smaller organization, because I actually feel like scale matters, and that's where the impact is real."

One future telecom executive had decided early on to focus his desire to help people into a career as a doctor. But this young man changed his mind one summer during college:

What led to my decision to go into business was I became very enamored with this idea of leverage. A doctor's contribution to society is limited to the 8 or 10 hours a day that they personally work. And I thought, if you're working toward the right set of goals, your contribution is multiplied by the number of people you have working with you to accomplish that set of goals. And that literally was the reason I went into business.

He was drawn to business because he saw that he could have the most positive effect on society by leading a large organization. The same is true of many in government and nonprofit leadership. These are leaders "attracted to scale," and institutions provide their kind of leverage. Another executive told me that his favorite thing about being a CEO was "building a legacy of a company that had already been around 85 years" and having a voice in national and international politics. This penchant for larger-scale influence is typical among the platinum leaders I encountered in this study. They want their lives and their leadership to count, and even if they are not CEOs, they prefer the access that comes from being tied to a major institution through a senior role.

Even the most seemingly unmovable institutions can be altered by the right leadership, as Marty Evans knows well. In 1991, Captain Marsha J. Evans had spent over 20 years in the Navy. She said, "I always thought I was on borrowed time . . . because women in the Navy in my generation were told fairly frequently that we were not wanted. We were not combat officers. . . . We were only support officers." As Evans's career progressed, more jobs opened up to women, but the Navy was behind the times concerning gender equality. This became abundantly clear when multiple charges of sexual assault were made against members of the U.S. Navy at the annual Tailhook Association symposium. The event was made worse by the fact that many attending flag officers seemed to have been aware of the assaults and did nothing. When the Navy conducted its own investigation, the episode was deemed simply a case of misbehavior by low-ranking enlisted men. The occurrence and its subsequent brushing under the table revealed to the public a startling sexism woven into the very fabric of the U.S. Navy. The inspector general of the Department of Defense would go on to hold his own investigation, which shed more light on the occurrence and resulted in the resignation and career demise of many admirals.

Evans was then tapped to chair a task force to change the culture and climate of the Navy and Marine Corps to one that would more greatly value and respect women. Or, as Evans put it, she was to "get the Navy off the front page of the papers." This was not just another assignment for Evans; it was personal. The ideal of gender equity was a norm in business and other sectors, and she was ready to see that same change in the military: "Gloria Steinem and her sisters forgot that we were there toiling in the vineyard with no support," Evans told me over coffee one afternoon. But she was a platinum leader, and platinum leaders are positioned well. Because of her senior role in the Navy, Evans had the opportunity to change an institution that activists from the women's movement could never reach. At this point in time, the Navy was coming around to the idea that "It's just not fair that people should have to be subjected to harassment or sexism, just like it's not appropriate or fair that we should denigrate blacks or Hispanics," said Evans, but there was still considerable resistance to change on the subject of women.

Evans knew that in order to make a change, she had to develop an argument based on more than the principle of social equality. At that time, the Navy had a cap on the percentage of women recruited, which meant that they turned away qualified women and often took lesser qualified men. There were also laws that prevented women in the Navy and Marine Corps from serving in combat units. This was the point that became Evans's logical fulcrum. If the mission of the Navy is "to conduct prompt and sustained combat operations at sea" as its primary function states, then it had a moral imperative to use the people who can do the job best, without regard for race, ethnicity, or gender. When Evans presented this argument to the Navy brass, they agreed. As she tells it,

> They were ready for the argument, and it resonated. That became the foundation for how to change the culture and climate to value and respect women. We have to change the law so that women serve on the same terms. We have to hold them accountable just like we hold men accountable. And then we have to fix these problems that prevent the whole team from working effectively. Because if you don't do that, then you might not accomplish the mission.

Evans's task force led the Navy to go to Congress and change the Title X code that prevented women from serving on combat ships, and subsequently women began commanding these vessels. Her work opened up Navy leadership to a new generation of women. Evans went on to become the second woman appointed admiral and the first to command a naval base. After her career in the Navy, Evans led the Girl Scouts of the USA and then the American Red Cross. She subsequently was the chief executive at the Ladies Professional Golf Association and currently serves on multiple corporate boards. Evans said, "Once a year or twice a year I go to the Naval Academy and speak with midshipmen. And today when you go out there and talk to women midshipmen, they just don't have any idea that they can't do this or that. It's really pretty exciting." Progress like this within the U.S. Navy could not have been made from outside the hierarchy.

Evans could have just gotten ticked off and started tweeting about it, but how would that have helped her future female cohorts? Lasting social change does not occur through people but through institutions. The most effective leaders, like Evans, realize that institutional momentum is far more powerful than individual, charismatic personalities. They work to make small changes to alter the course of an institution. Like a Navy aircraft carrier, these institutions move slowly and resist redirection. But in the right hands, once turned, they can change history.

CONNECTIONS

One of the most contentious and yet recurrent ways senior leaders exercise power in society is through overlapping board memberships, what scholars call "interlocking directorates"[2] or simply "interlocks." The term calls to mind the image of tightly fitting gears, where the slightest turn of one influences all the others. The tendency of boards of for-profit firms, policy groups, nonprofit organizations, and even universities is to share members. A CEO wants to fill a board with knowledgeable and trustworthy individuals, so she chooses people she knows and who are proven industry leaders; inevitably, there is overlap.

These interlocks can have important effects. On the industry level, some fear that competing organizations use interlocks to collude to hike prices. On the societal level, some think that members of the elite class use interlocking directorates to consolidate their control over the most powerful companies. It is not clear how intentional directors are in securing these advantages through multiple directorates. But the possibility for cohesion, or even collusion, certainly increases in this case. Interlocks can also keep out new faces, new perspectives. They can be pernicious and institutionalized forms of subtle discrimination.

Even though board affiliations mean relatively little to most directors, there is a group—an inner circle of directors who sit on multiple boards—for whom these networks are hubs of power, allowing them to exercise enormous influence, even in comparison to other platinum leaders. Consider the following irony.

There are hundreds of academic studies of interlocks from the past four decades. What has been little studied is what these interlocks mean to the board members themselves. For those in my study, contact with other boards allowed them to share information, consult each other for advice, act in concert to pressure for political change, find employees for high-level placements, raise money for charitable causes, and achieve countless other goals. Some have argued that the closeness of these networks allows for class cohesion and collective action among senior leaders, concentrating even more power in the hands of these already powerful people.[3] Others, however, say that while there is interaction through these interlocks, not much really gets done. I did not find evidence of much collusion or political unity emerging from these interlocking directors. I did find that interlocks limited the number of voices in the conversations at the highest levels of corporate and nonprofit life. They also keep some people from underrepresented groups from joining the global elite. For instance, black women—such as Ursula Burns (CEO of Xerox), Ruth Simmons (former president of Brown University), and Shirley Ann Jackson (president of Rensselaer Polytechnic Institute)—are among the most interlocked directors, serving on multiple boards. This at first appears empowering, but consider this irony: More boards are able to boast of the inclusion of females and underrepresented minorities, while because of interlocks, fewer women and minorities are received into the matrix as a whole.

COHESION AND TENSION

When institutional leaders are tethered to powerful organizations and connected to each other through networks, the potential for action and change is immeasurable. In the late 1960s, Thomas Frist cofounded Hospital Corporation of America (HCA), a revolutionary company that privatized health care in a for-profit environment. At its peak, HCA owned 347 hospitals and employed 175,000 people.

Frist had been mentored earlier in his leadership by a retired CEO who had instructed him to seek out board memberships at prominent universities and arts organizations to give him "the experience and the contacts to be better prepared rather than just be an entrepreneur." Frist was strategic, therefore, wanting to be involved not only with prestigious organizations, but also with organizations where he could have an impact in his hometown of Nashville: "You don't pick something that appears successful. How are you going to make your mark? . . . If you are going to be on the board, you don't want to just be a board member, you want to do something over and above what the primary role is." One of the boards Frist joined was United Way of Middle Tennessee. The organization was struggling, but Frist eagerly took on the challenge:

> *First thing is to turn around the United Way, in Nashville, for the good of Nashville, reestablishing its rightful way to be a major part of this community, the underpinning of it. Two is, if you can . . . do something that has some stickiness or lasting value to Middle Tennessee. I [didn't] know what it would be, but I set a goal to come up with it. And third is, if you are going to put all this time and effort into it, do something that is back-to-back walk-off home runs at whatever it is. That maybe has a ripple effect . . . for the whole nation.*

Not only was he aiming to help the local branch of United Way, Frist wanted a national impact. He came up with the idea of what became known as the Tocqueville Society, a leadership-giving program (named for volunteerism advocate Alexis de Tocqueville) whose members annually contribute at least $10,000 to the United Way. In addition to Nashville, Frist was able to convince four other United Way chapters to launch local Tocqueville Societies. That program eventually spread across the country and now is globally recognized as a major philanthropic success story. Today the society raises over $600 million a year through the program, and since its inception, it has raised, by Frist's estimation, over $7 billion. Frist's seemingly impossible goal of a ripple effect across the country became reality. Because of the successful launch of his effort, Frist was appointed chair of the national United Way board of trustees.

Frist came into the chairmanship of the board just after a scandal involving the CEO of United Way and misappropriation of the organization's funds.[4] Frist found himself in the tricky position of filling a CEO position. Through an executive search firm, Frist was able to hire a young woman named Elaine Chao. Chao would leave United Way four years later to become the secretary of labor, and she later served on the board of HCA.

Chao is just one of many powerful connections Frist mentioned in his interview with me. He described a business challenge that he resolved not through number crunching, but through network tapping: "Pick up the phone, call Jack Welch [CEO of General Electric]. Said, 'Jack, here's the situation: I think this would be a good investment for you.' And all of a sudden, there is a $600 million gap that is filled overnight." In addition to these business connections, Thomas Frist's brother, Bill Frist, is a former U.S. Senate Majority Leader. And Thomas referred to George W. Bush as "a good friend." This old boys' network is precisely the kind of thing that rightly causes outsiders to worry about elite cohesion and control. There is space for newcomers like Chao, but despite all good intentions, the matrix of power remains overwhelmingly white and male.

At one United Way meeting, Frist witnessed a conversation between John Opel (then CEO of IBM, on whose board Frist also served) and another board member, Mary Gates. Gates was telling Opel how worried she was about her son, Bill, who had left Harvard to start a "little software company" in New Mexico. Frist became good friends with Mary Gates, and they watched Microsoft's rise together. "It's fascinating, those relationships," Frist said:

> *Bill Gates would give me—after he started becoming a rock star over the next 10 years—he would give me two days a year to go over to Philadelphia, Houston, wherever, and he would help draw in the people who end up setting up and institutionalizing those Tocqueville [societies].*

Bill Gates did this for Frist out of loyalty to his mother, which illustrates that elite networks and interlocking directorates not only benefit people in power but also *can* advance the common good. Vast amounts of influence are wrapped up in this matrix; it is the intentions and passions of leaders that determine how this power is used.

Fractures

I've painted a picture thus far of platinum leaders, each existing as the powerful center point of a complex network of connections. These networks overlap, interweave, and, as described earlier, often interlock—to form a broad national matrix of elite power that can be incredibly efficient in its efforts. This is not to suggest, however, that the entire cohort of society's leaders is on the same page. Far from it. Sometimes networks are not enough to bring together disparate agendas. Jim Owens knows this better than most.

Owens spent his entire career with Caterpillar, the world's leading manufacturer of construction and mining equipment, diesel and natural-gas engines, industrial gas turbines, and diesel-electric locomotives. But his strong ties to Caterpillar have not isolated him from the rest of the business community; his ties to Peter Peterson (former secretary of commerce and former CEO of Lehman Brothers) and other executives have given him a place at many tables. Owens serves on the boards of Alcoa and IBM as well as being a member of the Business Roundtable, the Business Council, and the Council on Foreign Relations. Having many of these loose affiliations, or what we might call "weak ties," can be, in fact, more useful than a few "strong ties," because they allow for a more diffuse network. In the words of sociologist Mark Granovetter, "Those to whom we are weakly tied are more likely to move in circles different from our own and will thus have access to information different from that we receive."[5]

However, loose ties bring with them the potential for fractures in the matrix of power—points at which communication and goal-achievement can break down. In 2009, Owens was on the President's Economic Recovery Advisory Board (PERAB). Since Caterpillar is based in Peoria, Illinois, he had met Senator—now President—Obama, and had liked him personally. Still, Owens was surprised when he was asked to join PERAB, because he had significant political differences with Obama, especially regarding trade and labor policy.

Owens had a PERAB meeting in Washington just a week before a Business Council conference that he was set to chair. Owens invited the president to attend an off-the-record session with the Business Council at the conference. Owens told him, "It's a great opportunity for you to roll up your sleeves and shake hands with the top hundred business figures in the country. . . . It would be a really good give-and-take opportunity for you early in your administration." The president agreed and also asked Owens if he could visit a Caterpillar plant in Peoria that same week. Owens expressed that this was not an ideal time for the president to visit Peoria, because factories there were going to be closed soon due to lack of demand, and significant layoffs were expected. But the president insisted. He was trying to get his Economic Stimulus Bill passed, and he wanted to give a speech in a manufacturing plant in America's heartland.

So Owens flew with the president on Air Force One to Peoria. He took the opportunity to make sure the president knew the employment situation at Caterpillar:

> *Mr. President . . . a lot of industry is in free fall, and it's going to get a lot worse. Don't hang your political hat on having unemployment improve, because it isn't going to happen in the near-term."* *I showed him all the tables, he's looking at it, and then I said, "I know you said in Virginia that if we can get the stimulus bill passed, Caterpillar won't have to lay off people. You have to understand: the two plants you are going to go to—all of our plants in Illinois—65 percent of everything they build is for international markets. So if the stimulus bill passes, it will have almost no impact on my ability not to lay off people. These plants are in free fall. There are going to be more layoffs before we stabilize and can begin hiring again. You just need to be aware of that.*

The president conveyed that he understood, but later Owens was shocked when, contrary to the briefing Owens had provided, President Obama said in his speech:

> *When they finally pass our [stimulus] plan, I believe it will be a major step forward on our path to economic recovery. And I'm not the only one who thinks so. Yesterday Jim, the head of Caterpillar, said that if Congress passes our plan, this company will be able to rehire some of the folks who were just laid off.*

Owens told me, "I about fell out of my fricking chair. . . . I point-blank told him that was wrong on the airplane. I *just* told him." On that same day, Owens was in a press conference and was asked directly whether what the president had said was true. "I had to be honest with our community," Owens said. "I tried to endorse a fiscal stimulus in general . . . and at the same time trying to be polite and saying that we were going to have to have layoffs." Owens is still not sure why the president directly contradicted what he had told him. His guess is that the president got caught up in reading from the teleprompter.

The incident was a top news story, because, to some, Owens had called the president a liar. Trying to repair the damage, Obama invited the press to his "off-the-record" meeting with the Business Council. Unfortunately this prevented honest dialog there, further blocking the communication lines. Fractures like these, exacerbated by media attention, can disrupt the collective action of platinum leaders. The politics of networks mean that disagreements, misunderstandings, and disparate agendas can complicate even seemingly simple partnerships.

ACT PERSONALLY, BUT THINK INSTITUTIONALLY

The United States has always been the nation of the individual. Go West, young man. Pull yourself up by your bootstraps. Anyone can live the American dream. But in truth, this nation depends even more on strong institutions. We need the Navy, health-care systems, and companies like Caterpillar to provide infrastructure. A business executive cannot get things done on a major scale without a corporation where roles are differentiated and complex activities coordinated to bring goods to market. A scholar lacks funding and legitimacy without her university. A politician calling for change has little influence outside of a governing body. Even in the indiscriminate Internet age, one man can gain the attention of some, but a media institution can demand the attention of everyone. In this country, it's the powerful few who grace our magazine covers. But in reality, it's their institutions that should be the centerfold.

Individuals are not helpless slaves to soulless corporations. Most certainly, people can—and do—impact their own institutions. Personal relationships and principles can change the course even of institutional behemoths. Institutions like the U.S. Navy—with over 200 years of traditions and mores—might seem impossible to change, yet individuals like Marty Evans who are tethered to them can leverage their influence to move mountains. They do this by acting personally but thinking institutionally. While collusions (such as being brother to a senator) and tensions (such as disagreeing with the president's economic policy while serving on his economic council) are unavoidable within the matrix of power, success comes to those who wisely navigate their networks to direct power to the right places.

Both strong and weak ties connect these individuals and provide them with entrée to power across disparate sectors. That's how Richard Parsons' career started in the office of Governor Nelson Rockefeller and climaxed at the helm of the largest media company in history.

CHAPTER 2

Leadership Begins at 20

Beyond Bootstraps
and Boarding School

When most people think of powerful leaders, they think of someone like Bob Haas. His great-great-granduncle was Levi Strauss, the legendary businessman who first manufactured blue jeans. By the time Haas took the reins of the company, leadership of Levi Strauss & Co. had remained in family hands for at least four generations. While growing up, his father was the CEO, and the Haases vacationed every summer with the family of Robert McNamara, who would become secretary of defense. Haas told me that this early and regular exposure to people at the higher levels of society kept him from being starstruck as he ascended his own professional heights.

Certainly this sounds to most of us like a charmed life. After all, when you vacation with the secretary of defense, you doubtless also have the best health care, the finest education, and unmatched opportunities. But as it turns out, a privileged childhood is actually a poor predictor of becoming a senior leader. Bob Haas is, in fact, the exception to the rule. I found that virtually all formative experiences in the early lives of leaders are more ordinary than extraordinary.

Before great leaders reach the halls of power, they are "protoleaders," young people with talent and opportunity but yet untested. It is still up to them to make the most of what resources they possess. Some, like Haas, are born with lots of resources. More typical, however, is the life of John Mendelsohn.

THE PATH TO THE TOP

Dr. Mendelsohn, a cancer specialist, is educated and proficient on the latest medical research, can manage an enormously large institution, and can also dine with royalty and schmooze with wealthy donors. But his current high-profile life is a far cry from his childhood in Ohio. Mendelsohn's parents were squarely within the middle class; his dad worked as a retailer, and his mom was a homemaker. His early ambitions were modest—he simply wanted to do well in school, excel at tennis, and be a "good person," as he describes it.

Mendelsohn's horizons expanded as he took advantage of opportunities that came his way early on. He did well enough in high school to be admitted to Harvard (but, he confessed to me, it was not nearly as selective back then). He began by studying physics and chemistry but switched to medicine as he embraced, in his words, "a more liberal-arts approach to life." In medical research, he found the opportunity to combine a zeal for scientific discovery with a love for people.

Mendelsohn wanted to gain research experience, and he was tipped off that a new member of the biology faculty, James Watson, might be looking for an assistant. Mendelsohn followed the lead and landed the job. Watson was not your average new hire; in 1953, he and Francis Crick had modeled the double helix of DNA, a discovery that would go on to earn them a Nobel Prize. Not a bad start for Mendelsohn's career.

Between graduating college and starting medical school, Mendelsohn wanted to travel, so he secured a Fulbright scholarship to study biochemistry in Scotland. "I did some research and study," he said, "but most of the time, I traveled and hitchhiked, and I read *War and Peace* and did all the things I didn't do while I was . . . in Dr. Watson's laboratory for two years." After medical school, Mendelsohn completed his residency in Boston and obtained a research fellowship at Washington University Medical School in St. Louis. He looked well set for a successful, if unremarkable, career in medicine.[1]

Mendelsohn might have continued on this track had he not been willing to take a risk when he received an unexpected offer. While at Washington University, he was invited to help start a new medical school at the University of California–San Diego. He remembers his colleagues telling him, "It's going to be terrible. You're going to have to start new courses and teach, and you can't do your own research." But the opportunity excited him, so he took the ill-advised plunge. Mendelsohn moved to California and began building a new cancer center at UCSD. While there, he sharpened his administrative acumen and developed a reputation as an academic entrepreneur. Following a stint at Memorial Sloan-Kettering Cancer Center in New York, Mendelsohn was tapped for the presidency of the University of Texas M.D. Anderson Cancer Center. A few years into his tenure, M.D. Anderson surpassed Sloan-Kettering as the world's top cancer hospital, and virtually everyone credits Mendelsohn's leadership with spurring its ascent to the top.

Like Mendelsohn, most leaders start out with fairly normal childhoods, and they come from a wide variety of racial, socioeconomic, and geographic backgrounds. White males from better-off backgrounds do, indeed, start with an advantage over others, and a college education is important. As protoleaders grow, their life stories converge in college—only a miniscule number of leaders in this study did not earn a bachelor's degree. After graduating, protoleaders' paths diverge into their different fields of engagement, but they converge again around certain high-status institutions—graduate schools, consulting firms, law offices, and large corporations—where they build up records of successful performance, invest in relationships, and prepare to take advantage of opportunities that come their way.

OVERCOMING DISADVANTAGE

Hidden within the seeming normalcy of John Mendelsohn's life story are some of the first advantages he enjoyed—the benefits of race, class, gender, and a supportive family. In the United States, inequality has historically been largely about race, and the statistics show that racial and ethnic minorities are grossly underrepresented among America's leadership—91 percent of the leaders I interviewed were white, and this tracks with other quantitative examinations of the upper reaches of society. However, it is important to keep in mind that demography determines part of this. In the average birth year for the participants in this study, 1950, 87 percent of the babies born in the United States were white, while 13 percent were racial and ethnic minorities. Nonetheless, race entails a number of potential opportunities and obstacles.

Being on the Outside

Leaders with minority backgrounds face numerous unique challenges, especially the participants in this study, who largely grew up during the Civil Rights Movement. One African American described for me what he calls the "black tax": "The black tax is that you have to go earlier, stay later, run twice as fast to stay even. Don't complain about it, just do it; that's the black tax." Others recounted to me stories of shame and disgrace: teachers who believed that blacks were inherently inferior and should not strive for a profession beyond the rank of chauffeur; clubs and bars where white colleagues could enter with ease but they were not welcome. While we have today largely moved beyond such blatant discrimination, racial minorities still suffer numerous disadvantages. And we still have a long way to go in terms of equal representation in leadership positions. The college presidency, for example, is still the realm of 61-year-old married white men. Only 13 percent of college presidents are racial or ethnic minorities, and only a quarter are women.

Maryana Iskander, the COO of Planned Parenthood Federation of America, immigrated to the United States from Egypt as a child but, looking back, did not consider her race to be a barrier. For her, gender was the larger challenge. After capturing a veritable triumvirate of academic accolades—a Truman Scholarship, a Rhodes Scholarship, and the Paul and Daisy Soros Fellowship for New Americans—she entered Yale Law School.

Shortly after enrolling, Iskander found she could not get any attention from her professors. At first, she said, "I didn't associate it with gender at all. And so [a classmate and I] started this study, and I realized that . . . the institution had a problem, and it wasn't me. . . . The problem was that the faculty rewarded a set of behaviors that correlate with male behaviors." She described a scenario to explain her point:

> *A woman comes to office hours. Like me, she's done all her home-work, she's totally prepared, she wrote down her five questions, and she doesn't want to waste your time. . . . And you . . . tick-tick-tick answer her questions, and then she leaves. That's it. That was the interaction. A guy comes in, he hasn't read anything, he's not prepared. But he's there to talk about, I don't know what, and you're engaged. And you ask him where he went to college.*

*And then you ask him what he's interested in. . . . And then 20
minutes later, he has a relationship with you. And, then he has a
teaching assistant job with you, and then you recommend him to
go to the Supreme Court.*

A big part of the problem, according to Iskander, was the demographic makeup of the faculty. In her words, "Some of the older male
faculty were uncomfortable with . . . being alone with female students.
And so you can't build a relationship across that distance." It is not
only in law that women fall behind. Iskander was one of many women
in my study who felt the inequality of treatment and opportunities.
In fact, one of the few female CEOs of a Fortune 500 firm talked at
length off the record about her frustration with the old boys' club. Of
all the demographic skews of this group of 550 informants, the gender
imbalance is proportionally the most egregious. Only 12 percent of the
leaders I interviewed were female, despite the fact that they represent
half of the population.[2] In certain fields, the representation of women
is even less. Ten percent of the business leaders I interviewed were
women. In nonprofit life, the gender imbalance is not as bad (29 percent
of nonprofit executives are women). Clearly, women still struggle to gain
their place at the top.

The challenges that they face are manifold. Some, like the gender wage gap, are overt. The Institute for Women's Policy Research
found that the wage gap is most pronounced in the highest-prestige
categories—CEOs and financial managers. Female financial managers
earn 66 percent of what their male counterparts do, while among
CEOs, the proportion is still only 69 percent.[3] Moreover, the expectation that people who rise to the top must put work ahead of family
disproportionately affects women.

But not all the problems faced by female leaders receive as
much press as these. Recently, psychologists studying hiring practices in academia have shown that the relatively more "communal"
adjectives—"sympathetic," "helpful," and the like—are used more frequently in letters of recommendation for women and make women
less likely to be promoted than the "agentic" adjectives—"confident,"
"aggressive," and the like—which are applied more frequently for men.
The end result is that fewer equally qualified women are given the
glowing reviews needed to get to the top.[4]

Unequal Resources

According to scholars such as Harvard professor Robert Putnam, class—not race—is the major dividing line of inequality in the United States.[5] Proportionally speaking, this is true. Those like Bob Haas who were raised near the top of the social ladder are significantly over-represented among senior leaders relative to their prevalence in the general population.[6] Despite this disproportion, many more leaders in this study—59 percent of them—were drawn from the middle class, and a significant minority grew up in homes where one or both parents worked blue-collar jobs (28 percent) or were near poverty (4 percent).[7] Despite their lower- and working-class backgrounds, some overcame their circumstances through the aid of generous mentors, while others benefited from athletic or academic scholarships to college. In fact, these two items—support from benefactors and institutions of higher learning—serve as key equalizers for protoleaders who grew up in disadvantaged backgrounds. In other words, generosity, at both the individual and the institutional level, makes a big difference.

Poverty has sharpened the business acumen of a surprising number of corporate titans and financial tycoons. The private sector is often a sound choice for protoleaders in poverty. Half of the leaders I interviewed who grew up in poverty had earned a business degree, compared to only 21 percent of participants from more financially stable homes.

Family Challenges

One thing Bob Haas, John Mendelsohn, and Maryana Iskander have in common with the majority of other leaders I interviewed is that they came from households with two loving parents. This is an especially significant finding, because over the past half-century, the number of children born into single-parent homes has skyrocketed. Between 1960 and 2000, the percentage of children living with a single parent increased from 9 to 26 percent. Between 1980 and 2008, the percentage of children born to single mothers increased from 18 percent to 41 percent. Along the same lines, children growing up without both biological parents were twice as likely to be poor, to have a child out of wedlock, not to graduate from high school, or to have behavioral and psychological problems. Other studies have shown that children growing up with both of their biological parents do better on a host of indicators than those who do not. Children born to a never-married parent fare the worst. The critical factor seems to be the amount of time that they spend with their parents, which partially explains why the Platinum Study sample group had more than its fair share of firstborns—6 in 10—as compared to just over 4 in 10 firstborns in the cohort of children born in 1950.[8]

EARLY INFLUENCES

Early upbringing and the ascribed characteristics of race, ethnicity, and gender help us to understand why some have an easier time ascending to professional heights, but there is much more to the story. Leaders are made, not born, and though many talk about luck or serendipity, they are quick to add, as one oil executive did, that "certainly, putting myself in the position to have that luck was an important part of it as well," and "Once you're given that opportunity . . . you've got to make the most of it." Protoleaders distinguish themselves from their peers by taking advantage of their opportunities at every step along the way.

Self-Made Leaders

Kevin Plank showed an entrepreneurial streak early on: "I read stories about Carnegie, Mellon, and Vanderbilt, and the industrial revolution, and I wanted to be a captain of industry," the still-boyish Plank told me from his office in Baltimore. He had wanted to "be a part of building something greater than myself." The youngest of five boys and a competitor from the beginning, Plank had a zest for work. Just like many other platinum leaders, Plank developed a deep reservoir of energy from a very early age that he drew from to set himself apart from his peers. He first observed this one winter morning as a seven-year-old when Plank tried to rally his friends to shovel neighborhood driveways for cash. His friends were unwilling to give up their snow day, but it was a no-brainer for Plank, "We're getting $15 for this, are you crazy? We should be doing twice as much work!" he said.

His entrepreneurial energy continued into high school, when he started selling bracelets with his brothers outside a Grateful Dead concert. He made such a profit that he realized he was "good at [reading] people, feeling them out, knowing where to go, just kind of having a sense for knowing how to sell a product." In college, Plank ran "Cupid's Valentine," a rose-delivery service, from his dorm room. He ended up with seven phone lines coming into his dorm room, 50 drivers, and 1,200 dozen flowers delivered. He put away $17,000, which eventually became seed money for Under Armour, his most successful venture.

Unlike John Mendelsohn, who was always in the top 5 percent of his class, or Maryana Iskander, who graduated magna cum laude, Plank never felt at home in the classroom: "I've never felt like the smartest kid in the room, but I always felt like I could overcompensate with my ability to outwork anybody." He told me he did not apply himself in school and was kicked out of one school when he was 15 because he spent too much time partying and not enough time on his school work. He was a bit of a rebel, getting arrested several times for reasons including, in his words, "fights, jumping in a pool, driving cars before I had a license." As he reflected on these incidents, he noted, "I have always been kind of a knucklehead." Nothing serious seemed to come out of these indiscretions, though he told me he went to three different high schools.

His real passion in school was sports. In high school, he wrestled and played lacrosse and football. He excelled the most in football, playing on a varsity squad at Fork Union Military Academy, a high school known for developing first-rate athletes. He was disappointed when he was not recruited by the colleges he had hoped for and ended up playing as a walk-on for the University of Maryland at College Park. He was a fullback and a linebacker, and he captained the special-teams squad. He is especially proud of the fact that he never missed a practice in five years.

Although he was not a star athlete, there is no question that Plank's football career advanced his later career trajectory. Under Armour's marketing department proudly tells how the company's founder got tired of changing his sweat-soaked undershirt during football practices. He decided to invent athletic gear that would wick the moisture away rather than just absorb it. He set up headquarters in the basement of his grandmother's Georgetown townhouse and began building a business that would grow to over a billion dollars and attain worldwide reach just 15 years later.

But there is another story that does not get near as much press as Plank's sweat-soaked epiphany. The success of his company was not just dependent on his experience as a football player or his willingness to take risks. He also made very judicious use of his network of connections. When he first started Under Armour, he reached out to former college-football teammates who had entered the NFL for their help and endorsements. And he called every equipment manager in the Atlantic Coast Conference, trying to convince them to buy into his idea. His original business partners in the new venture were people he had connected with through high school or college sports. He maximized his network connections to catalyze not just his advance or the start of a company, but an entire industry of performance apparel.

Unlike most platinum leaders, Kevin Plank did not rise through a large institution. He did not go to graduate school, and he did not start at the bottom, working his way up. Instead, he gambled nearly everything for his entrepreneurial vision. Plank spent his last $500 on seven prototype microfiber fabrics. He was sleeping on his grandmother's couch and eating meals at home, because, in his words, "I was dead broke." Still, by building a good team, having a good product, and positioning himself strategically in the market, Plank has been able to build his *own* institution and lead it to one of the most successful ventures in the apparel market over the past two decades. Platinum leaders know that they need institutions. Sometimes, they just make their own.

Pierre Omidyar, the founder of eBay, remembered being under a great deal of pressure from his mother to go to business school, even as he was building eBay, because she saw that as the path to success: "Finally, I remember one day I said, 'Mom . . . I have six MBAs working for me. So, that's enough. I'm not going to go to business school.' That was the last time she said anything about [it]." Sometimes the rogues do reach the top.

Some activities—such as early employment, athletics, scouting, and student government—showed up again and again in my discussions. Working early is less common among leaders from minority backgrounds, though. Only 10 percent of minority leaders mentioned working before the age of 18, as compared to 28 percent of nonminorities. This may indicate that fewer people were willing to hire young people of minority backgrounds as these leaders were growing up, or it could simply indicate that they grew up without the expectation that they would hold a job early in life. A surprisingly large proportion of leaders were varsity athletes—41 percent in high school and 23 percent in college. There were also many Eagle Scouts in our study, and 58 percent of the leaders mentioned participating in student government in either high school or college.

While a record of early achievement is an important part of the leader's story, it comes with its own set of hazards. When leaders seem to peak very young, before their own sense of identity has fully formed, this can cause a sense of displacement and loss. Some who went to college early had depressive experiences. One said he got "too far over my skis," lacking the maturity needed to really get the most out of college experiences.[9] The Rhodes scholarship singles out promising protoleaders just out of college for a unique opportunity to study at Oxford. However, the prestige of the program and the high expectations placed on the Scholars lead many (including Maryana Iskander, who was a Rhodes Scholar before she attended Yale Law School) to have trouble at Oxford and experience failure for perhaps the first time.

COLLEGE AND BEYOND: CONTINUING THE LIBERAL ARTS LIFE

Although we often assume that the most direct path to national influence goes through major academic universities (such as Ivy League schools), nearly two-thirds of the leaders I interviewed attended schools that are not considered elite institutions. Further, recent studies have revealed that attending a selective college does not make a significant difference in future earning power.[10] Virtually everyone in the study graduated from *some* college. Only 3 percent of the leaders I interviewed did not graduate, and among this small group, most attended for some amount of time.

Even though it's not necessary to get a degree from one of the country's highest-ranking schools, there is some value in attending them. Many of the 14 percent of my informants who graduated from Ivy League institutions and the 22 percent that graduated from other elite universities lauded the intellectual training they received at these schools. But the real value of an elite education is in the social and cultural capital that students acquire while there.[11] Social capital relates to the value individuals receive from their involvement in certain networks; cultural capital deals with the acquisition of assets such as dress, manners, cultural knowledge, and education. Both are essential for advancement, and universities are a key location for gaining these necessary forms of capital.[12]

Top-tier schools typically do a better job than others in giving students a familiarity with the unspoken expectations of elite life— something that is elusive for most aspiring leaders. The CEO of a consulting firm told me that when he first arrived at Harvard, he felt terribly out of place: "I had classmates who had been on Wall Street. I didn't know where Wall Street was. Everybody, it seemed, in class knew how to tie ties. . . . They were by-and-large more East Coast." One day, a female classmate pulled him aside after class and told him that people were making fun of him for wearing white socks with dark pants. He was confused; it hadn't remotely occurred to him that his clothing mattered. He learned from that lesson, and he still looks back on his time at Harvard as an important time of socialization into leadership.

Another main advantage of elite universities is that their large endowments and significant research dollars generate more opportunities for students to work with leading scholars through research apprenticeships. Places like Harvard have a better track record of creating opportunity for people like John Mendelsohn, who had just decided to study premed when he knocked on the door of future Nobel Laureate James Watson to become an undergraduate research assistant in his genomics laboratory. Connections formed with classmates are important, too. The reason that Bob Haas's family vacationed with Secretary McNamara was that he and Haas's father had attended Berkeley and Harvard Business School together.

While the majority of leaders in this study did not attend a top-tier school for undergraduate life, experiences in graduate school concentrated around just a few institutions. Nearly two thirds of the leaders who received graduate degrees went to a top-10 graduate school in their field. Of those who earned a graduate degree, almost 3 in 10 earned a business degree, the most popular of the graduate degrees in the sample group. Six of the leaders in the study had graduated Harvard Business School between 1980 and 1983 alone, and eight of the current Fortune 100 CEOs also went to HBS, more than double any other business school.

Twenty-two percent of those in this study had earned a law degree and nearly a quarter of the graduate degrees that the leaders interviewed had earned were doctorates.

Even at the advanced level of specialization that graduate school requires, however, it is still important to platinum leaders to live a liberal arts lifestyle. For instance, even though a quarter of the leaders had earned doctorates or PhDs, only one-sixth pursued a traditional job path as a professor. Many leveraged their graduate degrees in unorthodox ways. Instead of narrowing their areas of specialization, they deployed their credentials to expand their expertise.

For most platinum leaders, this fork in the road appeared during or soon after graduate school. They began to separate from the herd by keeping a broad, liberal arts approach to life while continuing to develop the skills related to their fields. The ability to maintain a generalist orientation—one that sees beyond the narrow scope of the specialist—while increasing mastery in a specific field distinguishes platinum leaders from mere scholars.[13]

The most impressive leaders I studied tried out jobs in unfamiliar fields, acquired new skills, and developed a taste for a cultural cosmopolitanism. They became increasingly knowledgeable in all divisions of the companies they worked for, not just their own departments. Sometimes this came through structured programs, like management-trainee initiatives, but often it stemmed from their own intellectual curiosity and willingness to try new things, even as they were relative newcomers themselves. Through these boundary-crossing experiences within their own respective organizations, protoleaders develop a sufficiently large stage on which to act and build a record of successful performance. They might also impress a future mentor higher up on the ladder, who would shape not just their values and dreams, but their opportunities and careers. These older elite leaders would recognize their own ambitions in the fresh faces of the energetic protoleaders and respond with a willingness to personally invest. Sometimes a protoleader makes his way up the ladder rung by rung, but sometimes, in pursuit of the liberal arts lifestyle, his career advancement will look much more scattershot. In recounting his own looping career, one executive ruefully stated, "If you're successful, people say you're a Renaissance man. If you're unsuccessful, people say you're a dilettante, and the only difference is the outcome."

For Dan Bartlett, moving to Austin to attend the University of Texas changed his life. Bartlett had grown up in a small town in rural Texas, "where expectations weren't high." His move to the state's capital meant that alongside his realization that he had leadership skills lay leadership opportunities. He started looking for a job, and fortuitously, he found employment at the Texas State Capitol. There, he befriended a colleague who then left to work with Karl Rove & Company, a political-consulting firm in town. His friend sent word that they needed more help, and at age 20, Bartlett decided that he would try it out, since "it paid more than what I was making at the capitol." His work at Rove's Firm took him deeper into politics, drawing him into George W. Bush's first campaign for the Texas governorship. Eventually, he developed a close relationship with the candidate, which resulted in his becoming one of President Bush's closest confidants in the White House. Had he not moved to Austin, he would not have followed the same upward trajectory that took him to the White House.

Bartlett's experience illustrates a broader point that emerged from this study: location matters. People who grow up in large cities have a higher chance of reaching the top than those who grow up in rural areas. Fifty-seven percent of those I interviewed grew up in one of the 51 metropolitan areas with populations of over 1 million people in the 2010 census, even though these urban areas represented only 42 percent of the country's population in 1950.[14] The deck is stacked in the favor of urban protoleaders; living in cultural, political, and business centers provides them with more opportunities in their rise to prominence. Rurally raised platinum leaders tended to move to the city as young adults. In fact, 34 percent of respondents had moved into one of these metropolitan areas (having been born outside of them), while only 5 percent moved *out* of the country's major cities.[15] For people like Bartlett, moving to the city opened their eyes to bigger possibilities, which in turn enabled them to achieve more than did their siblings, many of whom were content to "get married, get a job in the mill, and make enough money to buy a car," to echo one business executive.

Broadening one's perspective was not just a domestic affair, however. For many of these leaders, young adulthood also entailed international travel. Sixty-five percent traveled for the first time between the ages of 16 and 30.[16] Bob Haas, who served in the Peace Corps in the Ivory Coast, told me that his time there made a significant impact on him: "I would say I frequently draw on the experiences I had in the Peace Corps and, even more particularly, in observing village life and activities in a small West African community, and thinking about interacting with people making difficult decisions."

Respondents were also significantly more likely than the general public to speak a second language. This underscores the importance of an early development of global awareness.[17] One university president shared with me how his international experience as a young man broadened his view on the world:

> When I was in the Middle East for a year and a half, I used to go into work very early, between 4:30 and 5:00. . . . The people who were on the road were people who were on their way to work. There were truckloads full of [immigrants]. Usually Bangladesh, India, Philippines. Day laborers. . . . And what struck me . . . is what people will do for a job. How hard people are willing to work. And if you can see the humanity in the world that's around you, then it certainly affects your leadership style and the way to manage people.[18]

Institutional Loyalty

While protoleaders are ambitious and always looking for new opportunities, they also tend to be loyal to the institutions they work for. Over half of this study's respondents had worked in the same company for the majority of their careers, and 69 percent were insiders to their first position at the top, a statistic that goes against the idea that senior executives are typically drawn from the outside.

The trend was not as strong, however, for *minority* protoleaders in large institutions. While 72 percent of whites were insiders to their first position, only 54 percent of racial and ethnic minorities followed such a path to the top, being less likely to be promoted up the chain of command to their leadership position.[19] Also of interest, ethnic and racial minorities were significantly more likely to mention having a specific mentor than were whites—71 percent of minorities I interviewed mentioned having a mentor, in contrast to 49 percent of whites. For leaders from minority backgrounds, who face the challenge of overcoming prejudice while establishing their reputation, investing in a relationship with a supportive mentor seems to provide the more reliable path to the top than relying on an institutional escalator.

Making the Most of Youth

By the time Dan Bartlett moved with President Bush to the White House as deputy assistant to advisor Karen Hughes (later to become communications director and counselor to the president), he had earned his fair share of confidence. Still, he told me that a significant challenge for him was that "most of the people who were my peers were at least a generation, if not two generations, older than I was." He did not actively try to hide his age, but at the same time, "I wasn't offering [it], because I didn't want them to look at me differently." Like Iskander, who became an executive at Planned Parenthood at 31, Bartlett quickly found himself far ahead of others in his age group, with people wondering whether he was up to the challenge. He told me about one interaction he had with Secretary of Defense Donald Rumsfeld, who was 39 years his senior:

> We're all waiting outside the Oval Office, and there was some decision that there was clearly a split view of. And so it's Powell, Rumsfeld, Cheney, Rice, Hadley, myself, and Andy Card. And the president's on the phone in the Oval Office with the door closed, so we're all waiting, cooling our jets. But Rumsfeld had done his homework; he knew I was on one side, and not his. And so he turns to me, and says, "Danny"—and remember, this is the guy who was [decades earlier] the youngest chief of staff, the youngest secretary of defense ever—and he goes, "Remind me how old you are?" And I go, "Well, Mr. Secretary, I'm 34 years old." "Good golly!" He's like, "I've got suits that are older than you, son!" It was kind of like, "Don't [mess] with me." And I said, without missing a beat, "Yes, Mr. Secretary, and this must be one of them." Powell was like, "Ooh, Rummy, he got you back!" So I kind of threw a brush back to him, saying, "Don't [mess] with me, either."

Leadership is not handed down, and there is not one right path to make it to the top. Does it help to be a Harvard legacy or the godchild of a CEO? Of course, but it is not necessary. The accumulated advantages of race, class, gender, supportive parents, academic success, and extracurricular involvement all help a protoleader, but the key time in a protoleader's development is her midtwenties. This is when the unique passions, skills, or connections that protoleaders have can be turned into a career, just as Kevin Plank turned his passion for sports into a new product and John Mendelsohn used his training and spirit of adventure to launch a new medical school. The best way parents can groom their children for success is to let them develop passions and perseverance through the normal challenges and trials of childhood. They don't need a silver spoon; they need the right mix of upbringing, opportunities, grit, luck, and drive in order to prime themselves for a leadership position at the top.

CHAPTER 3

More Breadth, Less Depth

Catalyzing Your Leadership

At age 23, Tom Johnson moved his wife and newborn son to the nation's capital with a newly minted degree from Harvard Business School—and little else. Johnson, from Macon, Georgia, had humble roots and had made it this far through hard work and the goodwill of the editor-in-chief of the *Macon Telegraph*, Peyton Edison. Edison had taken a 14-year-old Johnson under his wing when Johnson needed work to help support his family. He had such faith in Johnson that he paid for him to attend the University of Georgia—as long as the young man would work at the *Telegraph* not only summers, but also during the school year (despite the two-hour drive from the university). After Johnson graduated with a degree in journalism, Edison helped him attend Harvard Business School. After living in Boston, Johnson's wife Edwina was uneager to return to Macon, so Johnson applied for a brand-new program started in 1964 by President Lyndon B. Johnson called the White House Fellowship. The fellowship would take a dozen or so young professionals and give them secondary but meaningful positions in the White House for one year with hopes to "strengthen the Fellows' abilities and desires to contribute to their communities, their professions, and their country."[1] Johnson was interested primarily because, "I felt that as a person who wished to become a leader in . . . journalism, there is no topic as important as government." He had little idea what was in store for him.

One of the commissioners who made the selection during the fellowship's competitive admission process was John Oakes, the editor of the *New York Times*. Oakes must have seen promise in young Johnson, because he told him, "You know, Mr. Johnson, I think one day you will become the publisher of a major metropolitan newspaper." With this recommendation, Johnson was accepted into the program, where he worked under Press Secretary Bill Moyers. During this year, Johnson formed a very close relationship with President Johnson and remained in various positions in the administration until the president left office.[2]

I interviewed Johnson in 2009 in his Atlanta home, where he and Edwina talked with me for hours, telling me in turn humorous and tragic stories of his life of leadership. Yes, Johnson had retired in Atlanta, only 90 miles from his hometown. But he had taken the long way back, coming by way of (among other cities) Los Angeles, where he had served as the publisher and CEO of the *Los Angeles Times*. His return to Georgia had been at the invitation of the state's favored son, Ted Turner, to serve as the president of CNN's newsgroup. In this role, Johnson had ushered America through the Persian Gulf War. CNN was the only organization providing a live newsfeed out of Baghdad; people all over the world (President Bush included) were relying on the network for up-to-the-minute information. This established CNN as a global news organization. Looking back, Johnson credited his full life to the White House Fellowship:

> *My perspective was that of a person who was seeing the world through a prism that was largely focused on Macon, that town right in the middle of Georgia. . . . The window on the world for me was opened further by my undergraduate education at University of Georgia and by my graduate education at Harvard Business School. But nothing prepared me for the type of experience I had as a White House Fellow. . . . I don't think there's any chance [without the fellowship] that I ever would have become the executive assistant to President Johnson, publisher of the* Los Angeles Times, *or chairman and chief executive of CNN. So this was an unbelievably transforming experience.*

This kind of a catalytic experience is what growing companies and ambitious young people everywhere are trying to construct. Leadership development is a hot field, as organizations seek to train their next generation for oncoming challenges. But it is hard to pin down exactly what it takes to develop a leader. Most would agree that leadership is a combination of talent and training. But can leadership really be taught? Thomas Cronin, a former White House Fellow and former president of

Whitman College, gives this description of leadership training: "My own belief is that students cannot usually be taught to be leaders. But students, and anyone else for that matter, can profitably be exposed to leadership, discussions of leadership skills and styles, and leadership strategies and theories."[3]

By this theory, the key to any leadership development program is to give people the opportunity to *experience* successful leadership—up close and personal.

For Tom Johnson, this experience was found in the White House Fellowship. While the program has hurled many upwards—including Secretary of State Colin Powell and Secretary of Labor Elaine Chao—it is not the only catapult available. Among the most impressive leaders I interviewed, many have had a singular experience that elevated their early leadership successes and propelled them into elite circles. For some, it has been winning a Rhodes Scholarship, speaking at the World Economic Forum in Davos, or working on a successful presidential campaign. These transitional leadership experiences are what I call leadership catalysts. For most senior leaders, the presence of a catalyst is what takes the protoleader—an ordinary individual with a series of accumulated advantages—into a place where he can assume leadership of a major institution.

LEADERSHIP CATALYSTS

For the purposes of this study, a catalyst is either a program or a particular experience sponsored by a national institution that gives protoleaders the opportunity to develop a generalist mind-set, which is essential to leadership, and to connect with superior (elite) networks. Catalysts develop leaders by accelerating their comprehension of what is required to function in high-level positions and by stimulating their development. In a third of my interviews, leaders described a significant turning point—the kind that often occurs in catalysts like these. I also found that those who had mentioned turning points were more likely to have mentioned having a specific mentor or sponsor, suggesting a significant relationship between these turning points and the advisors who make them happen. In many cases, this mentor was someone the leader would not likely have met outside of the catalytic experience. And these turning points generally happen at a relatively young age; research suggests that the events and the decisions made in one's twenties and early thirties have a profound impact on the course of the rest of one's life.[4]

There are many programs, fellowships, and leadership development groups that claim to accomplish catalytic propulsion. Efforts by local governments and other organizations (such as the Southern California Leadership Network or the City Hall Fellows program) elevate the careers of protoleaders with varying degrees of success. A catalyst is a *targeted* program with a focus on propelling young people into the upper reaches of leadership. What distinguishes a catalyst (as I am qualifying it) is a very competitive admissions process, superior networks, and public recognition on a national scale. A true catalyst is not a career stepping stone; it's a career skyrocket.

While few programs command enough influence to be considered catalysts, they come in a wide variety. Catalysts are hosted within specific sectors (like business, government, or academia), but recipients do not necessarily remain in that sector over the long term. A Rhodes Scholarship, for example, is an academic catalyst in that it involves studying for a postgraduate degree at Oxford University. But Rhodes Scholars are not expected to remain in academia; the funding provides a broad and deep education through a life-changing experience. Many use the prestige of the program as an entry point to another field, because currency earned within a catalyst in one sector retains plenty of value elsewhere.

Programs

In academia, prestigious awards—like the Rhodes or Marshall Scholarship, the Fulbright Scholar Program, or National Science Foundation CAREER grants—operate as catalysts by distinguishing academics early in their careers and giving them coveted funding for travel, study, and research. Thousands of young Americans apply every year for only 32 Rhodes Scholarships, which send promising young people under the age of 25 to study for a post-graduate degree at Oxford University. Such scholars have the opportunity for an incomparable education before encountering the larger world. Not only is Rhodes a résumé pillar, but it gives young leaders a broader perspective. Alumni of the program say that at Oxford, they learn how to form good arguments and pierce through bad ones, to have "an intolerance of sloppy thought." "Oxford enables you to go deep," another scholar said. Army General Wesley Clark told me, "In a nutshell, the Rhodes Scholarship was, 'how to respect people from other cultures,' and the White House Fellowship was, 'how to deal with government and professionals.'" After serving as a Rhodes Scholar, said another leader, "I wasn't intimidated by the larger world."

Most professional fields also have established catalysts. This can be a top-ranked business school or a consulting or investment-banking development program. Others make the right connections through volunteering on a political campaign or serving in programs for young social entrepreneurs, like Ashoka or Echoing Green. Like a prestigious graduate program or postdoctoral program, these programs for young people offer them the opportunity to distinguish themselves from their peers.

But not all catalysts take years and significant tuition dollars to complete. For some, all it takes is a weekend. Attendance at an exclusive conference like the Aspen Institute, World Economic Forum, or Renaissance Weekends is another way young leaders gain entrée into elite networks. One of the hallmarks of these conferences is that they are hard to attain an invitation for, but once you are invited, you have easy access to attendees who, outside of the conference, would be beyond your reach. At Renaissance Weekends, for example, name tags for everyone except heads of state simply contain a first name. Even first timers can come across their idols in line for coffee and start a conversation.

One of the most exclusive conferences is the Bilderberg Group, a conference of only 100 to 140 invited guests from Western Europe and North America. In 1969, Vernon Jordan was the first African American to attend Bilderberg, and he has been a faithful attendee ever since. When he was originally invited by a professor at Harvard, Richard Neustadt, Jordan had made a career working with the NAACP and on voter education in the South. Jordan told me, "My whole concentration, my whole focus had been civil rights in the South. So Bilderberg became my window on the world. . . . It made me see a world that I virtually did not know existed." Through the Bilderberg Group, Jordan had entered the global elite, and he became an elite influencer in his own right:

I took Clinton to Bilderberg in 1991. He had never been, and these Europeans were saying, "Who is this guy, and where is Arkansas?"

I said, "He's going to be president." They said, "There's no way that's going to happen." A year and a half later, the steering committee met in March, and I had Clinton come over. They were stunned. And that has been professionally helpful.

Of course not everyone celebrates the exclusivity of these conferences (and indeed many other catalysts). Conferences like Bilderberg give power brokers the opportunity to establish policy behind closed doors, effectively cutting less privileged voices out of the process.

THE WHITE HOUSE FELLOWSHIP

I was introduced to the White House Fellowship (WHF) in 2008, when I served on its regional-selection panel in Washington, D.C. Impressed by the caliber of the applicants, I became increasingly curious about the scope and effect of the program. I was surprised, as a student of leadership, to have so little knowledge of it. The nonpartisan, year-long program assigns a small cohort of exceptional protoleaders to work as senior aides to top government officials such as the president, the first lady, the vice president, a cabinet secretary, or a member of the White House staff. It has operated out of the White House for nearly 50 years, and the alumni list is replete with prominent names from all fields of American life. Yet it has flown mostly under the radar every year, superbly training a new cohort of talented young people for American leadership.

As the vehicle for and goal of many ambitious men and women, the national government would seem like a natural setting for *many* catalysts. But because of bureaucracy and the democratic nature of American politics, there are no set pipelines to power when it comes to running for office or being appointed to a high-level position in government. In fact, catalysts themselves have relatively low success rates in placing participants into senior leadership positions. In other words, a catalyst is essential to a platinum leader's development, but not everyone who participates in a catalyst goes the distance.

The White House Fellowship, however, stands as an exception to this. Each year, approximately 30 candidates (down from 110 to 150 regional finalists) are brought in for final-round interviews. At this point, all the candidates are more-or-less equally qualified, so informal connections hold sway. According to multiple WHF commissioners I interviewed, the final selection is idiosyncratic—who connects with particular commissioners, who tells a funny joke over dinner, who is the best conversationalist. (All 30 are good enough to be selected.) From this group of national finalists, 12 to 19 are selected to become Fellows. When I studied the finalists who were not selected as Fellows, I found that 12 percent had gone on to become a CEO of a Fortune 500 firm or a similarly placed leader in another sector—a figure that demonstrates the high quality of these applicants. Astonishingly, however, when I studied the finalists who *had* been selected as White House Fellows, the percentage that then went on to such senior leadership positions was a much higher 32 percent.[5] At one point, then, the candidates are virtually indistinguishable. After the catalytic experience, however, Fellows are two and a half times more likely to reach the pinnacle of organizational life. Clearly, there is something about that one year that helps to bend the sharp angle of these young leaders' professional trajectories. I knew that this was indeed a program worth studying.

In order to learn how the White House Fellowship develops such leaders, I conducted the first extensive study of the program in its nearly 50-year history. This included a comprehensive survey of current and former Fellows and 100 interviews with former Fellows, directors, and commissioners who have been associated with the program.[6] Over the course of this study, I became more convinced that the White House Fellowship is the nation's premier leadership development program. While little known in the wider United States culture, the fellowship has been shaping the people who lead our country longer and more effectively than any other institution or program. It is an environment teeming with leadership life, giving a select few (the program has 683 alumni as of fall 2013) access to superior networks and the broad-minded perspective they need to direct a major enterprise.

The government official who supervises and (ideally) mentors a Fellow is known as the Fellow's "principal." Often Fellows attend meetings and travel with their principal and work on special projects in the office, department, or agency where they serve. Fellows also participate in an educational program consisting of seminars twice a week—including exclusive meetings with senior leaders—and several week-long trips, to explore policy issues both domestically and abroad.

The theory behind the White House Fellowship is that leadership is better caught than taught. In short, my research found that the Fellowship really *does* elevate the careers of protoleaders with demonstrated potential. And as leadership development programs proliferate, it emerges as a paradigm for success. I found four essential factors that lead to its incredible benefit: significant work, broadening education, a diverse cohort of peers, and public recognition. I have seen these four elements utilized to differing extents in other catalysts, but the White House Fellowship does the best job of combining them to give protoleaders the optimal investment in their future success.

Significant Work

One White House Fellow described his work assignment as an opportunity "to be able to sit in the cockpit of government but maybe not pull all the levers." Since Fellows are assigned to work for an individual cabinet officer or White House staff member, the kind and amount of work they get can vary greatly. But most Fellows I interviewed were satisfied by the challenge of their work. Jim Bostick wrote weekly activity reports and did advance work for the secretary of the Department of Agriculture. Marty Evans handled the Treasury secretary's weekly report to the president. In 1966, John Pustay spent a month in Vietnam studying anti-American sentiment. Bill Lennox helped the secretary of education develop an antidrug campaign. Wes Moore worked with USAID to consolidate U.S. foreign assistance. Peter Krogh negotiated with Vietnam protestors on behalf of the secretary of state. And in her role on the presidential transition team, Nicole Malachowski was responsible for creating an emergency plan in case of a crisis during President Obama's inauguration.

Regardless of what exactly a Fellow does, the work is important enough that these emerging leaders can demonstrate their talents, even in projects outside of their areas of expertise. To put it another way, the WHF gives Fellows an opportunity to actually work after years of learning how to work. "Even though I had gone to the Kennedy School of Government and had gotten my degree in public policy, I really didn't understand how the sausage was managed," one Fellow explained. As another Fellow put it, "I have come to a view that effective development of leadership has to include an experiential component. . . . There is no substitute for trying to *do* it. And the earlier you start trying to do it, the more likely you'll get good at it." John P. Kotter, a professor of organizational behavior at the Harvard Business School, would certainly agree:

> *Perhaps the most typical and most important [career experience for a leader] is significant challenge early in a career. Leaders almost always have had opportunities during their twenties and thirties to actually try to lead, to take a risk, and to learn from both triumphs and failures. Such learning seems essential in developing a wide range of leadership skills and perspectives.*[7]

Broadening Education

Kotter goes on to say that it is equally important to protoleaders to be broadened, "to grow beyond the narrow base that characterizes most managerial careers." The White House Fellowship achieves this through its education program. One Fellow summed up the program as "a year of extraordinary breadth and exposure and planting of questions." Another Fellow described the experience as "living in Disney World for a year, and you have a free pass to everything."

Twice a week, Fellows meet informally with recognized leaders from different fields. These off-the-record round-table conversations, which typically happen over lunch, cover a range of topics and are intentionally designed to introduce Fellows to issues and debates in fields ranging from architecture to zoology, from physics to filmmaking. Fellows gain access to a number of prominent leaders, including the president, Cabinet secretaries, and Supreme Court justices, and they meet with close to 100 of our nation's top leaders in fields such as business, the arts, science, media, and government. One Fellow pointed out, "It's some of the most famous people in the world from politics and business and journalism. And to talk to someone off-the-record for an hour and a half is a fantastic thing." Another Fellow said it was "an opportunity to engage . . . on a very personal basis, sitting in those lunches, asking questions, hearing their story, hearing what they did as young people and how they built toward Supreme Court justice, congressman, or senator."

Every Fellow I talked with could relate the story of at least one specific speaker, no matter how long ago their fellowship year had taken place. One Fellow described a particularly poignant conversation his class had had with a senator and his wife about the challenges of being a professional couple and raising children in Washington. The class of 1982 spent four hours with former President Nixon. One Fellow spoke about having lunch with Clarence Thomas just after his contentious appointment to the Supreme Court. Another recalled meeting with Jesse Jackson for five hours when he was running for president. Deanell Tacha recalled with wonder how New York Governor Nelson Rockefeller met with her class only days after the Attica Prison riot, which resulted in the death of 39 men as state police regained control of the prison at Rockefeller's order:

> *I watched a man who had power, money, influence—by all counts a leader—second-guessing himself, doing this amazing introspection about what he could have done differently at Attica. . . . I can still see his face; he had this great, craggy face, and it was just wild, and he clearly hadn't slept. I think anybody who was in that room that day, still to this moment, would be moved by this.*

This kind of access gives Fellows an unfiltered look into what life is like as a public leader. They learn how to get there, what to look forward to, and what to look out for.

The WHF's education program (both formal and informal) gives Fellows a broader understanding of the world around them as they gain intimate knowledge of the lives of prominent leaders and of complex policy situations. While their work for their principal gives them experience with (relatively) small-scale efforts, the education places their work in a larger context. Most graduate programs take someone deep into the minutiae of one particular field, but a catalyst opens leaders to wider knowledge of the world and their place in it.

A Diverse Cohort of Peers

Leadership isn't only "caught" from superiors but also from colleagues. The White House Fellowship is constituted by cohorts of 12 to 20 leaders from a variety of professional fields, and according to one Fellow that makes all the difference: "The other people are really what makes the fellowship a great thing. You meet lots of really interesting people who go on to do really interesting things. . . . It's really your peer group that has the biggest impact on you."

The WHF cohort has a unique dynamic. It is competitive and diverse—Army officers and public school administrators are placed in a cohort with investment bankers, lawyers, and artists. But it is also collegial; the Fellows become confidants during the intense year. In fact, 91 percent of Fellows surveyed described their relationships with their cohort Fellows as "friendship," compared to only 9 percent calling it a professional acquaintance. No one described it as a rivalry. One Fellow told me she was still in close touch with her class after having gone through the "shared crucible experience" of the fellowship the year before. Another Fellow said, "Through the experiences of other Fellows, you can exchange ideas with them about what they are learning in their experience and what they have learned prior to becoming a Fellow."

The original conception of the program envisioned a couple hundred Fellows each year. It has never grown that big, but one wonders if the small size creates an intimate setting with unique benefits. One Fellow told me she was enlightened by being in "close quarters" with different racial minorities.[8] Others—especially those who served in the early years of the program—mentioned to me that they had gained a greater perspective on not just racial but gender issues. One male Fellow came from working as an engineer at a company where "everyone was like [him]." Striking to him was his new exposure to talented women among his cohort; he "met the most talented women I think I'd met in my career at that point."

With their intense career focus, many Fellows come into the program with limited exposure to people on career paths that are similarly accelerated but on different tracks. They leave the program with a greater respect for other fields, having worked with parallel rising stars. In particular, the WHF changes its participants' perspective on the military. Thirty-seven percent of all Fellows have served in the military at some point. For many of the other Fellows, this is their first close and substantial interaction with a member of the armed services. I found that for every one additional member of a class of Fellows who had a military background, their civilian cohorts' confidence in the military grows exponentially.[9]

Doris Meissner came to the Fellowship in 1973 after working at the National Women's Political Caucus. She said, "One of the most valuable things about the year was to get to know career military people close up, because I would have to say, I probably never had met one." Meissner described her perspective:

> I'm not sure that I could say that I was open-minded about it. I think a lot of it was just lack of any contact, but it also was having a real attitude that was rampant during the 1960s that was a [hallmark] of the Vietnam era. . . . And so getting to know these people and understand how extraordinarily well-trained they were [by] the institutions that they worked in was a real eye-opener for me. And I continued to believe that if you look at, across the society, the single public institution . . . that invests the most in people as human capital continues to be the military.

After her fellowship year, Meissner remained in the Department of Justice and eventually became the commissioner of the Immigration and Naturalization Service. Meissner was in this role for seven years and dealt with several emergency immigration situations (including the placement of Elian Gonzalez) that required her to work with the Department of Defense. She was thankful for the WHF program, which "did prepare me also to have a sense of how to work with the Defense Department and how to work with the kinds of capabilities and mind-set that military people have."

Many of the Fellows I talked with had similar stories about changing their perspectives, and it is no surprise. Numerous studies have shown that wider exposure to people who are different from you gives you more tolerance for diversity.[10] While Fellows come from different sectors, they are alike in their ambition and diligence to their work. When they see similar qualities in people in different fields, from different backgrounds, and in different political parties, they gain greater respect for one another. This respect and understanding help them to make more thoughtful choices once they ascend to leadership.

Public Recognition

As important as what the Fellows learn from their work, the education program, and one another is the confidence they gain that they are on the fast track for professional success. The prestige of the program endows Fellows with respect and special opportunities rarely afforded young leaders. This extra push of public recognition is often what it takes to propel protoleaders to higher levels of accomplishment.

Not only does the fellowship's prestige give Fellows greater confidence in their own abilities, it signals to future employers that the Fellow is a standout and furnishes for them a respect equal to many years of job performance. One Fellow told me that it "compresses 15 or 20 years of life experiences into a very brief period of time."

For example, before becoming a White House Fellow, David Beré was the brand manager of Cap'n Crunch at Quaker Oats. He described himself as a "solid performer" but not a "superstar." Beré was accepted into the program on his second try and was surprised and embarrassed that Quaker Oats "made a little too big of a deal," including a press release, out of his selection. Thankful for their support, Beré returned to work at Quaker Oats at the end of his fellowship year. But now he had the attention of his superiors. Beré said that the program "kept my name in front of senior people so that it was easier to be recognized." He went on to become the president of the breakfast division before leaving Quaker Oats and eventually becoming the president and COO of Dollar General. Sometimes a catalyst is just what a protoleader needs to catch the boss's eye.

For David Neuman, the youngest Fellow in the history of the program, participation gave him something no other 23-year-old had. After the fellowship, Neuman used the connections he had made to get a place in NBC's management-training program. "As I was looking for job opportunities, it put me in a very elite category," Neuman explained. "People looked at me different. They returned my phone calls and letters. They paid attention to my candidacy for a job in a way that they wouldn't have before." Neuman went on to serve as the president of Walt Disney Network Television, chief programming officer of CNN, and president of programming for Current Media.

From Microscope to Telescope

When I met with Sanjay Gupta in his office at the CNN World Headquarters in Atlanta, it was easy to see how he has gained the trust of millions of Americans as CNN's chief medical correspondent. But without the White House Fellowship, the telegenic smile that is familiar in homes across America might have remained behind a surgeon's mask. Gupta started college at 16 and completed his undergraduate and medical degrees in six years. He took a year off during his neuroscience residency to take part in the WHF, expecting to go back afterwards and pick up where he had left off in his training. But the White House Fellowship, and in particular his work for his principal, First Lady Hillary Rodham Clinton, gave him new connections and an interest in media:

> *I literally had* [*an*] *epiphany. . . . I realized that both literally and figuratively, I had been living under a microscope. In the operating room, I'm using a microscope all the time, and my worldview was pretty closed. . . . And as much as we fancy ourselves as sort of more Renaissance citizens, especially neurosurgeons do, the irony is that so much of our training almost beats it out of us. . . . All of a sudden, I got this chance to run to this notion . . . that we could actually be more Renaissance, learn about a lot of different things. So I* [*went*] *from the microscope to the telescope.*

Gupta did go on to become a neurosurgeon; he works as the associate chief of staff at Grady Memorial Hospital in Atlanta and serves on the faculty of the Emory University School of Medicine. But he has influenced the most people through his work outside of the operating room, reporting on medical situations in the United States and during crises abroad.

Gupta is certainly not the only one who made a "microscope to telescope" transition through the White House Fellowship. A major result of a catalyst's broadening education is that people who have spent their lives up to that point developing skills in a specific field or subset are taught how to approach their work with a more generalist orientation. A well-designed leadership development program produces people who are capable of thinking about and understanding broad issues outside of the organizations they lead. Consider the words of Fred Benson, the president of the United States–New Zealand Council:

The education program . . . [led me to ask] questions about a broader range of subjects than I had been exposed to. . . . It changed my outlook. It internationalized my thinking, and it made me much more aware of our country domestically [and] its issues and problems. Candidly, I was a fairly successful, but narrow-minded, infantry colonel when I started the program. The program changed all of that.

Many leadership commentators (including White House Fellowship founder John Gardner) bemoan the rise of the specialist as drawing "most of our young potential leaders into prestigious and lucrative nonleadership roles."[11] Young people are trained in school to know everything about one field or subfield, but many are not trained in operating as a generalist. A generalist mind-set, however, is essential for leadership, and promoting it is the mission of liberal arts schools, which seek to educate young people through interdisciplinary and adaptive learning.[12]

One Fellow compared leaders to jugglers; in order to lead, you have to manage to keep multiple balls in the air. Another Fellow likened the intellectual variety of the White House Fellowship to "weight training and aerobic training for the brain."

The liberal arts emphasis of a true catalyst facilitates a leader's transition to a different sector afterward. Two out of five White House Fellows, for instance, switched fields after their fellowship year, trading on the prestige of the program to gain entrée into foreign territory. The fellowship inspired Diane Yu to make such a switch. She went into the White House Fellowship as a lawyer and was assigned to work with U.S. Trade Representative Clay Yeutter. "When I came out," Yu said:

I had a lot more confidence that I could take on a new challenge, a new position, a new field, a new industry, a new business. And as long as I worked as hard as I could and gained an understanding of what the mission and goals of the organization were, I had a reasonably good chance of doing alright in the new setting.

Yu moved from law to academia, eventually reaching her current position as chief of staff at New York University. Steve Poizner left the field of technology and prepared to run for governor of California. Many Fellows switched to work in government—rising from 22 percent in government before the fellowship to 38 percent afterwards—and Ron Lee, a West Point grad who took part in the fellowship in its first year, was asked to stay on after his fellowship and served as the assistant postmaster general.[13]

The liberal arts attitude that must be adopted by senior leaders is evident in the fact that out of 51 people in the study who had two distinct positions senior enough to qualify them for this study (that is, a CEO of a Fortune 1000 company or its analog in government and the nonprofit world), 86 percent shifted not only companies, but between completely different sectors. The most gifted leaders master the ability to organize and lead—talents and abilities that are moldable, even when moving from business to government or government to nonprofit life.

Cultural and Social Capital: The Golden Web

Catalysts like the White House Fellowship act like social and cultural capital investment firms, bringing protoleaders in contact with existing leaders willing to build relationships with them and help them learn to interact at their own level of seniority. Unlike economic capital, social and cultural capital cannot be transferred instantaneously from one person to another.[14] Building the trust that forms the basis for social capital takes time, as does building up one's base of knowledge, skills, abilities, and familiarity with valued cultural commodities.

General Wesley Clark remembers realizing this on a WHF-sponsored trip to New York: "We sat there in New York City with George Balanchine of the New York City Ballet. And see, for someone like me, to go to New York City and see George Balanchine—I mean, that's a long way from Fort Riley, Kansas."

Many Fellows looked back and chuckled over social faux pas they had made early in the Fellowship. When one Fellow saw that the door of the lead car of her principal's entourage was being held open, she assumed it was for her. She sat down inside only to realize the courtesy had been meant for her principal. Henry Cisneros, a Fellow in 1971, would go on to become the secretary of the Department of Housing and

Urban Development, but he had little experience in the upper echelons of government at the time of his fellowship. Cisneros ruefully related to me his ignorance of norms:

> *I remember having a green suit and I thought the right thing to do was to match it up with a light green shirt and a green tie. I must have looked like the jolly green giant or something. But I had absolutely no comparison. It was a very cheap suit, too; it was something I bought and thought I had a real bargain. . . . But these were people who wore Brooks Brothers and had been at the highest levels of Massachusetts politics—Boston and New York. [But] after a while, you learn.*

Knowing where to buy a suit and how to talk about ballet are examples of the kind of cultural capital that protoleaders need to collect in order to feel at home in top circles. For those who don't learn these finer points growing up, programs like the White House Fellowship provide an essential tutorial on the hidden curriculum of elite life in the upper echelons.[15]

Sixty-one percent of the Fellows told me that contacts they had made through the WHF program helped advance their career. One went so far as to reveal to me that his principal had been instrumentally involved in securing every position the Fellow had held since leaving the program. One Fellow told me that the key to catalysts was the "accumulated advantages because of networks." A congressman described how members of his fellowship class not only supported his campaign financially but would "show me around where they knew people who could help out politically." Even the Fellows who initially told me that the Fellowship had little impact on their careers would go on to spend the rest of the interview inadvertently describing the vital connections they had made through the fellowship.

Colin Powell's is one story of success that can be tied back to the people he met as a White House Fellow. His principal had been Frank Carlucci, who was working in the White House at the time. Later, when Carlucci was Ronald Reagan's national security advisor, he asked Powell to be his deputy. When Casper Weinberger, then the secretary of defense, resigned in the wake of the Iran-Contra scandal, Carlucci took his position and, in the words of Powell, "came into the Situation Room one day with Reagan and handed me a note and said, 'You are the new national security advisor.'" For Powell, being the national security advisor (and subsequently, the chairman of the Joint Chiefs of Staff and the secretary of state) would not have been possible had it not been for the relationships he had formed as a White House Fellow.

Peter Krogh tells the story of his interview for the position of dean of the School of Foreign Service at Georgetown University. Krogh was not only being stared down by a 15-member search committee but also a row of dour cardinals lining the wall in Georgetown's Hall of Cardinals in historic Healy Hall. The interview had been going on for quite some time, and Krogh could not tell if it was going well; the search committee was as stone-faced as the cardinals in their portraits. Then, suddenly, the interview was interrupted by a knock on the door. A secretary poked her head in, saying, "Dr. Krogh, there's a call for you." Krogh blanched; who was calling, and how had they reached him here? Embarrassed and confused, Krogh tried to turn down the call. But the secretary insisted: "It's Secretary of State Dean Rusk." Krogh looked around the table and said, "Ladies and gentlemen, if you'll excuse me, I think I should take this call."

The interruption had been purely coincidental. Years earlier, Secretary Rusk had served as Krogh's principal, and the two men remained close. Needless to say, when Krogh returned to his interview from the five-minute phone call, the mood in the room had shifted. He had the job.

Krogh told me, point-blank, "I would not have become the dean of the Foreign Service School had I not been a White House Fellow, just as simple as that."

This sort of "lifetime supply" of social capital was the norm among the many Fellows I talked with. One from the very first class of Fellows shared how he can still trace its impact:

[*The White House Fellowship*] *just continues to reverberate 'til today. I mean it's not just an event that happened [and] then you look back on it historically. It just continues to impact and influence my life, my work, my activities yesterday, what I'm about to do today. All the interlacing. It's really a golden web, rather than a tangled web, that has developed as a result of this. Because one leads to the other.*

Leaders take all kinds of paths to their eventual positions, but a catalyst like the White House Fellowship is the key gateway to this "golden web." As ever, achieving platinum leadership requires a combination of the right opportunities and the right person to take advantage of them.

CHAPTER 4

The Essence of Leadership

Driving Productivity, People, and Culture

In 1971, when first-term congressman Paul Sarbanes told a friend that he had decided to join the House Judiciary Committee, his friend was incredulous. It was a boring committee, he told Sarbanes, and he wouldn't see much action there. But just a few years later, Sarbanes stood before Congress and made history as he read the first article of impeachment of President Richard Nixon.

This was only the beginning of Sarbanes' 36 years in Congress—three terms as a congressman and five in the Senate before he retired in 2007. Sarbanes grew up on the eastern shore of Maryland, and he was the first in his family to go to college. "My parents were immigrants from Greece who ran a restaurant," he told me. "They were determined that their kids were gonna get educated, and that we would go to college. But our horizons for college were all local." Looking to diversify its admissions pool, Princeton University sent a recruiter to Sarbanes' public high school, and he was encouraged to apply. Sarbanes was accepted, and after Princeton, he went on to earn a Rhodes Scholarship, graduate from Harvard Law School, and work briefly in law before pursuing his greatest passion, politics. In 1966, Sarbanes ran for the Maryland House of Delegates, and from that point on, he never lost a race, going on to defeat two House incumbents, a sitting senator, and two former senators.

I interviewed Sarbanes on Capitol Hill in the office of his son, Representative John Sarbanes, who replaced his father in Congress in 2007. At 77 years old, Sarbanes had a full head of coarse, gray hair. He was the very image of an elder statesman, speaking with a slow, deliberate pace. We talked for an hour and a half, and at the end of the interview, Sarbanes gave me a ride back to my hotel, driving me himself.

Despite his long tenure in the Senate, Sarbanes was little known on the national stage for most of his career. An article in the *Washington Post* described his style as "almost averse to cameras and attention. . . . He is a straight arrow who largely disappears for the six years between each election, letting scrappier politicians hash things out in Annapolis, Baltimore, and elsewhere while he studiously tends to his senatorial duties."[1] Sarbanes cannot understand politicians who are unable to restrain their impulses, getting caught up in scandals. "It reflects a basic character weakness, and then they expect to be excused for it," he said.

LEADERSHIP AND POWER

James MacGregor Burns is an emeritus professor at Williams College and a giant in the field of leadership studies. In his seminal work, *Leadership*, Burns defines power "not as a property or entity or possession but as a *relationship* in which two or more persons tap motivational bases in one another and bring varying resources to bear in the process."[2] We all exercise power and have power exercised upon us through relationships. According to French thinker Michel Foucault, power is a force that works *through* people rather than something that operates directly on them.[3] Top organizational leaders are in a position to wield this power not only as they relate to individuals, but also to whole groups and organizations. For this reason, they must necessarily be circumspect in how they employ it. Burns would say that those who use their authority to control others or simply for their own gain are not leaders at all, but only power-wielders.

Susan Ivey, of Reynolds American, the second-largest tobacco company in the United States, makes an interesting distinction between true leadership and the power that arises from rank: "I construe power to be using your position, not necessarily your character, to influence culture or outcomes or decisions, whereas leadership is more formative, and it can be more collaborative." She compares leadership and power to salt and pepper, which, as every informed dinner guest knows, should not be separated but should also not be applied equally. In Ivey's words,

"Salt adds flavor . . . context, and it enriches food . . . whereas pepper is strong and sharp." Both leadership and power are necessary, but in the proper balance—plenty of salt, but only a sprinkle of pepper. In other words, positional power accompanies good leadership, but it should be used only when needed.

To Sarbanes, the right seasoning is a mix of knowing the beliefs of his constituency and using his own judgment to navigate the legislative system. "There's an art or a craft to legislating and putting together a legislative passage and mustering support for it," Sarbanes said. "You have to put together enough votes to carry the day." While the "whole loaf" of a bill typically does not make its way all the way through Congress, usually, Sarbanes said, "what you're voting for is better than what the alternative is."

The irony of Sarbanes' career is that while he largely maintained a low-key presence, he is now known globally as the cosponsor of the Sarbanes–Oxley Act of 2002. As the chairman of the Senate Banking, Housing, and Urban Affairs Committee, Sarbanes initiated and pushed through the bipartisan bill that raised the standards for public boards and accounting firms after the accounting scandals of Enron and others. Sarbanes–Oxley went into effect in 2002 and made "Sarbanes" one of the most repeated names in my interviews. Despite domestic and international praise, the legislation has many critics, particularly along partisan lines. It is a complicated legacy. Shortly after enacting Sarbanes–Oxley, Sarbanes announced his retirement, "I had been in the fight for a long time, and it was time for someone else to pick up the fight and bring a fresh viewpoint."

In the words of one businessman I interviewed, "The highest form of leadership is when you come to know it's not about you. It's about the organization that you're responsible for and even being willing to sacrifice yourself for that organization." Organization heads who do not see themselves as stewards of their institutions are simply manipulating their power, not leading.

In my research, I found three basic responsibilities that institutional leaders master if they are successful in their leadership: they are productive with their time and energy; they motivate and manage people well; they build an organizational culture with a vision for human flourishing. As one leader put it, "It's about leadership; it's about culture; it's about values. And if you get those things right, and pick the right people, and let them do their thing, and reward and recognize them for their results, it's really not that hard."

PRODUCTIVITY

Heads of organizations are not only required to be leaders and managers but, as one university president described her job, "You've got to be a mayor; you've got to be a priest; you've got to be a scholar; you've got to be a clown." So the mantle of leadership is not only heavy, it comes with about a thousand hats. "The biggest challenge was never feeling I had enough time to do what I knew would be useful," she explained. "Going to dinner with students would've been great, sitting down with faculty would've been great, meeting with alumni, talking to the architect. Every day, there were 15 things I could do that would've been rewarding . . . and I could only do 7 of them." This challenge of managing so many different responsibilities was consistent across the leaders I interviewed. One former governor described his work as a "blizzard of daily information, challenges, information, questions, decisions." "We all have infinite jobs," one telecom executive said. "I could work 24 hours every day and never be done." With so much on their plates, leaders need to have systems in place to make the most of their limited time.

No Typical Day

The frequent travel and myriad duties of top leaders make every day different. Many thrive off of the diversity of tasks. One construction executive said:

> *The beauty of the job was that there was no typical day. It was very eclectic. . . . One of the things a good CEO does is learn to dial in and really focus on the opportunities of the day. That could be [for instance] going to a factory and talking to the hourly workforce and trying to help them understand what our vision means and how collectively as a team we work and how we all have a role in getting that done across the whole enterprise. That could be in any country of the world or in one of our large traditional plants with strong union focus.*

Steve Ellis, the worldwide managing director of Bain & Company, gave me a sample rundown of one of those rare days when he is in the office. The work of leaders varies across the disparate sectors, but I found his description to be representative of most others I interviewed.

His day starts at 5:30 or 6:00 A.M. Indeed, over two-thirds of the leaders I interviewed started their workdays before 8:00—some started as early as 4:30. Many found that morning hours provided uninterrupted time to get work done before their subordinates arrived. One nonprofit executive, for example, gets to work at 6:00 A.M. every day in order to have two hours to work on correspondence before the rest of her office arrives. Ellis starts his day with a call—usually received at home—from one of the various leadership groups around the world that he manages. Other leaders begin their day by reading newspapers (or, for those in government, intelligence briefings). A few start in solitude and spiritual reflection or prayer. Others exercise. Getting into a rhythm that is not interrupted by others helps these leaders build up a stock of energy for their jobs.[4] As one of my informants reported, "I've never met a really, really, really great leader that didn't have a lot of energy."

After two to four calls in the morning, Ellis said, "Then I'll usually have one or two client-related issues that I have to deal with." This means a half-day meeting on the phone or, if the client is local, a face-to-face in San Francisco or Silicon Valley. As for later in the day, "The afternoon is typically [filled by] connecting with individual members of the leadership team or key partners around the firm."

After a day packed with meetings, Ellis tries to make it home for dinner with his family. But the day is not over yet. Ellis then works from 8:00 to 10:00 P.M. on email, "just trying to keep ahead of the avalanche." (For some, this can mean as many as 800 emails a day, which is the highest number reported in this study. However, several hundred emails is typical.) Sometimes dinner with the family or late-night work is impossible, because a leader will have a work-related reception or dinner—some leaders attend these engagements more nights than not, so the pace can be grueling and relentless.

For leaders like Ellis, there is much to do and only so much time to complete it. The most productive leaders, I found, develop time-saving habits, manage meetings wisely, set aside time for the intellectual labor of the job, stay accessible to their direct reports, and build a thriving organizational culture.

Saving Time and Managing Meetings

Leaders apply myriad strategies to keep details from eating away their time. Jamie Dimon of JPMorgan Chase tries to return every email and phone call the day he receives them so that they don't bog him down later. Another CEO of a Fortune 100 company with nearly 100,000 employees makes a point to respond to every single email—regardless of who it is from. On the other hand, a more common response to the inbox overload was for leaders to delegate their correspondence work so that they can "have time to focus on the big things," as one college president put it. Assistants are also helpful for scheduling, but one university president retains total control over his calendar as, "only I can tell what I think is or is not important and how to rank it." Before one leader goes on a trip, his assistant will place the materials he needs in his car in bags color-coded according to content. A banking executive intentionally sets aside 25 percent of his time to do miscellaneous tasks like read mail, make calls, and walk around the office. Otherwise, such tasks could take up much more of his day. Platinum leaders devise strategies to overcome the avalanche of the minutiae.

One trend that came up repeatedly is that platinum leaders write things down. Many leaders make to-do lists at the start of the day. One leader takes down her own handwritten notes throughout the day to help her remember things. An airline executive keeps notecards on him so he can jot notes of things that he wants to accomplish in a given time. By keeping their own notes or lists, leaders are able to make sense of and organize the overwhelming amount of information they are presented with every day.

One of the biggest time-sinks leaders face is meetings. Modern organizational leadership means meetings—lots of them. In fact, Michael Duke of Walmart estimated he spent as much as 80 percent of his time in meetings. Hence, every effective leader I met had addressed this potential problem. Some scheduled processing time between their meetings to make sure they were able to focus exclusively on the content of each one. "I would try generally to separate meetings by at least enough time so that I could get the last horrible news out of my head or the last obligation jotted down someplace so that I could move onto the next," said one leader. With so much going on, a leader has to be careful that all his time is not dictated by other people. Thus, some meetings should simply be skipped. One college president told me, "I learned that it was not in the college's interest for me to be at every meeting. It was in the college's interest for me to set agendas for meetings and call meetings when I needed them, rather than them call me."

John Whitehead, former co-chair of Goldman Sachs and former deputy secretary of state, had a highly developed approach to meetings. Whitehead's years at Goldman, the New York Stock Exchange, and the State Department had taught him to avoid becoming bogged down with small talk or endless discussion. Instead, he emphasized control and preplanning:

> Before you had a meeting, you better be sure you knew how it was going to turn out. So I didn't like long, public-discussion meetings at all. Because I thought they sometimes resulted in the worst decisions of all. . . . I like meetings that everybody knows when they come what's going to be discussed. . . . I believe in short meetings where you announce at the beginning the time that it will end.

This isn't to suggest that Whitehead didn't value meetings at all; he just kept them short and useful. He typically scheduled four 15-minute meetings back-to-back as a way of meeting with four sets of colleagues in the most efficient manner. Aware of the time constraint, constituents policed themselves on side banter or irrelevant talking points. In a similar way, another person I interviewed talked about how holding meetings while everyone remains standing helped curtail unnecessary discussion. These gatherings also provided regular opportunities to generate positive emotional energy among colleagues. They were as much about strengthening workplace relationships as about making major decisions. Dick Kovacevich, former Wells Fargo CEO, confirmed that such face-to-face encounters were minutes well invested when decisions or changes were to be made: "Why waste all this time? . . . Because the result would be much more accepted" by employees who perceive "a fair process, rather than getting even a better result [when] the people think the process wasn't right." This wise use of interpersonal time and energy can significantly increase a leader's social capital in the most efficient manner.

Time to Think

With so many meetings and commitments, leaders have little time to accomplish the necessary tasks of thinking through the ins and outs of their decisions and reflecting on the consequences of their actions. Many leaders set aside time in their office to focus on these tasks undisturbed. South Dakota Senator Tom Daschle set aside an hour of "desk time" every day so he had a chance to go through all the major materials that he needed to focus on. Heavy travel schedules actually come in handy for substantial thinking time. One leader told me, "I use my airplane time as a way to catch up on all my reading, email, and any sort of writing I need to do, whether there's a speech I have coming up, or there's a key communication of some kind." For many leaders, "the sanctuary of those 12-hour flights" is their best chance to get work done.

Some leaders see a need to periodically emerge from the minutiae of their work and reconnect with the broad vision of their institution or think through recent developments in their field. Former Harvard president Derek Bok shared with me that in academia, there is seldom grooming for a presidency. "[New presidents] know something about what academic life is all about. They understand something about students. But they don't understand what has become a large and complicated body of information about the different parts of the university," Bok said. To run a large university, presidents need diverse knowledge on the many areas and fields they supervise. In order to educate himself, Bok wrote a report on a different school of the university every year, usually before he had to choose a new dean for that school. In taking time to write these reports, Bok reminded himself of the broader mission of Harvard and educated himself on how to achieve it within the context of particular departments. On a similar note, every year of his presidency, Charles Vest of MIT wrote an essay about an issue confronting MIT or higher education in general. He then shared his thoughts with the campus.

For seven years, George Shultz had one of the most important and consuming jobs in government, serving as secretary of state under President Ronald Reagan. In the midst of the whirlwind of incoming information and outgoing decisions, he purposefully paused for undisturbed intellectual labor:

It's easy to get totally dominated by the events—something is always happening. So I would try—at least twice a week during the day when I was still fresh (not at the end of the day)—to take three-quarters of an hour off. I said, "If the president calls or my wife calls, put it through, but no other calls." And I make a pact with myself not to look at the stuff in my inbox, and I go over and sit in a comfortable chair with a pad and paper, take a deep breath and say, "What am I doing here? What am I trying to achieve? What are the main problems?" So you try to get yourself out of all of the details of day-to-day stuff and try to look a little more broadly from your own perspective.

By routinely taking the time for personal reflection on the major problems he was facing, Shultz was able to stay sharp and focused on the important issues in the midst of chaos. Another executive used his daily 10-mile run for reflection.

MANAGING AND MOTIVATING

Leaders need to know how to wield their authority in a way that motivates their employees. In the words of one businessman, "You can't be effective technically as a leader until you're effective relationally, because we're too interdependent." A Washington insider told me that people are the real challenges in leadership, that "the soft stuff is the hard stuff." In order to accomplish anything, a leader needs to get the people of the organization on her side, which is about much more than popularity. Gordon England, who served as deputy secretary of defense and twice as secretary of the Navy during President George W. Bush's much-maligned tenure, at one point reminded the beleaguered Bush:

You know Mr. President, keep in mind that leadership is not about being popular. It's about being respected. . . . There's a tendency in Washington to take opinion polls on how well the president is liked [to mean] how effective he is as president, but his current popularity is only a small aspect of his leadership.

While popularity is simply the quality of being liked, emotional intelligence is the ability to understand and manage effectively the emotions of yourself and others. This, I determined after studying hundreds of leaders, is *the* vital component of leadership. "You can always find smarts," one leader told me. "I want to know who really knows how to work with people and get things done, and you just try to do your best to find those intangible qualities in people . . . that emotional intelligence."

Emotional intelligence, popularized by Daniel Goleman in 1995, is "the capacity for recognizing our own feelings and those of others, for motivating ourselves, and for managing emotions well in ourselves and in our relationships." Goleman's work adapts the work of earlier psychologists and includes five primary competencies: awareness of one's own emotions, regulating one's own emotions, being able to motivate oneself, sensing the feelings of others, and handling emotions in relationships well.[5] In his book, *Working with Emotional Intelligence*, Goleman claims that "IQ takes second position to emotional intelligence in job performance." In a comparison of competence models for 181 organizations, Goleman concluded that 67 percent of the abilities deemed essential for effective performance were emotional capacities. On the basis of a similar analysis of competencies for U.S.-government jobs and research he commissioned on executive leadership positions, Goleman observed that "the higher the level of the job, the less important technical skills and cognitive abilities were and the more important competence in emotional intelligence became."

High emotional intelligence means knowing how to relate to coworkers in a way that does not alienate anyone, including the person in charge. "If you put walls between yourself and others," one businessman told me, "those walls will come back to haunt you. In my position, the last thing I need is people who are only telling me what they want me to hear or only telling me the good things. I need people to believe that I'm approachable." As another leader observed, the phone rings a lot less when you are the CEO. Executives are at the small end of the funnel; information comes through only a few sources. One aspect of being approachable is being even-keeled. Many leaders told me about prior bosses infamous for their tempers and yelling fits, but most in this generation of leaders endeavor to communicate frustration in gentler ways. A professor shared, "I had learned early on as a faculty member if you ever shoot down a student, no matter how dumb the comment, no matter how aggressive the question, you freeze the whole class, because they fear the day that you do that to them." The same is true in the office realm.

Of course, knowing how to relate to someone means getting to know him personally to some extent, too. For instance, while United States senators have unique leadership in their own states, they find themselves among equals in the Senate chamber—equals hoping to persuade one another on a daily basis. To be successful at this, one senator shared, he had to know his colleagues well and to employ appropriate tactics to get their consent: "You get to know people really well in ways that you have to know them in order to work through them to get things done." The senator described sitting next to a colleague during an important vote; even though it was a secret ballot, his presence was a subtle pressure and ensured the victory.

Using relational influence rather than mere positional power like this senator and executive described, allows a leader to get what she needs by using her unique understanding of each of her coworkers and constituents.

Staying Connected to the Ladder

There is a tendency for senior leaders to grow distant from the day-to-day running of the organization, and their position often makes it intimidating for others at the firm to approach them. But this is a recipe for confusion and frustration. They must take action to overcome this difficulty, both through formal, scheduled mechanisms with direct reports, and through less formal connections with those farther down the ladder. The rhythm of a productive leader's workday is set by his routine daily, weekly, or monthly meetings with subordinates.

The first key to positive interactions with subordinates is hiring the right people. Former Coast Guard commandant Thad Allen told me that his first rule when hiring direct reports is that, "Number one is that they shouldn't be me." He described the necessity of what he called "cognitive diversity," having people on his team from different perspectives and parts of the organization. He applied a Coast Guard metaphor to the situation. "When you're out trying to fix your position," Allen explained, "you'll take a bearing of one lighthouse, another one, another one. Where the lines cross is where you're at. It's called a fix. The wider those angles are, and the more of them you have, the more fidelity you have in your position."

This connection to those below and valuing of divergent perspectives are essential for leaders to gain the information they need to make decisions. Condoleezza Rice shared, "At least two, three times a week . . . I would have a staff meeting where I expected people to give me quick bursts on what they were doing." Rice would ask them, "What's keeping you up at night?" Like the meetings with colleagues and constituents described earlier, this regularly scheduled accessibility builds trust and confidence, social capital, and, ultimately, productivity.

Chase Untermeyer, who served as head of presidential personnel at the White House and later as U.S. ambassador to Qatar, had an experience early in his career that changed how he managed his direct reports later in life. While Untermeyer was serving a deputy role in the White House, he found he had trouble getting time with the secretary of his department. When he confronted the secretary about this, the man smiled and responded, "If you think you need an appointment to see me, you will always need an appointment to see me." Untermeyer eventually learned that the best way to see the secretary was to wait around his office at the end of the day:

> *Inside the secretary's office, he was sort of holding court with some of his intimates. . . . And then the executive assistant would say . . . "Do you want to see Untermeyer?" . . . [I] would be able to come in and give a burst of a question or some nugget of information that was needed and get an answer and go forth.*

Untermeyer found this method "appalling" and inefficient. "I decided," he said, "that . . . all the principal people who reported to me would always have a regular time on my schedule every week." This gave Untermeyer the chance to give them his thoughts and gave his reports a chance to share necessary information with him. It was also a way for Untermeyer to tell them, "I really care about what you do." Untermeyer understood the necessity of being open to the needs of his staff and obviating his boss's cronyism. "I truly believe," Untermeyer said, "that those executives who . . . hold them[selves] apart from sources of information, have only themselves to blame if they are caught by surprise or if things occur that were predictable or preventable."

Another senior government official shared a similar routine; around 6:30 P.M. every evening, her office would be open to any of her deputies who wanted to talk with her. It was an informal time that would allow her direct reports to update her and "feel that we were in this together and moving in the same direction." Many other leaders described to me the importance of their constituents having easy access to them, and some had even more creative ways to accomplish this. In order to incorporate access into his administration, one university president invited any interested students and faculty to join him on his biweekly four-mile run. Anyone who could handle the distance not only had an opportunity to bring ideas or concerns to the president, but also was able to interact with him in a relaxed setting.

Another university president communicated her respect to colleagues by stepping out of her office: "One of the things I was most praised for was going and visiting people in their offices when I was getting to know them." This is because subordinates are usually called in at their boss's leisure and on their boss's turf. By visiting her deans in their own offices, she communicated not only humility but also an interest in their working conditions. An energy executive shared how he made regular visits to his 18 refineries during which he would have dinner with the local management, host a barbeque with all the employees, give out company hats, and go on a walk-through of the refinery. He said, "The most important thing is [for it] to be visible to your people that you care about what they're doing." Every leader has to figure out what works for her. But across the hundreds of interviews I completed, virtually everyone found one way or another to stay in regular contact with direct reports, and surprisingly, it often occurred outside the context of formal meetings in the corner office.

Developing a Shared Vision

By working collaboratively with the people in her organization, a leader—especially a leader new to the organization—can develop a vision that springs naturally from the current community. Some leaders I talked with developed a shared vision by engaging purposefully in lateral leadership, making sure others play a significant role. As one

CEO put it, "You are driving an aircraft carrier here, not a speed-boat." One nonprofit leader described the long-suffering and relentless collaboration crucial to development of a strategic plan:

> *Fifteen hundred volunteers and staff across this country have their fingerprints on that plan: small meetings, time. And it's a slow way to work; it's a messy way to work. But at the end of the day, if the stakeholders feel they have ownership—and that's how nonprofit charities have to work—[it succeeds].*

Leadership can be shared in for-profit settings as well. Steve Odland has been the CEO of Office Depot and AutoZone, but he spent much of his career at Quaker Oats, where he learned much of the leadership he exercises today. Some of it was interpersonal—Odland learned to say positive things in front of a group and to give individuals criticism privately. He also noted that "if people trusted you, you had a lot more room to make mistakes." Odland carefully garnered trust among his peers, and when a cross-brand promotion came up that required all the division heads to be on the same page, Odland was prepared to work laterally to achieve agreement:

> *It required almost like, being the ambassador for a foreign country; you get to go with ideas, take ideas, but be open to listening, modifying ideas, and really working. It was brutal work. It was long; it was inefficient as can be. But it ended up with a good product. And you only do that through influence and willingness to concede—diplomacy, essentially. . . . But the interesting thing is that that skill set and that process is actually the best process for leadership, even if everybody reports to you.*

Odland called this process "gaining enrollment." He wanted not only to sell an idea to his peers, but to have them totally commit themselves to the idea, "enrolling" in it in the same way students enroll in a college course. He acknowledged that this process was time consuming, but it produced much stronger work cohesion than would a simple directive from the top. Odland brought this belief in lateral leadership with him to Office Depot where he led alongside an officer coalition of the top 100 vice presidents.

On the other hand, soliciting input can go too far. A university president warned me of the dangers: "We aim for consultative decision processes, not consensus decision processes, because with consensus decision processes, you'll never get there. You'll never make decisions. . . . That's, I think, what paralyzes many universities." Former Senator and U.S. Attorney General John Ashcroft told me:

Consensus is the enemy of leadership. If you're only taking people where they're already going, you might as well be a bus driver. . . . A leader does more than just drive people to a destination to which they are already headed. . . . A leader either takes you where you weren't—where you hadn't had the idea of going—or gets you to a previously understood noble destination at a pace which would have otherwise been impossible.

Many other leaders whom I talked with also endorsed a middle ground between consensus and top-down command.

BUILDING A THRIVING CULTURE

Shane Tedjarati moved to China with his family in the early 1990s. The consulting company he started there was so successful that it was quickly bought by Unisys, a U.S.-based technology firm. Unisys was impressed by Tedjarati, and asked him to head the company's offices in China when he was only 31 years old:

I got my rude awakening when, on a Friday afternoon, somebody came to my office . . . left 12 contracts—which were about, you know, three- or four-foot-high—and he said, "All the banks that we sold [information] systems to, these would now be your responsibility." And I realized they'd sold systems and they'd never done anything with it. I went to visit the first one in Changsha, and I was very politely arrested. And the public security took my passport. . . . They said, "The bank has got the money, but nobody has come to install for 14 months. We've paid all the money—millions of dollars. Nothing has happened, so we would like you to stay here until [we] can call people to come and sort this thing out." So I went for a one-day trip, and I stayed two weeks.

Because Unisys was an international company, most of the senior managers in China were expatriates like Tedjarati. "They only looked at China as a place—like leeches—where they can make quick bucks, without really understanding what's going on in the country." With his unique background of living in Iran, Canada, the United Kingdom, and the United States, Tedjarati was used to working with diverse people. "So I decided that 'I'm going to understand the locals.'" He ate in the cafeteria with the workers, unlike others who brought their own food. His attitude and willingness to learn Mandarin quickly made him friends. Tedjarati's actions not only created easier relations within Unisys, but they changed the perspective of his employees toward the country where they worked. He changed the culture of the place. For leaders like Tedjarati, this culture change is less like laying fresh sod for manicured lawns and more like cultivating the soil for maximum growth. It takes longer than a cosmetic fix, but it's an investment in future prosperity. Sometimes engendering this prosperity means shifting cultural norms in surprising ways.

Paul O'Neill served in the George W. Bush administration and was CEO of Alcoa, one of the world's largest producers of aluminum. When he took over at the struggling Alcoa, everyone expected him to focus on increasing productivity as a way to increase profits. But they didn't expect that his first priority would be worker safety. This countercultural move turned out to be just the thing that Alcoa needed. Its profits skyrocketed in the next year, stunning industry gurus. What was the connection? As O'Neill said at the beginning of his tenure, "Safety will be an indicator that we're making progress in changing our habits across the entire institution."[6] A focus on something as seemingly arbitrary as workplace safety transforms worker habits and nurtures capable attitudes that can lead to increased profits. O'Neill knew that workers who feel valued naturally bring value to an organization. When I interviewed him, years after he left Alcoa, he was still extremely proud of his safety record, mentioning it several times. He told me a story about how prevalent the safety emphasis was:

The Wall Street Journal *sent a reporter out to Davenport, Iowa, where Alcoa's got this huge facility that makes wing planks for*

Boeing airplanes and everybody else with airplanes. And when the reporter got there, it was raining. So he jumped out of his car and started running across the parking lot to the office building, and a voice yelled out to him, "Stop!" And it was such an authoritative voice, he stopped. And this big guy who'd just come off shift in his overalls came over with an umbrella and said, "We really care a lot about safety here, and jumping out of that car and dashing across this concrete could cause you to slip and fall. So let me walk you over with the umbrella so that you don't fall." This is an hourly worker who had no idea that this guy was a Wall Street Journal *reporter, but it said more about people buying the safety idea than I could have ever accomplished with all the speeches in the world. Somebody that far away [from the top] not only understands the idea but has the courage to act on it even with a stranger. That's pretty good!*

While every employee plays a part in making a positive company culture, ultimately it is the leader who is responsible for initiating and guiding these efforts. Sometimes to fulfill this responsibility, a leader needs to step back, as was the case with Donald Kennedy. With public expectations piled on top of work responsibilities, the line marking where the job ends and the person begins can become pretty hard to see, often to the detriment of the leader. Kennedy was president of Stanford University for 10 years but stepped down in 1992 after a scandal emerged regarding the university's spending of federal research money. In describing the situation, a Stanford insider said:

The people who were holding those hearings weren't holding them to seek truth. They were doing them to prove that they had a way to embarrass the high and mighty, and Stanford was part of the high and mighty. And I think Don and some of the people around him played into that, and I think they then created an entanglement [and] he became personally associated with what he had defended. . . . The government ultimately agreed that we had fulfilled the contracts, but that was four years later or five years later when no one remembered any of that. And by letting it go on, by becoming personally identified, the only way then to ever resolve it was to start with a clean slate, and the only way to have a clean slate was to have a new leader.

The university recovered quickly, but some of the backlash was personal to Kennedy and even his wife. He told me, "We got some pretty bad publicity, and of course, that's singularly unattractive to a spouse. There was one cartoon in the *San Jose Mercury News* showing the two of us reaching into a cookie jar." Granted, some of the funds in question had been spent improving the president's house, which may have inspired the personal attacks. Kennedy saw these home expenses as justified because of all the university events at the president's residence, but onlookers viewed the action as an indulgence. Kennedy was in the hopeless situation of being not closely enough affiliated with Stanford to justify his personal spending, but too conflated with the institution to avoid taking the fall. So Kennedy stepped down. He saw that the fastest way for Stanford to recover was for him to fall on his sword. His sacrifice allowed Stanford to move forward and reconstruct its institutional pride.

Institutional Reconnaissance

Before they can change the culture, leaders have to gather information on the state of their organization. Two effective ways they do this are through the "shipboard tours" technique and the "special ops" technique. The master of the first method is Clifton Wharton, who has held leadership positions in government, business, and academia, making him no stranger to starting fresh at an unfamiliar organization. In the days before commercial flights, a young Wharton traveled with his family by ship. Fascinated by the operational complexities of the vessel, he would canvass the whole ship. He was allowed extensive access, likely because he was a little boy, and the sailors took a liking to him.

As a man, Wharton turned this early experience into "shipboard tours." Whenever he started work at a new institution, he would begin by exploring it at every level. "For me to be able to operate effectively," Wharton explained, "I want to know where everything is, what's going on, what it is." So once Wharton was elected president of Michigan State University, he interviewed all of the top officials and most of the trustees before starting on the job. Then, as chancellor of the State University of New York, Wharton visited all 64 SUNY campuses in his first 10 months. When he finished, "I had insight of all the agenda items I was going to undertake. I knew what needed to be done, and I knew all the campuses." Wharton followed the same plan when he became

CEO of the pension and financial services behemoth, TIAA-CREF. He walked every floor of its three buildings and met every employee over the course of two days. After his shipboard tour of TIAA-CREF, Wharton said he was able to correctly guess the departments that were giving the company the greatest trouble and make changes that dropped TIAA-CREF's personnel turnover rate from 26 percent to 5 percent.

Shipboard tours are ideally suited for just after a leader takes office, but leaders need to know what is going on at their organizations throughout their entire tenure. Ironically, the higher up one gets, the harder it is to take the true pulse of an organization. So some leaders get more covert with their reconnaissance—they implement "special ops." And as any SEAL or Green Beret can tell you, to gather the best intel, you have got to blend in first. As president, CEO, and chairman of AT&T, Randall Stephenson knew he was far removed from the day-to-day interactions of his employees and customers. So he secretly requested removal from the executive telecommunications plan and became just another AT&T customer. "I start receiving a bill," he said. "And if I want to have service changed, or I have a service problem, I call one of our call centers. . . . Over a period of years, the word started getting around, so it's becoming harder." But Stephenson still tries to get the normal AT&T customer experience. He described walking into an AT&T store in a cap and sunglasses to buy an auxiliary cord for his iPhone. "So I watch how they're taking care of customers, and then you just engage with the employees, and you can do that in ways that they don't know who they're speaking to." At one point, Stephenson made a call to the AT&T service center on behalf of his mother and was so impressed with the representative who handled his request that he drove to her office, introduced himself, and interviewed her to learn how she did her job so well.

This interest in the customer's everyday experience even led Stephenson to reverse a policy decision. To cut costs, he initially had decided AT&T employees who install broadband in customers' homes would no longer hand out business cards. But his brother, who is a broadband installer, explained that the card was actually an important part of their business. Without it, customers who have trouble after the installation have to call the automated system for help, and they might be on hold or transferred several times before they reach their installer. When the installers leave a business card, it's much easier for the customers to reach them with any problems. "Most of them never call me," Stephenson's brother explained to him, "but the ones that have a problem, I can just show right back up and fix any issues that have lingered—it's huge." So Stephenson reimplemented the business cards.

A few leaders go even deeper into foreign territory, dabbling in a little espionage. This form of institutional reconnaissance was commercialized into a reality TV show in 2010, *Undercover Boss*. The CBS show disguises CEOs and sends them among the ranks of entry-level employees to see how they fare (and what they can learn) away from the executive suite. For executives, the show—which averages 17.7 million viewers[7]—is largely a publicity tool. But it also gives participants a fresh look at on-the-ground life within their companies. Two leaders in my study had participated: Joel Manby of Herschend Family Entertainment and Rich McClure of United Van Lines, the largest moving company in the United States. After participating in the show, Manby, a friend of McClure's, advised him to take advantage of the opportunity to gain a unique perspective on his business. So over the course of nine days of filming, McClure went undercover. He worked as a household mover, in a warehouse, and alongside his company's most highly rated packing team. McClure's experience on the frontlines led him to implement a new web-based tool to help meet the needs of the household movers. He provided financial incentives and training to help some of those he worked with move up the ladder, and he arranged for retraining of an employee who did not seem to be taking his work seriously enough. His wife talked with a female trainer from the claims department and found that she thought of the company, particularly the claims department, as an "old boys' club," where women did not have much of a chance for advancement.

Leaders do not really need TV cameras or false goatees to find creative ways to cross divides in their organizations. But it does require time and initiative. Ed Whitacre was the chairman and CEO of AT&T and General Motors—two companies with high numbers of unionized employees. He led both companies through years of remarkable success, in part due to his ability to connect with union leaders. "I grew up in a union family," he said. "So I was about as comfortable, if not more so, with the union workers and the so-called blue-collar workers than I was with the management." Whitacre related to me that on his second day as CEO of General Motors, shortly after the U.S. government's bailout of the automaker, he visited the head of the United Auto Workers.

The union president was shocked; no automobile CEO had ever been to his office. By making this connection with the unions a priority, Whitacre turned his natural friendliness into a major asset for General Motors. Platinum leaders leverage their personal backgrounds and individual strengths for their organization's benefit.

Reconnaissance, company-wide inspections, hiring, vision-casting, scheduling, traveling—it certainly is a lot to handle. But platinum leaders thrive on the diversity and high-stakes nature of their work. When a leader acts, she does more than just the work of one woman. Her passion and habits trickle down throughout the organization to have tremendous effect. This is the challenge and the advantage of platinum leadership: Everything you do is magnified. John Ashcroft described to me the unique challenge and potential of organizational leadership:

> *It may be more difficult to turn a big ship than it is to turn a rowboat, but I think you have to decide where you want to go. And if you're going to go with the flow, neither is hard to turn. If you're going to go against the flow or you're going to change the direction, they're both going to be hard to turn. If you're in the rowboat, you probably can turn it by yourself, and that's a solo activity, and that's not leadership. It may be noble, but it's solo. If you're in a larger craft, you're going to have to have help to do it, so people are going to have to be convinced by the nobility of your objective and the intensity of your activity.*

CHAPTER 5

Strength in the Crucible of Crisis

For Bud McFarlane, 1986 was the year lightning struck.

On October 12, the *New York Times* ran a short story giving a few details about a plane that had been shot down over Nicaragua, allegedly carrying weapons to Contras, anti-Sandinista rebels engaged in guerrilla warfare against the ruling communist government. The story might have blown over, had it not been for what happened a few weeks later: A Lebanese newspaper, *Al-Shiraa*, printed an article based on the testimony of an Iranian informant, detailing a U.S. scheme to sell American antitank and antiaircraft missiles to Iran to use in its war against Iraq. The scheme, which had been approved by National Security Advisor Robert "Bud" McFarlane, had carried with it the hopes of future release of Iran-held U.S. hostages. Over time, the situation had degenerated into an unsavory weapons-for-hostages deal run completely undercover. Further investigation revealed that the money from the arms deal was going to support the Contras. The arms sales to Iran had been carried out in secret, and the support of the Contras had illegally circumvented Congress's prohibition of Contra support. The so-called Iran-Contra affair became the biggest political scandal of the Reagan administration.

In the midst of the disgrace, McFarlane fell into a clinical depression driven by his deep regret of having embarrassed President Reagan and shamed his country. On the morning of February 9, 1987, the day he was supposed to appear before the panel investigating the scandal, McFarlane attempted to end his life by overdosing on Valium. He was rushed to the hospital, and doctors were able to save him. Just over a year later, he pleaded guilty to four misdemeanor charges of withholding information from a congressional investigation. He and the 13 others indicted in connection with the incident took the fall for a scandal that stretched from West Asia to Latin America.

Up until this situation, McFarlane's life had appeared to be charmed. After studying at the U.S. Naval Academy, he spent 20 years in the Marines, earned a master's degree in strategic studies at the Institut des Hautes Études in Geneva, became a White House Fellow, then served for three and a half years as the military assistant to Secretary of State Henry Kissinger. He was one of the men who helped put together the Strategic Defense Initiative, dubbed "Star Wars" by the media.

Like other public leaders, McFarlane served as a lightning rod for those under him, at times collecting the shining adulation when the organization was favored—at others bearing the brunt of the public's rage when he and those he led violated the nation's trust. We expect our leaders to take responsibility not only for their own actions, but for the actions of the institutions they lead. Even if it is not within their power to make things happen (or keep them from happening), the mantle of responsibility accompanies the privileges that leaders enjoy.[1] The men and women I interviewed were those who had taken up the call to leadership with all its benefits—and burdens.

SURVIVING FRUSTRATIONS AND FUTILITY

We want our leaders, like lightning rods, to heartily handle whatever strikes the organizations for which they are serving as sentry as well as commander. And we expect them to remain unscathed. Otherwise, we want them replaced. What good is a lightning rod that can't stand tall in severe weather? Further, the public assumes that leaders can really get things done—that they are agents of action. But do leaders actually believe this cultural narrative of their own capability and invincibility?

Robert McFarlane believed it, and it nearly cost him his life. His chain of early successes took him to the very pinnacle of achievement. However, as he tells it, his own sense of agency outgrew his actual power:

> *The notion of bringing down [the Nicaraguan] government, even though they deserved it, is far too ambitious a goal, and*

inappropriate when you don't have the staff or resources to really get it done. And thinking that we could was a hubristic overstretch and one which ended in great embarrassment for our country, let alone for me personally.

McFarlane's glorious past had not fully prepared him to cope with the sense of powerlessness he felt as all his efforts, even his attempt to end his own life, seemed increasingly futile: "This new failure [of not pulling] off the suicide, deepened the depression."

A high sense of personal capability is not limited to those in government. One CEO told me about his long-standing belief on the matter: "If you work hard at something, you can make something good happen. . . . You make your own luck." While he acknowledged that there had been others who had contributed to his success, he did not spend much time talking about their roles and seemed to feel that he had paid off any debts he might have owed to them for their help along the way. He told me, "Obviously a lot of people helped me. . . . I helped them, they helped me."

While McFarlane was recovering in his hospital bed, he received an unexpected visitor: former President Nixon. Also in poor health, he had taken the time to come down and encourage McFarlane. He told him:

"You are blessed with intellect and opportunity, and you vindicated much of that, but there's a lot more you could do. . . . This trust, this special trust given you as a person of above-average intellect must be vindicated. You have a blessing that you cannot ignore, and to ignore it is to sin." And then he was quite stern. He said, "You are similarly blessed. You have had a huge endowment of love of others, of your parents, mentoring, in scholarship, to bring you to an ability to do great things." And he said, almost verbatim, "Get your butt out of bed, get back into mainstream life, and find a way to do something worthwhile."

McFarlane is an example of the heights *and* depths a leader can reach as a result of the unique role of leading an institution. Like Icarus flying too close to the sun, leaders in crisis can plummet quickly. These crises can result from their own pride and misconduct or simply the unavoidable events of the world around them. But the crucible of crisis does not always destroy. It also provides an opportunity for leaders to prove their mettle and emerge stronger than before.

Leader Knows Best

Many times, the toughest decisions and crises occur totally off the radar. In 2000, Warner Music Group made a bid to buy EMI Group, which would have "created the best music company in the history of the world," as former CEO Richard Parsons described it to me. The attempted merger occurred at the same time as the AOL merger, and it largely fell under the radar, even though it would have substantially changed the music industry. The deal never went through, as the European Commission denied the merger amid concerns of market dominance. Parsons put a tremendous amount of time and energy into trying to appease the European Commission and make the merger work—only to watch it fizzle into obscurity. The failure will not be mentioned in histories of the recording industry, but to Parsons, it's the big catch that got away.

Indeed, I found that platinum leaders spend a plurality if not a majority of their time working on projects that go entirely unnoticed by the public. Sometimes they are working extra hours to keep bad news from becoming public scandals. The situation can range from legal challenges to disgruntled employees to major blunders committed by executives. Often the top leaders have to marshal all their political and relational resources to keep a lid on the boiling pot. The other category of work that drains their time is good things that never materialize. Leaders can spend months pursuing an acquisition that falls apart at the last minute, like Parsons. Or their work could entail a massive restructuring that, in the end, is not feasible for one reason or another. They never announce what they had been working on, because, why bother? It failed. This is one of the biggest burdens of senior leadership—receiving no appreciation for some of the things that you put your heart and soul into.

Ralph Waldo Emerson said, "To be great is to be misunderstood."[2] Leaders sense a huge communication gap between themselves and members of the public—who do not have their knowledge base, experiences, or inside information, and who are being directed by the media. Many of the factors that go into a leader's decision-making cannot be easily explained to the masses in a sound bite. Dozens of the people

I talked with long for the chance to set the record straight on particular issues that had affected their reputations, but because of confidentiality standards, they are not able to speak freely. This is another cost of leadership—knowing more than you can share and enduring the uninformed who think they know better.

For example, in the mid-1980s, a major issue on many college campuses was student pressure to end apartheid in South Africa. At the time, Nannerl Keohane was the president at Wellesley College, her alma mater. Regarding South Africa, Wellesley had adopted the Sullivan Principles, a set of human rights standards for companies, and the list included things such as nonsegregation of employees. But this was not enough for Wellesley students; they wanted total divestment in places like South Africa while apartheid was still active. After a "very upbeat, positive teach-in" hosted by Wellesley faculty, Keohane herself became personally convinced that total divestment was the right thing to do. But the decision was in the hands of the trustees, not hers. At a trustee meeting, Keohane tried to sway the board:

> Quite a few trustees came over to this view, but not enough. We lost by one vote. The students were all gathered out in front of the library where we were meeting, waiting for the news, because they were all hoping for divestment but sort of expecting we wouldn't do it. So when I announced that we were sustaining the Sullivan Principles, this great groan went up from the students, and they all dispersed according to a plan. . . . They immediately dispersed and blocked both exits to the campus [by lying in the road].

Meanwhile, the trustees escaped campus by a footbridge at the president's house and had cars pick them up. While Keohane was sympathetic to the students' cause, she could not let them close off campus in this way. Campus and local police joined her in trying to persuade the students to move off the road, but they refused. Having no other choice, the police arrested the students. Had the students cooperated and given their names, they could have been released, but the students all claimed to be named "Winnie Mandela."

"The real challenge," Keohane said, "was if we arrested them and they won't give their names, according to the law, they had to be held overnight." There were not enough jail cells in Wellesley for the dozens of arrested students, and Keohane thought that the female students would have to be sent to the Framingham women's prison, which Keohane said was "as bad as it sounds. . . . The idea of putting 56 Wellesley undergraduates in that prison was one of the most horrible things I've ever contemplated." But the chief of campus police arranged for the students to stay overnight at the Massachusetts National Guard armory, where Wellesley provided them with cots, blankets, hamburgers, and breakfast the next morning.

"I think in retrospect, I made a wise decision at each stage," Keohane told me. But the crisis was made all the more complicated—and agonizing—because she did, in fact, agree with the students. She was both their advocate and jailer, ultimately subject to the board of trustees. The trustees had made the decision and then sidestepped the students' protest, leaving Keohane with the responsibility of managing the mess. Sometimes leaders are forced by outside circumstances to act against their personal judgment, but because of the responsibilities of their symbolic role, they cannot make their real sentiments known.

THE CRUCIBLE REFINES

A dramatic, unexpected event that throws an organization into chaos will either prove or refute a leader's strength. Senior leaders constantly work to maintain the value systems of their organizations, develop strategies to deal with uncertainty, and find ways to maximize the efficiency of their decision-making process. A crisis differs from a leader's everyday tasks more in degree than quality, and thus it serves as an intense test of the systems these leaders have already put in place.

Ronald Heifitz and Marty Linsky define the life cycle of a crisis in three stages: the preparation phase, the emergency phase, and the adaptive phase.[3] The preparation phase is the time before the crisis, when a leader has the opportunity to lay the groundwork for response and to anticipate what is needed for what looms ahead. In the emergency phase, leaders deal with the immediate problems through short-term solutions, focusing on the momentary survival of the organization. In the adaptive phase, the leader charts the long-term course of the organization to bring it back to stability.

No crisis in our lifetime has impacted American life as dramatically as the 9/11 attacks. The stories of the leaders involved show us how executive habits and the organizational cultures they build come to the fore during crisis.

As national coordinator for security, infrastructure protection, and counterterrorism in 2001, Richard Clarke, who had served in one senior leadership position or another in the White House for 16 years and through four presidential administrations, was known informally as the counterterrorism czar. It was his responsibility to anticipate and prepare for the possibility of terrorist attacks. Clarke later claimed that he had communicated fears about a terrorist attack from al-Qaeda but that his warnings had fallen on deaf ears in the Bush administration. He was unable to prevent the crisis during the preparation phase, but as will be seen, he was certainly up to the task during the emergency phase.

Clarke was away from the White House when the first plane hit the World Trade Center, but upon hearing via phone what had happened, he had his assistant convene an emergency videoconference with the various Cabinet departments, to be underway upon his quick return. When Clarke arrived, the principals of the National Security Council (NSC) had gathered in the Situation Room, and the deputy national security advisor, Steve Hadley, had taken charge. But when Clarke came in, "still [with] his overcoat on" (in the words of a person present), Vice President Cheney and National Security Advisor Condoleezza Rice gave him the authority to manage the proceedings: "There was no dissension; there was no combativeness. It was just that Dick [Clarke] had been there for nearly 12 years; he had been through many different crises, so [everyone was clearly] deferring to him." Cheney and Rice hurriedly moved through the White House corridors to join the other upper-level staff in the President's Emergency Operation Center (PEOC), in a bunker under the East Wing. Meanwhile, Clarke led the NSC staff in information gathering in the Situation Room.

The NSC was anticipating that another plane would hit the White House. As we now know, this crash was ultimately forestalled by the brave actions of the passengers of United Airlines Flight 93, but the expectation at the time added an additional layer of tension to the NSC's work. In his interview, Clarke told me they were "beyond being nervous" and that nothing could have truly prepared them for that experience.

"No matter how much you make those exercises realistic, you know they're not," he said. "People were dying; people I knew were dying, had died. [We in the White House] thought we would. But it focuses the mind."

Clarke had the experience and the know-how to lead the National Security Council—and indeed the White House—in its important work of gathering information for the decisions that needed to be made. In the midst of a crisis, leaders like Clarke, with a lifetime of preparation, take control and keep their staff focused by deploying necessary authority. Most of their influence in that moment, however, has already been secured through the *moral* authority they earned over years of hard work and diligent preparation.

The authority that Clarke easily assumed in the hours after the tragedy did not extend into the adaptive phase of the crisis. While he continued to work in the Bush White House for two years, he was a contentious figure in the post-9/11 conversations. Clarke resigned from the Bush administration in 2003, published a book detailing his perspective, and testified at the public 9/11 Commission hearings. He denounced what he considered the president's disregard for his repeated early warnings and criticized the administration's decision to go to war with Iraq. Many Republicans and members of the Bush administration responded by attacking Clarke's credibility. While Clarke was the obvious leader in the midst of a national terrorism crisis, when the moment of crisis had passed, such stark authority was no longer required (or wanted), and Clarke became a more ambiguous figure, moving from hero to scapegoat. He was unable to transition his authority from one phase to another. The most effective leaders are ones who transcend single phases of a crisis and lead through multiple stages.

The Emergency Phase

Clarke was just one of many people in the White House who responded on September 11. Mike Fenzel was an Army major serving under Clarke as a White House Fellow from 2000 to 2001. While the 32-year-old did not have such a high-profile role as Clarke, he still served an important purpose. Starting out the day with Clarke and the other NSC staff in the Situation Room, he helped manage the information as it came in. But eventually Fenzel realized that Vice President Cheney, whom he could see in the PEOC through one of the videoconferencing screens, was not getting the information required for his duties:

I knew I needed to go somewhere where I could be more useful in creating an open line of communication and to possibly be the translator for the vice president [and] the national security advisor for what was transpiring in the subgroup meeting (it was called the Counterterrorism Security Group). Because all of the information for all of the decisions that had to be made was bubbling up through that subgroup, with Dick [Clarke] pulling it out of people, demanding information, needing answers to questions that he had. And it was amazing how effective he was at getting it. I mean, it was very streamlined. And so here you have all this great information, and it was not going anywhere.

Fenzel left the Situation Room and—after some trouble—gained access to the PEOC: "I got down there, to what is basically a large safe door, and there's four guys all with submachine guns and suits on. It was surreal. And it's sort of when the gravity of all this is striking you." Once in the PEOC, Fenzel turned up the volume on the Counterterrorism Security Group meeting feed and turned down the volume on CNN. He also established a phone connection between Cheney and the Situation Room. Fenzel introduced himself to Cheney and explained that he would take notes and help provide the vice president with the relevant information he needed. Fenzel realized that he was playing a unique and necessary role. "Here are all these important people. This is what struck me," he said. "Amazing talent. Great leaders. But they can't make a decision if they don't have information. So I realized my job is going to be to provide them the information they need." Fenzel stepped up in a variety of ways that day—from penning lines for the president's national address to crawling under the table to retrieve Mary Matalin's glasses. He did not wait to receive orders but stepped in to ameliorate the situation in which he found himself.

Another person who stepped forward in the emergency phase of the 9/11 crisis was Brenda Berkman, a New York City firefighter. In 1977, 24 years earlier, Berkman had been one of hundreds of women who first tested to become NYC firefighters. Like all the other women, she failed the physical test. Berkman, who had recently passed the bar, issued a lawsuit against the state of New York, claiming the exam was discriminatory toward women in that it required the testers to perform feats of strength that were unnecessary in actual firefighting. Berkman won the suit and was in a cohort of 41 women who became the first female firefighters in the state of New York. As she told me when we sat down for an interview, Berkman's life has been defined by this accomplishment:

Most of my adult life revolved around that event, and because there was such an intense and long-lasting opposition—which continues to this day against women firefighters in the New York City Fire Department—it isn't something that I just sort of did for two or three years, and then it was an issue that resolved itself and I went on to something else. No, it was always in the background and in the foreground no matter what I was doing in my professional life. So I would say that that event certainly is my proudest accomplishment.

While Berkman has received a good deal of attention for her commitment to gender equality in firefighter ranks, her commitment to the field is about much more than taking a stand. "I don't consider myself to be particularly heroic," Berkman said. "I just think that I'm a person who is very stubborn, and I had an idea that . . . I believed in, and so I wasn't going to take no for an answer." For her, this is not just another career made open to women, but it is the opportunity to fulfill her life's calling. She remained a New York City firefighter for 25 years after the lawsuit, long after most of the initial female cohort had retired or moved on. She worked her way up to captain in the New York City Fire Department, but she loved being a simple firefighter; she avoided roles that would take her away from the physical challenges and daily labors of the job.

So when the towers went down on September 11, Berkman responded in the way that was instinctive for her—as a firefighter. That historic morning, she was off-duty but borrowed the extra gear of another firefighter—a man who would die that day—and joined the fray as she made her way to the burning World Trade Center complex. When Berkman saw the smoke from the towers, she did not sift through possible responses and their various repercussions. She did what she had been doing every day for the past quarter-century. When sacrificial actions such as pulling people out of burning buildings are repeated daily, they become automatic. They cause a firefighter—whether man or woman—to run toward the smoking tower rather than away.

In times of crisis, organizational leaders must similarly look to the needs of their community over their personal needs. And as long as an emphasis on the common good has been well entrenched, this response will feel automatic, not foreign.

But as a crisis switches from the emergency to the adaptive phase, leaders have to make sure they maintain a healthy balance of care for the community and care for themselves, in order to thrive over the long haul. Berkman described to me how many firefighters never sought help for emotional and psychological struggles caused by the event. "The organization was completely unprepared to handle both the event and the aftermath of the event, and so the damage just sort of continued along, rather than being helped," she said.

The Adaptive Phase

While Berkman spent the days following 9/11 sifting through debris, Andy Rosenthal was working 10 blocks from the scene at the Times Square Building. Today, Rosenthal is the editorial page editor at the *New York Times*. Not only has he worked at the *Times* for more than 20 years, but in Rosenthal's words, "I've been at the *New York Times* since I was born." His father, A. M. Rosenthal, was executive editor, giving Rosenthal a long and personal history with the paper.

In 2001, Rosenthal was the assistant managing editor at the *Times*, and he was responsible for what appeared on the front page. After 9/11, "The biggest part of my job," Rosenthal said, "was editing the special section we created called 'A Nation Challenged,' . . . and that was the best and most important journalism I've ever been involved in." In the months after 9/11, "A Nation Challenged" covered all aspects of the tragedy and profiled every one of the victims. "I worked 'til 9, 10, 11 o'clock at night, almost every night, and it was very consuming," Rosenthal said. He decided which pieces made it in the section, a responsibility he took so seriously that he stayed away from the Ground Zero site in order to prevent his emotions from clouding his judgment.

During this period, the work was hard and the hours were long, but it also revealed something to Rosenthal that he had not realized in his whole length of service to the *Times*:

> *For the first time in my professional life, I get it. People are waiting for this paper to come out every morning. They need us. They need the news; they need the comfort. . . . This is the service that journalism provides. . . . I had a pivotal job to do, and it was thrilling.*

The staff of the *New York Times* won the 2002 Pulitzer Prize for public service for "A Nation Challenged," and the Arthur L. Carter Journalism Institute at New York University selected the section as the top work of journalism in the 2000 to 2009 decade.[4] Even though Rosenthal had dedicated his career to journalism, it took a crisis (specifically its adaptive phase) for him to realize the true meaning of his life's work.

Like Rosenthal, Gerard Arpey had dedicated his career to one company. But Arpey spent his time in the travel business, rising up through the ranks at American Airlines. By 2001, he was the executive vice president for operations after spending 20 years with the company. His ascent had been slow, but Arpey was in no hurry:

> *I was always a hard worker, always driven in good ways to do my best, so I think the progression of my career was not some arc of ambition. . . . I was just someone who . . . used their God-given abilities to do their best, and that just resulted in bigger jobs along the way.*

Arpey was at American's headquarters near the Dallas–Fort Worth Airport early on the morning of September 11 when he got a fateful call from the airline's Systems Operations Control (SOC). He was told that someone alleging to be a flight attendant had called American's SOC and claimed that Flight 11 out of Boston had been hijacked. Arpey was incredulous at first; false reports are common in the airline industry, and the identity of the caller had not yet been confirmed. But right before he hung up the phone, his colleagues mentioned that the caller had said that the "bad guys" had taken control of the flight deck. Arpey had never heard that phrase used in this context; he immediately felt a strange chill.

That sense of foreboding prompted him to head directly to the SOC, where his fears were confirmed: that flight had indeed been hijacked. American Airlines was in the midst of reporting the incident to the FBI when they heard the reports of a plane hitting the World Trade Center.

Things moved rapidly from that moment: American confirmed that the first plane had hit World Trade Center One and that United had lost communications with two aircraft.

"I think instinctively I started thinking like a pilot," Arpey told me. A licensed pilot himself, he decided that if he had been scheduled to fly that morning, "I wouldn't want to be in the air." He made the call to divert all flights in the air and ground the entire airline without waiting for a directive from the government or American's CEO, Don Carty. Arpey recalled the intensity of the moment: "That was the first moment when I thought to myself, truly, 'What the hell am I doing?' But Don arrived at the SOC right after we made the decision and immediately concurred." They then received word that American Flight 77 was hijacked and that the second tower of the World Trade Center had been hit.

When we discussed the events of that day, Arpey was remarkably low-key about it, insisting that he did not play a particularly heroic role and declaring that he did not want to dramatize his experience in light of the day's tragedy. "I did what anyone with any common sense would have done," Arpey said. "It was the wise, natural thing to do under the circumstances, [but] I don't think it was anything extraordinary."

Extraordinary or not, things changed that day for slow-and-steady Arpey. Within two years, he was the president and CEO of American, and his outlook had been radically altered:

> [*Before 9/11*], *I had drive, but I think a tremendous amount of passion came along with that drive after 9/11. And I just became even more determined, convinced that I wanted personally to do everything I could to help this company, that these murderers would not destroy our company. . . . It's given me something beyond just my business career, beyond just doing my job. It's given me a passion and a drive to try to do something to help this institution and its employees and its constituents.*

A crisis can spiritually or existentially wound some leaders as they struggle with questions of identity and purpose.[5] But the best leaders—like Rosenthal and Arpey—emerge stronger from the crucible, leveraging crisis for greater strength, personally and organizationally.

MAKING DECISIONS IN THE CRUCIBLE

Andy Card, one of the longest-serving White House chiefs of staff in U.S. history, summarized his position for me by saying, "Most of the job is putting out fires." Card defined his primary role as making sure the president was never "hungry, angry, lonely, or tired." As gatekeeper for the world's most powerful man, Card fiercely protected the president's time. "I don't believe," Card said, "the president should ever make an easy decision. If the president is making an easy decision, the chief of staff probably hasn't done his or her job. Presidents make only tough decisions."

This is true not only for the president of the United States. A leader is someone to whom the hard decisions fall. While everyone in an organization has important responsibilities, a leader must focus on the toughest decisions and leave the smaller ones to be handled by others. Indeed, decision-making (and knowing when not to make a decision) is the most vital activity of a leader.

Of course, getting the right information is fundamental to making good decisions in the crucible. "With the ascendency of leadership there are the development of blinders," one U.S. Navy admiral told me. "So the way you take information and look for answers requires a lot more initiative and ingenuity maybe than what you were thinking about as a subordinate." Leaders must "sort through what is noise and what's an indicator of a real problem, and that oftentimes means that you rely on instincts in judgment," he said.

At this intuitive level, judgment has a lot do with who the leader is—is she naturally a risk-taker? Does he prefer to avoid conflict? Former Purdue University President Martin Jischke started as a physicist and engineer, and as a result of his background, he said, "I tend to think of things technically and quantitatively." But he acknowledged that decisions on the executive level are rarely technical or cut-and-dry matters. "Very bright, hardworking people would often have to make a value judgment or a leap of faith. That is, at some point you couldn't reduce this to a calculation." Jischke learned about the challenge of making these executive decisions when he worked with Judith Connor, an assistant secretary of transportation in Washington, preparing for a presentation on emissions and noise issues. The presentation was to be given to the secretary, who would decide the proper course of action. Connor taught him the best way to help senior leaders when they need to make a decision:

> *She said she was looking at this strategically from the perspective of the secretary. She was asking herself, "What would I want to know if I were the secretary making this decision? And how do we, in writing this report, shape it so that he has real options that he might have to exercise?" It was such a revelation to me as a young professor of engineering who thought you get all the facts down, you do the analysis, and that information will just point you in the right direction. I thought at that time what we had to do was help the secretary come to the right decision—that is, to find the decision, whereas Judith was saying, "No, we have to present him with options. There's no [correct] decision or single answer; there are multiple answers. And he may have to bring to bear a set of considerations that either we don't know about or we can't fully understand."*

As a college president looking back on that experience, Jischke told me that Connor had been absolutely right. It is the job of a leader's inner circle to provide all the information they have and to present choices, and it is the leader's responsibility to decide what to do. Effective senior leaders train their subordinates not to make the tough decisions, but to bring them viable options when a tough decision must be made.

Robert Rubin's work as U.S. Treasury secretary in the Clinton administration is widely admired.[6] Describing his approach to decision-making, he said to me:

> *The more time you can allow to gather from others— information, analysis, points of view, and everything else, the better. But then at some point you have to make a decision. . . . The real trick is to know when you've got to the point where deferring the decision has more marginal disutility than utility.*

When I asked leaders about the hardest decisions they made at work, 41 percent—a plurality—told me they involved personnel matters. That response was nearly double that of every other decision type. No matter how black-and-white the credentials or offences of a subordinate, each hiring and firing decision is not only subjective; it's personal. New York Public Library Chief Tony Marx said that his most agonizing decisions had involved denying tenure to faculty when he was president at Amherst College. At the small institution, Marx knew all the tenure candidates personally. But, as he explained, "In order for the college to keep getting better, its standards have to be maintained, if not raised. And that means that in cases that are on the edge, my job is to go negative on them." Marx put the long-term health of his college over personal connections, but with such talented professors, those borderline cases were never clear either way. "You don't tenure based on promise; you tenure based on delivery," he said. "But it's hard when you see great promise."

One senator admitted to losing sleep over big decisions, as did over half of the leaders I interviewed. Many others had trouble eating. But periods like these were usually brief; leaders knew the anxiety was getting them nowhere. Once a decision is made, the leaders I interviewed tended not to look back. The vast majority told me they do not apply a lot of hindsight to their own decision-making. One university president put it directly: "I don't look back. If things go wrong, or didn't work out quite the way I thought, I try to learn from that mistake and think about what I would do differently next time. But I don't spend a lot of time second-guessing myself." It is not worth their valuable time to feel self-regret or to wonder what might have been. Senator Tom Daschle said, "I have a philosophy that the windshield is bigger than the rear-view mirror, which means that you always do most of your best effort looking forward rather than looking back."

This face-forward perspective is prevalent in large part because top leaders have very high self-confidence. They need it to do their jobs. A leader with a ready catalog of mistakes and transgressions would be too doubt-filled to take the risks associated with decision-making. One CEO described his "mental defense mechanism" as saying, "Well, I can't think of where I made a real mess of things." Leaders cannot move forward if they are mired in the past. As one military leader told me, "I don't spend a lot of time in the regret locker. . . . I'm careful about what I let rent space in my head." But sometimes, under intense criticism or personal guilt, a leader has to admit that something has gone wrong—even if it is not his fault. I found over two-thirds of the leaders I asked were willing to accept blame for personal and collective failures under their leadership even if the issue did not happen as a direct result of their actions. Leadership means taking responsibility, regardless of whose actions are at fault, and then moving on. Former Housing and Urban Development Secretary Henry Cisneros left office after a sex scandal and found he still faced challenging decisions:

> *When you make a mistake, whatever it is . . . you face a decision. Do you hide under a rock the rest of your life in embarrassment? Or do you turn cynical and angry and pursue just private interests? Or do you understand the tension in the world, and try to either overcome it or use it to continue to do the good things you were trying to do under more favorable circumstances? I think I've tried to do the latter. It's not as glorious, rewarding, high-profile an existence, but we do the best we can.*

Cisneros left politics, and he now works in the private sector as CEO and chairman of Cityview, an urban institutional investment firm.

Sometimes the toughest decisions are the inevitable ones, where all a leader's efforts and talent cannot stem the tide of fate. September 11 was not the beginning of troubles for the airline industry. It was a dreadful blow in the larger drama of a decades-long downturn. Things had been tough for the so-called legacy carriers since the Airline Deregulation Act of 1978, as they had been pulled in opposing directions by customer demands for lower fares and labor demands for higher wages. The events of 9/11 further shook up the industry, and they were closely followed by the oil crisis and the recent recession. As airlines reported record losses, American Airlines' Gerard Arpey did not back down from these challenges. He translated the passion inspired by 9/11 into a specific goal for the airline: "If possible, the word bankruptcy would never be associated with American Airlines."

His goal was lofty; since Congress had deregulated the industry, every legacy carrier had either ceased operation or regrouped under the temporary shelter provided by Chapter 11 bankruptcy. Continental had filed in 1983 and 1990, United in 2002, US Airways in 2002 and 2004, and Delta and Northwest in 2005. In each situation, bankruptcy had given the airline the chance to cancel its debt, eschew responsibility for employee pensions, and renegotiate more favorable contracts with labor unions. "[American] and Alaska and Southwest are the only airlines that have not gone bankrupt," Arpey told me when I interviewed him in the spring of 2011.

"Our bankrupt colleagues all made net profits, good net profits last year, and we didn't," Arpey acknowledged. "And you can mathematically pinpoint that to termination of pensions, termination of retiree medical benefits, changes of work rules, changes in the labor contracts. That puts a lot of pressure on our company, not to be ignored." Despite the pressure, Arpey remained convinced that bankruptcy was not the right choice for American:

> *Many people view [bankruptcy] as a business tool, but I have a view that if you borrow money, you should pay it back, and that if you can fund your employees' pension plans, you should do it. . . . We want to be successful; we want to reward our shareholders. But we also want to be mindful of all of the stakeholders in the company.*

But after being the only major airline with a net loss in 2011 and with dismal prospects ahead, American joined the rest of its major competitors when the board voluntarily declared bankruptcy in November 2011, only six months after I interviewed Arpey. Given what I knew of Arpey's personal convictions about bankruptcy, I was unsurprised to hear that the declaration was immediately followed by Arpey's resignation as chairman, CEO, and president. The American Airlines board requested that Arpey remain at the helm, but as he wrote to American's employees, "Executing the board's plan will require not only a re-evaluation of every aspect of our business, but also the leadership of a new chairman and CEO who will bring restructuring experience and a different perspective to the process." Arpey resigned and stepped away with no special severance package and nearly worthless stock holdings.

When I spoke to Arpey again after the bankruptcy, he was gracious about American and positive about the leadership of his successor, Thomas Horton: "I really believed then, as I do now, that he was a better man for the job."

While Arpey was able to translate the devastating impact of 9/11 into moral purpose, the subsequent crises his airline faced were too much. This is the reality of leadership in the crucible; it is complicated and does not always end well. But Arpey's efforts were not in vain. He is remembered as a leader who held true to his moral convictions, perhaps the only airline CEO who regarded bankruptcy not simply as a financial tool but also as a moral failing. In a day and age of outrageous executive compensation and protest movements justifiably spawned by the self-serving nature of the elite, it is refreshing to see a CEO leave a position with honor even as he loses a long-fought battle.

CHAPTER **6**

Lead with Your Life

Because It's Much More than a Job

When Steve Jobs resigned as CEO of Apple in 2011, Apple shares immediately dropped 5 percent. The reaction was so strong because Jobs had embodied Apple's ethos. His creative, controlled persona had begotten the cultural DNA of his organization. That doesn't mean he was an ideal leader or someone we should model our lives after. Leading with your life is not a normative platitude. It is a descriptive reality. Leaders like Jobs don't just tell their organization's story; they live it. And in this way, they communicate a narrative to their employees, consumers, and the public—whether it be the plight of the underdog, a history of innovation, a period of frugality before a return to full strength, or a dedication to employee care. Extraordinary leaders do more than verbalize; they personify.

While the majority of leaders today are not as closely identified with their organizations as Jobs was, every leader who aspires to make a significant difference in her firm, industry, or society must inspire her constituents not only with her words but her actions, habits, and traits. The quickest way to bring down a political opponent is to uncover marital infidelity; voters surmise that a politician unfaithful to his wife will be unfaithful to his political promises. Similarly, when CEOs institute layoffs and pay cuts while simultaneously raking in millions, employees, shareholders, and the general public resent the hypocrisy.

Glenn Tilton is a case in point. After graduating from the University of South Carolina and rising through the ranks at Texaco, Tilton was named the CEO of United Airlines in 2002—the airline's third chief executive in one year. The entire airline industry was struggling in the wake of September 11, but United's case was especially dire. To complicate matters, the employee stock-ownership plan enabled the two major labor unions at the airline to fire a CEO. This arrangement produced, in Tilton's words, "a ridiculous situation." His assessment—one shared by many outside investors—was that the actions required by the CEO to turn United around were the very ones that would trigger his dismissal.

Tilton, however, succeeded in leading United through the industry's largest-ever bankruptcy. To get the company back on its feet, he exacted deep cuts in employees' wages and canceled the airline's pension plan through the bankruptcy proceedings. Yet Tilton underestimated the importance of symbolic issues such as executive compensation and pay packages for top employees. Indeed, he was the highest-paid airline executive in the industry the very year that United's employee pensions were canceled.

He saw nothing wrong with that scenario: "My view of attracting the right people to a bankrupt company was they should be paid a virtual premium. People—including myself—who weren't a part of decisions that put this company into bankruptcy should be well paid to come sacrifice the possibility of advancement in another company." During tense negotiations with aviation workers in New York, Tilton and the United board stayed at a Ritz-Carlton hotel, and when United finally emerged from bankruptcy, Tilton and senior management were awarded large pay packages. In 2008, company pilots called for Tilton's resignation, citing improper management. They created a website for their cause, and flight attendants wore orange bracelets that said, "Glenn must go."

Their efforts were to no avail. Tilton remained at the helm, all the while raking in significant paychecks—he landed on the *Forbes* list of top-paid executives in 2009 and 2010. Through his comments, Tilton communicated United's dire financial straits. Yet he did not see how his rising pay contradicted this overall narrative. No doubt, his individual pay package was insignificant in the grand scheme of United's finances, but it was highly significant in the eyes of United employees. Tilton may have saved United from financial collapse, but he eroded any goodwill that existed between the employees and upper management.

While many leaders make similarly alienating choices, the best leaders recognize the power of their actions—even if they are symbolic—and they use this knowledge to get more things done in and through their organizations. Mike Birck, the former chairman of the telecommunications giant Tellabs, could not be more different from Tilton. Birck founded Tellabs in 1975 and led the company to its height in 2001, when it had nearly 9,000 employees and record sales of $3.4 billion and earnings of $730 million. After the telecom industry bust in the early 2000s, the road was not easy, but Birck was committed to doing right by the firm's workers. Rather than instituting layoffs right away, Birck asked workers to report to work only four days a week and cut the pay of senior management by 20 percent. But there was only so much that could be done. In the end, he had to downsize and contract out Tellabs' manufacturing, shrinking the company to one-third its original size.

Much like Tilton, Birck made major changes to his organization that resulted in layoffs. And like Tilton, Birck made a lot of money. But Birck was honored rather than castigated by his employees. He retained enormous moral authority, because he understood the symbolic nature of leading—that we lead as much with our lives as with our actions.

Many leaders I encountered made token gestures such as refusing bonuses or traveling by the subway instead of by limousine in order to communicate economy to their constituents. Depending on the individual leader, these self-denials may come out of a genuine respect for their employees, or they may simply be a manipulation of public perception. Especially in a climate of recession and layoffs, leaders recognize that conspicuous modesty reflects well in the eyes of the public.[1] Whether under scrutiny from their employees or the larger populace, leaders like Birck are aware of social attentiveness to their actions, and this attention constrains them. Platinum leaders attend to dynamics such as these.

As the first woman to lead her institution, one nonprofit executive certainly feels the scrutiny. She recognizes that there are benefits as well as costs to having such a public platform. Everything she says and does is amplified because of the world's interest in the institution she leads. As much as her presidency gives her a platform to speak and be heard, it also gives her the platform to be *mis*heard: "I worry about how what I say is going to be printed on the front page of the *New York Times* and how what I may want to give as a nuanced answer . . . can be tweeted or recorded partially or transmitted in a way that doesn't have what I would see as the full story. . . . That makes me anxious."

In effect, her role as a symbolic actor means her words and actions, for better or worse, become a part of the cultural public domain and are subject to different interpretations and representations by those who reproduce them. While leaders can control what they do and say, they cannot control how their actions and words are disseminated and perceived.

All this attention affords leaders great power but also creates personal burden. In Dallas, businessman Morton Meyerson feels self-conscious every time he pulls out his credit card, as people recognize his name from Dallas's Morton H. Meyerson Symphony Center, which his friend and former colleague, Ross Perot, named in his honor. Likewise, leaders who live in small towns—like Jim Owens, whose construction company, Caterpillar, supplies many of the jobs in Peoria, Illinois—become local celebrities. The attention makes Owens feel a bit "like Robert Redford": "Everywhere you go and everything you do is noted, observed. Your compensation, of course, is front-page headline news when it happens. If you lived in Chicago or New York, nobody would care, but here it is headline news."

When John Donahoe stepped into leadership at eBay, he instituted major changes that moved the site away from its original auction model. eBay users were furious with Donahoe, and they posted hate-videos on YouTube that compared him to the Nazis. To diffuse the tension when he appeared before 15,000 eBay sellers at a conference, Donahoe started his presentation with pictures from his childhood. He had to show them part of his humanity, moving beyond the state of merely being a figurehead without a personal story.

Leadership means representing your institution to employees, board members, customers, and the media—but also to your waitress, your housekeeper, and your mailman. A leader must consider how everything he does reflects on his organization. In fact, great leaders manage their personal actions with the same care as they manage their work. Most people have no idea of the toll this takes on leaders as individuals, on the people around them, and on their families. One of the great challenges of a leader is to be able to compartmentalize this toll so that she can carry on with her job.

Each spring, the president hosts the White House Correspondents' Dinner, a special event for White House reporters, media figures, and politicians that includes a "roast" of the president and his administration.

On April 30, 2011, President Barack Obama was responsible for maintaining the light-hearted nature of the event by sharing the podium with comedian Seth Meyers. Hours earlier, Obama had come from a phone call with members of SEAL Team Six, during which he had wished them Godspeed in their mission to capture or kill Osama bin Laden. On the Sunday morning after the dinner, Obama would be gathered with his advisors in the White House Situation Room to watch the events unfold in Pakistan.

While President Obama was agonizing over the decision to send SEALs into harm's way a full day before he could announce anything to the country, he had to maintain a light-hearted, jovial demeanor for the public. This partitioning of emotions that was required of the president is unfathomable to most of us. Even on a smaller scale, intense situations often occur outside of the public's eye—a secret deal is on the verge of collapse, internal personnel issues have exploded, or a covert operation is being carried out—and yet leaders must maintain a demeanor of confidence and serenity.

THE TOLL IT TAKES

In addition to being named the seventeenth national security advisor under President George H. W. Bush, Brent Scowcroft achieved an even more selective honor during his tenure in the White House: He was the first recipient of the Scowcroft Award, which the president then bestowed annually to "the person who fell asleep most frequently in meetings, and woke up pretending he'd never been asleep." To this day, the award is proudly displayed in Scowcroft's Washington office with a picture of him sleeping on Air Force One. He was no narcoleptic; he was simply too busy to sleep normal hours. Indeed, the greatest toll on the lives of leaders I interviewed was the number of hours they work every week. Their *average* workweek is 68 hours, with a range of from 40 to 106 hours. As national security advisor, Scowcroft worked from 7:00 A.M. to 9:30 P.M.—more than 14 hours per day, week in and week out. Scowcroft's story is not unique among presidential appointees. While many of these leaders are government careerists like Scowcroft, serving for many years in public life, the four-year term of the presidency and the fast-changing tides of U.S. politics mean that practically every position in Washington is temporary. Most presidential appointees stay in their positions for an average of only two-and-a-half years, but with workdays that exceed 12 hours and little time for families, much less personal rest, who can be surprised with these short tenures?

Andy Card was chief of staff under President George W. Bush for five years. From Monday through Saturday, he was in the office at 5:30 A.M. and left at 7:30 P.M. at the earliest—sometimes staying until 10:30 P.M. And he was never the first to arrive or the last to leave. "There's always people at the White House," he told me. A former deputy secretary of Homeland Security shared:

> *I usually headed home around seven, knowing I had an hour in the backseat of a car before I got home. So I was leaving home at five-thirty in the morning, and I was getting home about eight o'clock any given day. And that was six days a week and often a seventh day. At the end of that experience, I was physically, mentally, emotionally, exhausted. It was an endless, endless, demand on every facet of what you could bring to the table.*

This heavy work schedule was consistent across the senior government leaders I interviewed; 88 percent worked all seven days a week. This is significantly higher than what I found among leaders in the business and nonprofit sectors. Fifty-seven percent of senior government leaders worked over 70 hours (that includes leaders from the last nine administrations) compared to only 43 percent of nonprofit and business leaders.

Leaders in government may work the longest hours overall, but the pace of life for leaders in business and nonprofit life is far from leisurely. New information technologies like smart phones and wireless Internet give the workplace more and more access to the private sphere.[2] This accessibility makes it hard for leaders to escape the pressures of their jobs or the responsibilities of their roles.

Everett Spain, a White House Fellow from the Class of 2008 and former aide-de-camp to David Petraeus in Iraq, explained some of the reasons work becomes so all-consuming: "Usually one of my inner self-identities is to be able to outwork people. . . . I don't outwork them to outwork them; it's how I really contribute on a large scale. I'm not really smarter or more perceptive than a lot of people but I have been able to put together large quantities of useful work—productive work that makes an impact long-term." The demands of these jobs are high, but the leaders I interviewed often had a unique drive to be productive. They also often associate their jobs with a moral purpose. Nearly a third of the leaders I interviewed described having a vocational calling of some sort. These people tended to be more likely to also mention making decisions with a broader picture in mind. On one hand, this means that these individuals have a powerful ability to contribute to human flourishing, but they do so in a way that takes a tremendous toll on them as individuals.

So the hours of the workweek are only part of the story. After a long career in the United States Navy, Admiral Dennis Blair was appointed director of National Intelligence. I interviewed Blair a year after his resignation from the post, and he described the many stresses of such a public and important role. Blair had been working 12 hours a day, but he shrugged off the time commitment:

> *That pressure you feel is not hours; it's responsibility. You can never do enough to try to do the right thing by the organization that you're in charge of. So any time that you have that spare mental minute, your mind is working on, you know, "What's something that we can do better?" or "What's an opportunity we can take advantage of?" . . . What people notice physically is when you get out of the job, you look so much younger and more refreshed.*

Blair recalled living with this pressure as far back as when he commanded his first ship in the 1980s. The weight of responsibility seemed to increase with his rising rank, eventually manifesting itself physically. "I had terrible leg cramps in the middle of the night," he told me, "maybe twice a week. I mean, just eye-watering pain." Assuming that these might have revealed an underlying medical condition, I asked him how he was doing now (at the time of our interview). His response summed it up: "I haven't had them since I left."

Another factor contributing to and resulting from stress is the aforementioned lack of sleep; two-thirds of the leaders I interviewed sleep six or fewer hours a night. During a string of student demonstrations, one college president I talked with averaged four hours of sleep a night and lost 30 pounds.[3]

TAXING THE PERSONAL LIFE

The majority of leaders say their professional success has cost them something personally. One leader poignantly realized just what he had lost at his son's wedding rehearsal dinner: "He's talking about a memory of his mom teaching him to play catch and playing catch with him in the front yard. And I'm sitting there thinking, 'That should have been me.'" In addition to the long hours, these positions come with heavy travel commitments. A surprising number of these top leaders work in a different city, state, or even continent from where their families live. Even leaders whose offices are in the same cities where their families reside can travel for as many as half the days in a year. When leaders travel this much or commute between cities, they can feel like "a person without a city," as one put it, restless and never truly at home anywhere.

The combined forces of long hours, travel, and constant scrutiny leave leaders with little time or energy to invest in their personal lives. For women leaders I interviewed, this strain is particularly pernicious. In addition to their workload, women have centuries of traditional gender roles pushing them to be the chief relational investor in their families. So women in leadership positions find balance even harder to achieve than men do, and many chose to focus only on their careers. Only 64 percent of the women I interviewed were currently or had been married, compared to 96 percent of the men.

Early in her career, a female television executive I interviewed decided that she could not have it all—or more specifically, she could not have it all at the same time: "If I were to be married with kids, I could not do this job. And you can lie to yourself, but I know I couldn't. Right now I have the liberty to get on a plane whenever I want." Whether most of these women in top leadership roles consciously choose career over family, the numbers compared to women in other jobs reveal that these high-profile careers inhibit their chances of being wives and mothers.[4] One nonprofit executive explained to me that women professionals have to work harder, longer, and better, which "didn't leave a lot of time for other things." When I asked if her professional success ever cost her something personally, she was quick to respond, "Oh sure, you mean like the day I woke up and realized I didn't have any kids? Seriously, yes." Sixty-nine percent of the women in this study have children, compared to 94 percent of men. While feminism has paved the way for women to hold senior positions in our society, they still lack the personal freedom that allows men to manage both a high-powered career and a family. In *The Second Shift*, Arlie Hochschild reports that in marriages where both partners work, women are the ones who work "the second shift," as primary caregivers on top of their work.[5] If women in leadership positions are working both harder and longer than their male counterparts and more than other working women, they have little time or emotional energy to take on this second shift. And so women who manage to break the glass ceiling in the corner office can still find themselves trapped by traditional gender assignments at home.

A few women, however, appear to somehow manage it all. Anne Mulcahy, former CEO and chair of Xerox and mother of two told me, "I'm always really clear about this, that is, there's room for a big-time job, and there's room to be an active and engaged mother. There's just room for nothing else." Indeed, among the few women I encountered who had very senior jobs and who had traditional family lives, practically all of them talked about having no hobbies or outside activities. In their estimation, there simply was not time.

Some women leaders spoke of rewarding marriages, but many more spoke of marriages that fell apart as their careers advanced. Women were nearly three times as likely as men in our study to have been divorced. Women were also less likely than men to mention a supportive spouse at home in our interview (even when accounting for the fact that fewer of the women were married). Marriage was also less likely to be mentioned as a part of the overall narrative of a woman's career path. This suggests that women in leadership continue to feel concerned that prevailing cultural norms about gender do not thwart their upward mobility or account for their ascent.

Family Matters

Leaders' families also feel the strain as their father, mother, or spouse is pulled away by a demanding job. One day, as Bill Roper left for his job as head of the Centers for Disease Control and Prevention in Atlanta, he was shocked to hear his three-year-old son send him off by saying, "Thanks for visiting, Daddy." A surprisingly high number of leaders I interviewed have similar stories of realizing that their absence led their children to have extremely low expectations of them. *New York Times* editor Andy Rosenthal's son told Rosenthal that, "He understood that the *New York Times* was more important than he was. And that was what got me." Nearly all the leaders I spoke with acknowledged the need to find balance between their families and their work, but they addressed the challenge in different ways and with varying degrees of success.

Many leaders strictly keep their work and personal lives separate. By compartmentalizing their stress, they protect their families from concern over work issues. The CEO and chairman of General Electric, Jeff Immelt, said, "What I like about my wife and my daughter is that they are not plugged into work-ish type things":

> *I can't tell you the number of times my wife has said, "You didn't tell me you were going to do this deal where this person was going to get fired," and I said, "I don't tell you a lot of things." Because that's helpful to me that I don't have to bring work home.*

In a similar vein, football star Kurt Warner has a policy that he does not sign autographs for fans around his family, because he wants his family to know that when he is with them, he is focused on being "Dad" and not an NFL star. These leaders feel that by protecting their families from their work, they preserve the sanctity of family time.

But other leaders find it far more helpful to integrate their work and family lives, intentionally blurring the lines between office and home. One executive shared with me that he frequently arranges to have his wife and children come with him on work trips: "I just try and involve them as much as I can, so that it's not seen as this scary thing out there that draws their dad away; it's actually something that they understand."

Kevin Plank, the founder and CEO of Under Armour, is on the extreme end of the spectrum. Plank considers his personal and professional life "all one." Not only does he consult his wife on things like personnel decisions, but he also involves his kids in his trade. Plank described a Saturday with his son: "Come on, we're going to stop by Dick's Sporting Goods, and I'm going to buy an arrow set for the house. Later we're going to go shoot bows and arrows, but we're going to sit there and watch people, see what kind of shoes they buy for two hours."

For Plank, Under Armour is his mission (he's "building something great"), and he expresses his devotion to his family by involving them in it. Plank (and others like him) believes that he preserves his family by involving them in the preservation of his work. But there are painfully obvious trade-offs involved. He may be more present to his family than many whom I interviewed, but his presence is obviously sometimes a partial one.

To obviate these potential problems, leaders I interviewed engineered a number of strategies to preserve space for their families. Two things emerged across the interviews I conducted as the defining factors of parenthood: attending kids' sporting events and performances, and being home for dinner. Attendance at special occasions like kids' recitals and sporting events was usually not too difficult to swing, since these events come with advance warning. As the heads of their organizations, these leaders have a great deal of control over their calendars as well as access to tremendously helpful resources—like corporate jets—that the rest of us do not. But being home for dinner signifies their presence in their family's day-to-day lives and is much harder to achieve on a consistent basis. While some try to set aside the weekend as sacrosanct family time, three-quarters of these leaders still work seven days a week, meaning their presence at home is even more pinched. John Donahoe of eBay, however, has created a tradition of making pancakes for his family every Sunday morning.

Another businessman purposefully structures his meetings for early morning in order to come home sooner to be with his kids: "One of the things I learned early on is my teenage children didn't care where I was at 5 A.M." But being home for dinner was paramount.

A majority of the leaders I interviewed cannot make it home for dinner every night or to every soccer game, even if they feel it is expected of them as parents. Many, then, are compelled to rework the definition of "father" or "mother" into something they can actually achieve. Like Donahoe with his Sunday morning pancakes, they create rituals and routines that allow them to continue in their demanding jobs and still feel good about their parenting involvement. By fulfilling regular expectations, they attempt to both satisfy their work requirements and demonstrate love and respect for their spouses and children. For example, one leader had a weekly date night with his wife and drove his kids to school every morning. During a career lull, one publishing executive took six months to take his kids on individual vacations around the world. Another businessman works in San Francisco but calls his family in Chicago every night at dinnertime. Another works out with his wife every morning. These are simple things—mere snapshots of family life. Yet by making rituals of them, leaders hope to elevate a nightly cross-continental phone call or a morning workout to evidence of fidelity and devotion.

THE PRIVILEGED LIFESTYLE: "THERE'S SOMETHING WRONG HERE"

Parenting requirements are not the only perceptions refracted by leaders' proximity to such consuming work. The lifestyle allowed by these high-paying jobs puts many out of touch with reality. Today's elite leaders enjoy personal benefits such as expensive houses, travel opportunities, and interactions with celebrities. And they share all these benefits with their families. As one businessman described, it really is the good life:

> *My personal success has enriched my life tremendously. My wife and I and my daughter have been around the world. I've taken them on trips with me. I've made so much money that we can do anything we want. My daughter can go to the finest school; we live in a beautiful house; we can do things for our parents and people that we love that otherwise couldn't be done.*

Few leaders I interviewed talked so directly about the lifestyle perks of their jobs, but the evidence was all around us during the interviews: their expensive suits, mammoth homes, and expansive office suites high above the fray of America's metropolises. When one executive visibly revealed his frustration with my tardiness to our appointment on a rainy afternoon in New York City, I asked him about the last time he had hailed a cab in lower Manhattan in the middle of a storm. He immediately retorted, "That's why I always have a car and driver . . . so I don't have to keep important people waiting."

The best leaders I encountered in this study recognize the symbolism of their actions, but even the most impressive ones I interviewed have become largely distant from ordinary people. They forget how unusual are the lives that they lead. One CEO ruefully related to me the story of meeting a man at a dinner party, and upon hearing that the man worked at Pepsi, asking if he knew Steve Reinemund (then the company's top executive). The man, who drove a delivery truck for PepsiCo, had never heard of Reinemund, and the CEO, embarrassed, quickly changed the subject. It is easy for these leaders to get so entrenched in the exclusive world of the global elite that they forget that most of us do not run in such circles. Nowhere is this entrenchment more obvious than around the touchy subject of executive compensation.

Debate about social equality well predates the birth of our nation; Jean-Jacques Rousseau wrote 250 years ago about the social contract that holds modern society together.[6] Even though class distinctions have always divided us, the great accomplishment of the modern economic system has been the emergence of a robust middle class that did not exist in the medieval era or earlier. Economists such as Paul Krugman and Larry Summers and writers like Ben W. Heineman, Jr., have spoken out against excessive executive compensation as a particular threat to this system. They attest to its erosion of the moral cohesion that used to keep executives and laborers working for the same goal—profitability of the firm. The "Protestant ethic" that once facilitated Western capitalism has little to do with Protestantism today, nor is it much of an ethic when determining the divide between a firm's top-paid and lowest-paid employees.

And now, in an era of high unemployment and movements such as Occupy Wall Street, millions of everyday Americans are expressing their anger about the growing divide between rich and poor in our society. Since 1970, the share of income going to the top 1 percent of Americans has steadily increased, and in the economic boom from 2002 to 2007 that preceded the latest recession, incomes in the top 1 percent grew 62 percent while those of the bottom 90 percent grew only 4 percent. Even with the recent economic downturn, executive compensation has grown by an average of 4 percent per year for the past decade.[7] Citigroup made headlines in the spring of 2012 when shareholders voted to withhold a $15 million pay package from CEO Vikram Pandit, "marking the first time that stock owners have united in opposition to outsized compensation at a financial giant."[8] Executive compensation packages include more than cash. Perks like country club memberships and personal use of corporate aircraft are highly valued.

Significantly fewer of the leaders in this study, however, endorsed such a cap. And opinions on the issue fell clearly along party lines. The

Republicans—both inside business and out—were far more likely to resist government intervention in setting compensation guidelines. In fact, of the leaders I interviewed, three-quarters of those with Republican views believed there should not be a cap on compensation, compared to less than half of non-Republicans.[9] According to a recent Gallup poll, 59 percent of the American public favors government action to limit the pay of executives.[10]

I conducted my interviews on the eve of the Occupy Wall Street movement, but compensation was already a touchy subject for the leaders I talked with. Many of them have been on the Forbes 400 list, the definitive register of personal wealth in the United States, and they used a variety of excuses to defend their positions. Most blamed the system.

Business leaders defend their high pay packages by citing the importance of economic incentives in a capitalist system. The founder of Home Depot and a former director of the New York Stock Exchange, Kenneth Langone described it simply: "It's capitalism, and if you leave it alone, it'll work. It'll work like a charm." As the major stockholder at Yum! Brands, the world's largest fast-food company, Langone also makes sure CEO David Novak is very well paid—in 2012, Novak's pay package was valued at $29.67 million.

Novak, like other executives with high compensation, deflects responsibility for his pay: "I can't explain why I make so much money; I didn't create this system." They attribute their sizable income to share value. As it rises, so also does executive pay. "If you have the right leader at the helm, it pays off in spades," he explained. "I've made an awful lot of money, but I've also been blessed to be in a company that's grown our stock six times over the last 12 years."

One banking executive says he understands people's frustration, but he disputes the Rousseauian notion of a social contract where compensation affects social solidarity: "We don't have a social responsibility, other than to conduct ourselves in compliance with the laws. . . . What I would say is that the better we do (living within the rules, obviously, and conducting ourselves in an ethical manner), the more jobs we create, and that serves America well." So in this way of thinking, high executive pay *should* accompany economic growth. And it does, when CEO pay is based solely on stock value. But practically all executives receive base salaries as well, and over the past four years, those base packages have not followed the economic downturn.

Other business leaders say that CEO pay should not only be based on stock value, but also on the significance of the CEO's performance in determining that. Former secretary of the Treasury and CEO of Alcoa Paul O'Neill puts it this way:

> *I like the idea of stock options that produce significant value if the enterprise significantly outperforms the competition. . . . A company can make a lot of money, but it may just be in a virtuous cycle for the industry. That's not a good reason to pay an executive a whole lot of money. . . . They should get paid for the difference that they make, not for the good fortune they have in happening to be in the right place at the right time.*

Dozens of business leaders talked about the complexities of setting executive compensation, citing the role of outside consultants, executive search firms, compensation committees staffed by board directors, and performance-incentive packages. This process of diffusing responsibility for executive pay has not only spawned a number of cottage industries around compensation questions but has also produced rampant growth in CEO pay. Whereas earlier generations of capitalists set their own income—and therefore had to take public responsibility for it—the current generation has been able to depersonalize its involvement in the process, allowing pay packages to continue to grow despite increasingly strict disclosure obligations of public companies and subsequent public outcry. In essence, we have created a mechanism for tremendous growth in CEO pay without individual accountability.

The trend toward higher CEO pay has even infiltrated the ranks of the country's leading nonprofits. In 2010, four U.S. senators refused to approve a large package of federal grants for the Boys & Girls Clubs of America after discovering that the organization's CEO, Roxanne Spillett, had earned almost $1 million in compensation in 2008. Senator Tom Coburn was one of many who criticized Spillett: "A nearly $1 million salary and benefit package for a nonprofit executive is not only questionable on its face but also raises questions about how the organization manages its finances in other areas."[11] The senators' critiques were especially poignant, because at the same time that Spillett was receiving this pay package, Boys & Girls Clubs were closing across the country as philanthropic dollars evaporated in the economic downturn. Spillett, who has worked various positions at Boys & Girls Clubs since the 1970s, was chastened by these criticisms. She told me, "I feel a huge sense of responsibility for our local clubs, and so, if [my compensation and the news attention it generates] is in any way, shape, or form hurting our clubs . . . it's like a punch in the gut." In response, Spillett asked her board to discontinue all retirement payments, which were a large part of her total compensation package. Actions such as hers have helped to calm some of the criticisms of nonprofit executive pay, but they are virtually unheard of in the private sector.

Other leaders revealed little understanding of why their compensation would be perceived as a problem. When I interviewed 55-year-old Jamie Dimon, he had gone totally gray, but he still had ruddy cheeks and was teeming with energy. He is warm, engaging, and incredibly smart. After spending time with him, I understood why he is the most respected and liked bank executive around.

Dimon first made history when he helped his mentor, Simon Weil, build CitiGroup, the first behemoth financial-services conglomerate. He made history again when, after a break with Weil, he rose to become JPMorgan Chase's chairman, CEO, and president and guided the bank through the previous decade's financial meltdown. Legend has it that when Dimon was a boy, his father asked him what he wanted to be when he grew up, and Dimon was quick to respond, "I want to be rich."[12] He had certainly achieved that goal when I met with him, sitting in the conference room of the executive suite on the 48th floor of 270 Park Avenue. The wealth of the place hung in the air as I asked Dimon about his pay package—which had neared $110 million over the previous five years. He compared executive compensation to the pay packages given to celebrity athletes. From his perspective, the high income of executives was in no way to blame for the low wages of others. As he put it, "I think a bigger crime isn't that CEOs make a lot of money but that inner-city-schooled kids don't have the chance to compete." Dimon has been vocal in many news outlets about his right to wealth as a result of hard work and success; wealth has, after all, been his goal since he was a boy. But Dimon, like other executives, is unable to see what the situation looks like outside of the gilded halls of Wall Street. Years ago, when Dimon told his family that he had been fired as the president of CitiGroup, his young daughters were very concerned, asking if they would have to live in the streets and if they could still go to college. Dimon reassured his daughters—bank executives, even those who have just been let go, do not have to worry about living in the streets.

Randall Stephenson of AT&T also sees little wrong with the system if an executive generates wealth for shareholders: "The only morality issue I perceive is, 'Is there an executive taking advantage of [the system]? Is there an executive whose performance did not warrant that level of compensation?'" Yet even Stephenson recognizes the need for limiting some executive perks. In 2008—at the start of the recession—he waived his $3 million bonus. It is a matter of "fairness . . . equity," said Stephenson. As long as employees "believe you're in the boat with 'em, I don't think there's a big resentfulness [about] how the shareholders choose to pay me. But I think if they see me [getting a bonus] and they're getting hammered [by lower pay], then that's not right. I just kind of think we're all in this together."

One businessman struggles because he knows intuitively that the system is wrong, but he does not know what to do about it. He blames the marketplace for determining executive compensation, explaining that he would've done his job if the compensation were one-tenth of what it was, because he found the work interesting. "But I would not have felt good about that," he admitted, "if everybody else was making 10 times more than me doing the same job. That's where the human nature part comes into play." He was refreshingly forthcoming in his personal thoughts, "We all sort of know it intuitively. We know it in our gut, there's something wrong here. But we don't know what to do about it."

Other business leaders also acknowledged problems with the current system, but most of these leaders do not see their compensation appears to the rest of their fellow citizens. Their work requires so much of them—more time, more commitment, more sacrifice—that they become accustomed to this excess in all areas of their lives.

THEY LOVE TO WORK

The common conception is that these leaders are in it for the money. But I found that while money and status probably play a bigger role than leaders verbally acknowledged, the overwhelming majority are driven by much stronger forces. These leaders embrace their work much more than they do the leisure and freedom allowed by their paychecks. As one person explained, "It wasn't about making money . . . I didn't even think about it. It wasn't about going up in an organization. I always just wanted to make a difference in people's lives."

Eighty-six percent of the leaders I interviewed specifically expressed that they loved their jobs. In the words of Jim Turley, chairman and CEO of Ernst & Young, "It's a relatively intense life, and if I didn't love it, then I couldn't do it, because it takes a toll. . . . But I get more out of it than I feel like I put in." Rather than being drained by the hours, the attention, and the responsibilities, these people are inspired by them. They love the larger-than-life role they are called to take on. They have to love it in order for it to be worth the sacrifice. A U.S. senator told me, "People ask, 'So what's it like to be a senator?' and my answer is that it's more. M-O-R-E, more. It's more of everything. More fulfillment, more reward, more frustration, more stress, more of the best and the worst of life in every way you can imagine."

Other leaders communicate their vested passion in their work as an ingrained trait. "If you're high-octane people, you're high-octane people," said Doris Meissner, former Immigration and Naturalization Service commissioner in the Clinton White House. "I work hard. Well, I've got to face the fact, I must love it. And if I wanted more balance in my life, I probably could have it. But . . . if you like intensity, you like intensity." Apple chairman Arthur Levinson works because he is afraid of wasting his limited time: "Ever since [I was] a little kid, if . . . I've wasted the day, I'll dream about it. . . . There's something deep-seated in my brain that does not allow me to live a casual life."

After graduating from the Wharton School, former University of Pennsylvania fullback Robert Wolf had every intention of becoming a doctor. After taking the MCAT, he decided to go on a few practice interviews in preparation for interviewing for medical school. But everything changed for Wolf when he walked onto the Salomon Brothers trading floor at 1 New York Plaza. "Huge electricity in the air, a lot of energy," Wolf described it. "I'm a naïve 20-year-old kid, and I'm thinking, 'Oh my god, what a great environment to work in.' . . . It was just an environment where I said, 'This is where I belong.'" Wolf recalled leaving the interview and calling his mother to tell her, "Med school was a great dream, but I found what I want to do."

Wolf abandoned his medical school plans and took a job at a different bank-holding company that offered higher pay, but he found the environment a far cry from the excitement he had experienced at Salomon Brothers: "I get there at 7:00 A.M., and no one's there till 9:00 A.M. And [later] it's like, the bell rang at 5:00 P.M., and everyone was ready to leave." Wolf wanted to experience the long hours and intensity of investment banking. So after nine months, he "literally begged Salomon to get into their next training class."

He spent 10 years at Salomon Brothers before joining UBS AG, a Swiss global financial services company and one of the largest managers of private wealth assets in the world.[13] Wolf rose through the ranks at UBS, becoming president of UBS Investment Bank in 2004 and chairman and CEO of the UBS Group Americas division in 2007. When I asked him if he still loved his work in the industry that had lured him away from his intended career, he paused for a long time before replying with the reason why his answer is yes:

> *There isn't a day I don't open the paper [and] relate it to something in our industry. Whether it's with oil or there's a war going on, or whether it's what's going on in a political party or where we are with taxes, or currency, or what we're doing in China, or free trade. There is not another industry, in my opinion, that can tangentially be part of everything that's going on in this world.*

These factors—the energy and excitement, the people at the top of their game, and the relevance to world events—are what many platinum leaders love about their work. And it does not always require personal sacrifice. Instead of seeing his busy work life as a detriment to his marriage and family, Wolf considers aspects of it a blessing. "If you are financially secure, it probably removes 80 percent of the tension points in a marriage," he pointed out. While the 2008 recession hit everyone, rich and poor, to some extent, Wolf said his family avoided feeling its sting since they have always lived well below their means. He and his family only have one home, and it is the same first house they bought in 1993.

It is clear that the intense lifestyle of leading a major enterprise is too costly to be about something as small as money. Leaders lead because they are passionate about what they do. As Jeff Smisek, the CEO of United Airlines succinctly put it: "I don't really *not* work. I don't have a life. . . . With telecommunications as they are, and BlackBerries, you're pretty much working around the clock. But that's okay, because my kids are grown, my wife has a job, my dog is okay—and I love this business."

CHAPTER 7

Lead for Good

Motivations and Outcomes

The people we know, the events we experience, and the places we visit leave an immeasurable impression on us and, in turn, on what we contribute to the world. So it should come as no surprise that platinum leaders' greatest contributions to society are highly influenced by their personal histories, inherent motivations, and private influences. One mother's 15-year battle with breast cancer left an indelible impact on her daughter's life and ultimately, the lives of millions:

> *Extending my mother's life from the first time she had breast cancer, when I was 15, to the time that I was 30 mattered. It mattered because she got to see her daughter grow up and become a professor at Stanford and go into womanhood, and it mattered for me to have my mother in those years.*

Millions of people could share a similar story, but what makes this one particularly important is that it was spoken by Condoleezza Rice in 2002 at a meeting of President Bush's inner circle. They were considering the launch of the President's Emergency Plan for AIDS Relief (PEPFAR), a global health program of unprecedented scale to provide relief from the AIDS pandemic. At the time of this meeting, the question on the table was whether PEPFAR should provide antiretrovirals, which do not cure AIDS but extend the lives of people who have contracted the disease. This is when Rice spoke up. "If you can extend the life of a mother long enough to see her child graduate from high school, it matters," she said.

Michael Gerson, a Bush aide who was present at the meeting, told me that this was one of the most poignant moments he experienced in his years at the White House. He was affected not only by the true and moving story but by the fact that one woman's experiences would help to shape the fates of millions of suffering people in similar situations.

Platinum leaders like Rice are indeed poised to leverage the good from a single life or a single experience 100-fold. Spurred by Rice's own story, half of PEPFAR's funding went toward providing antiretroviral drugs. From 2003 to 2007, PEPFAR averted an estimated 1.1 million deaths in Africa and reduced the death rate by 10 percent in the targeted countries. Despite criticism of PEPFAR's requirement that one-third of its prevention funds be used to promote abstinence programs, PEPFAR has been called "the most lasting bipartisan accomplishment of the Bush presidency" and has received widespread praise.[1]

The stakes do not have to be life or death to be important. There were other ways, for example, that Rice drew upon her personal experiences to make decisions that affected millions of people. While serving as secretary of state, she would watch the *local* news every day when she exercised at 4:30 A.M., believing that "if a foreign-policy issue made the local news, it was salient to the American people." When she saw a news story about a woman being unable to follow through on vacation plans because she had not received her passport in time, Rice thought, "Uh-oh, passports. That's me." She had known that the new Western Hemisphere Travel Initiative (which required passports for Americans to enter countries like Canada, Mexico, and Bermuda) would put a strain on passport application processing, but she was unaware that people were having to wait six months for a passport. So Rice got to work reducing the backlog to three weeks.

It is easy to imagine that high-profile, powerful leaders are only concerned with their own interests, devoting their resources to their own comfort and advancement. They are caught up in the world of executive suites, town cars, obsequious insiders, and consuming jobs. And there certainly are those who never make it beyond Narcissus' pool. But for platinum leaders—the ones who really stand out for the impact they are having—their work is personal.

Of the hundreds of business leaders I interviewed, Barry Rowan articulated the most compelling and succinct statement on the purpose of business. For him, "the fundamental purpose of business is to serve." He described four ways that business serves the larger community: through strengthening the economy, bettering the lives of customers, creating a work environment "that enables people to grow into full expressions of themselves," and being a responsible citizen of the community. After the 2011 tsunami hit Japan, Vonage (where Rowan served as CFO) offered free calling to Japan as a goodwill effort to increase communication to and within the struggling nation. This measure cost them, but they saw it as the right thing to do to support a struggling community. While businesses can't always afford to give away their goods, there is value in occasional, strategic philanthropy like this.

MOTIVATIONS

With so many resources and opportunities both at work and away from it, how do leaders who are pursuing the common good choose among the many options? And what drives them? In his 1918 lecture "Politics as Vocation," sociologist Max Weber analyzed two ethical frameworks held by leaders.[2] First, the ethic of responsibility takes the big picture view, calling for the sacrifice of principles in order to achieve the necessary ends. The ethic of conviction, on the other hand, maintains that we should do the right thing in each particular moment, regardless of the long-term consequences. Both frameworks have their strengths and weaknesses. Sometimes—and as a society, we hope for this—leaders are able to access both their personal convictions *and* their public responsibilities for the good of many.

The Ethic of Responsibility

The ethic of responsibility is all about outcome. Leaders with this ethic value the ends over the means, and they frequently feel an obligation toward a specific institution or goal. The ethic of responsibility is most concerned with taking practical steps to achieve tangible results.

Dick Kovacevich is known as the wildly successful (albeit understated) chairman and CEO of Wells Fargo, one of the largest banks in the United States. In the mid 1990s, Kovacevich was running Norwest Corporation, a large bank based in Minnesota. He knew that in order to grow, Norwest would have to expand into other regions. So in 1998, he led a merger of the regional bank with Wells Fargo. Kovacevich became the CEO of the new company, which kept the Wells Fargo name to avoid the regional connotation of the name "Norwest."

One of the first decisions Kovacevich made was to move the company headquarters from Minneapolis, where Norwest had been based, to San Francisco, where Wells Fargo's headquarters was situated. This was a very unpopular decision; many people were angry that Kovacevich was pulling out of Minnesota, which is home to only half as many Fortune 500 firms as California. The bank would, of course, still have a presence in Minneapolis, but the local business community was worried it would downsize its business in Minneapolis to the detriment of the community. Kovacevich, however, was adamant that the move needed to happen, even though it meant depriving the Minnesota economy of the company's headquarters. He knew that he needed to learn more about the Wells Fargo side of the organization, whose business in California was 10 times that of the firm's business in Minnesota.

Kovacevich was not deaf to the cries of the business community; he has a personal ethic of community development, but his decisions are more informed by practical considerations. "There aren't any tough decisions," Kovacevich told me. He went so far as to take out pen and paper and draw a graph laying out how to judge the costs and rewards of a particular decision. "There's only one way you can solve this one," he said. "It's very simple; you test. Let's say there are only two answers. Test one of them. If it turns out well, then that's the one. If it doesn't, then you know it's the other one, right?" This was when Kovacevich's background in industrial engineering was apparent. In the lab, decisions are made based on facts of outcome, not people or politics.

Lynn Elsenhans is well known in the oil industry as being the first woman to lead a major oil company; she was CEO of Philadelphia-based Sunoco for four years. Before leading Sunoco, Elsenhans spent most of her career at Royal Dutch Shell. At the start of our interview, Elsenhans shared with me some of the core expectations of her childhood. Among them, she said, "There was the expectation of what I would call 'responsibility'; being the kind of person who took accountability for your own actions, was a responsible person, someone who maintained their commitments." As she ascended to leadership, this accountability to commitments grew into an ethic of responsibility to make sacrifices in order to protect her organization's long-term health.

For example, Elsenhans told me a story from her time at Shell when she travelled to personally close down a plant in Odessa, Texas. "This was a plant that did everything right," she said. "They had the best safety record. They had great productivity. . . . How do you go and tell people [who have] essentially done everything that you've asked them to do that you have to shut them down?" The small plant had to close because it could no longer compete with larger plants in the Gulf of Mexico. "So their world got completely changed on them through no fault of their own," Elsenhans said. She continued:

> *I went through it with them, explained why it was happening. I explained what the company was going to do in terms of offering them employment at other plants, but that meant that they'd have to move. . . . They took it so professionally, and I didn't get booed, I didn't get people storming out, and to this day, it just stuck with me. . . . I really felt badly about it and they really did everything they could to make me feel less badly about it. [There was] a certain humanity about it that was very touching.*

Across the board, leaders said layoffs were their hardest periods, and platinum leaders acknowledge their part in the layoffs and regret their necessity.

But the ethic of responsibility is not idealistic; it acknowledges the necessity of making decisions that, in the immediate term, call for significant sacrifices. Its adherents make decisions one step at a time, obligated to act to achieve specific outcomes, no matter the cost.

Ethic of Conviction

The success of Sunoco and Wells Fargo make it clear that Elsenhans and Kovacevich made the right decisions on behalf of their companies, but sometimes the ethic of responsibility can be inappropriately employed. In the fall of 2011, the world was shocked as the details of the Pennsylvania State University child-sex-abuse scandal unfolded in appalling detail: the years of repeated abuse, the awareness of Penn State administrators, and their deplorable inaction. President Graham Spanier, Coach Joe Paterno, and others involved had chosen to look the other way, because they believed inaction to be the best decision for Penn State in the long run. They privileged the ambition of a reputable and successful football team over the immediate need for justice for the victims.

I interviewed John Surma, the recently retired CEO and chairman of U.S. Steel, in the spring of 2011, but today Surma is unenviably known as the face of the Penn State trustees at the time of the scandal. Surma was the vice chairman of the board and was asked to handle the university's response. While Surma and the board certainly wanted what was best for the university in the long run, they also knew that action had to be taken on behalf of the victims. In the face of intense criticism from die-hard fans and alumni, Surma insisted on the dismissal of both Spanier and Paterno, facing the resulting media storm head-on. While board chair Steve Garban would go on to resign for his involvement, Surma was widely lauded for his even-keeled handling of the situation.

The ethic of conviction holds that leaders should be true to their moral principles, regardless of the outcome. "Let there be justice, though the world perish," is one age-old motto along these lines.[3] Basically, leaders who hold tight to an ethic of conviction prioritize faithfulness to an ideal above practical steps for problem solving. Surma has a history of maintaining an ethic of conviction.

U.S. Steel is the largest producer of steel, with a revenue of $17 billion and more than 42,000 employees. As U.S. Steel's CEO and chairman, Surma has reached great heights. But one of the challenging aspects of Surma's position today is that he is responsible for the pensions of U.S. Steel's retirees, which total around $500 million a year—almost as much as U.S. Steel's capital budget. "I think about what I could have done—we could have done—since 2001 with an extra $500 million a year. What we could have done, it's unbelievable—where we could be right now!" Surma acknowledged. His personal convictions, however, have superseded any thoughts of default: "These people retired with a deal. It's nobody's fault; it's the way life is, and we have to take care of it. And hopefully we'll get through at some point, and over time it will work its way out." This is a classic ethic-of-conviction reasoning—we can't be responsible for the results of doing the right thing. Despite the financial detriment these pensions mean to the company, Surma remains committed to his moral duty.

Current employees also feel the effects of Surma's convictions. When he first came into his position, U.S. Steel's safety statistics were near the best in the industry, but Surma considered this pitiful praise. He compared it to "being the valedictorian at the reform school." Before Surma's safety initiative, U.S. Steel had 105 employees seriously injured in one year. The next year, it had dropped to 13. Further, Surma incentivized safety in his own contract and those of his managers in order to provide additional accountability. He lost 20 percent of one bonus because of one incident where six people were injured.

Early on in Surma's tenure, U.S. Steel came to a crossroads. Essentially they would either be bought out by a private-equity firm or they could buy a recently bankrupted company called National Steel. Surma decided to take the risk and merge with National Steel. Tensions were running high between company management and the steelworkers union that represented the majority of both U.S. Steel and National Steel's workers. Surma got in the weeds with the union workers to ensure a successful transition. "I sat through the whole negotiation," Surma said. "[It] took about three weeks, all night. And I figured that I wouldn't have understood the soul of the company until I did that." He was the only U.S. Steel president to ever go to such lengths for labor negotiations, and he told me that the experience changed his life: "It was a big deal, really hard, and it was probably the best thing I've ever done." Continually, Surma has set aside what has traditionally been considered good business in order to hold true to his moral convictions. Thanks to Surma's actions, Penn State is slowly recovering, but the same cannot be said for U.S. Steel. The stock price has fallen 90 percent since 2008, and Surma and much of his executive team were replaced in late 2013.

Sometimes a leader's moral convictions can cause an internal conflict difficult to solve. Cheryl Dorsey developed such a conviction during her year as a White House Fellow in the Clinton administration. Having a front-row seat to the Monica Lewinski debacle opened Dorsey's mind to ask questions about character and accountability. "I don't consider myself partisan," she told me. "I don't consider myself ideological, but I just think . . . there is a moral and ethical dimension to leadership, and I do think there is a solid North Star and you have to serve as an example." Dorsey had shared with her colleagues her conviction that if she had been in the president's position, she would have resigned as a matter of principle. They called her naïve. Ultimately, Dorsey decided that politics was not the best place for her. Instead, she went on to lead Echoing Green, a nonprofit hub that encourages and launches social entrepreneurs, and a better fit with her understanding of leadership as moral example-setting.

Even though Dorsey could have accomplished good outcomes as a politician, she was not willing to do so at the expense of her convictions. When applied wisely, personal convictions can lead to lasting and flourishing good. However, just like the ethic of responsibility, the ethic of conviction can be taken too far. Thankfully, Dorsey and Surma show that leaders driven by conviction are not necessarily dogmatists.

Combining Conviction and Responsibility

In his original lecture, Weber described the two motivation systems as "fundamentally differing and irreconcilably opposed maxims."[4] He also stated that the best leaders operate alternately out of both systems, deciding in each situation whether it is best to relinquish control of the outcome for the integrity of the process (the ethic of conviction), or to compromise principles for the sake of the ultimate objective (the ethic of responsibility). The give and take of these two ethics can be seen in the life of Michael Maudlin. Maudlin has been driven by conviction since his conversion to Christianity, which now provides his *raison d'être*: "I was almost like a knight in my fantasy literature who had no purpose, and Arthur finally came up and said, 'Here is your mission.'" Maudlin exercises that mission as the editorial director and vice president at HarperOne, an imprint of HarperCollins:

> *Being part of something bigger, contributing to a nobler and grander cause is very important to me. And that's my primary motivation in publishing. . . . It's an incredible privilege to work in publishing, because I think it's the skeletal system of the human enterprise of being at our best.*

Maudlin's love of the exchange of ideas leads him to endorse what he calls "robust publishing," a sometimes intuitive, sometimes pragmatic approach to acquiring a *range* of manuscripts. His choices have brought him in conflict with some of the evangelical Christian community, but he persists.

Maudlin told me about two books that came before the publishing house. One, by a celebrity psychic, was about the "afterlives of the rich and famous." Maudlin knew there would be a market for the book, but he winced at the idea of publishing it, because "it just feels like a fake book." But since Maudlin knew it would be successful, he took it on. His responsibility to HarperCollins trumped his personal ethic of conviction.

A second book came to Maudlin's desk that he was passionate about—an academic book that proposed a new way of looking at faith in the current culture. But he was unable to get any interest in it from his colleagues, so he had to turn it away: "I *could* insist and get people to get it approved, or negotiate—I've done that before—but it's always a mistake. Because unless you have buy-in from the house, it's hard to get energy." In occasions like these, Maudlin prioritizes his responsibility to the organization first. Still, a balance between the two forces—profit and worthiness—is necessary. Maudlin explained that if HarperOne only printed easy moneymakers, its reputation would suffer:

> *There are some books that we do that I feel a little embarrassed about our contribution to the noise out there, so that was one agonizing part. It makes me all the more work harder to make sure that the good books are successful, so we can keep having a mandate for doing those.*

Both conviction and responsibility are needed for a successful enterprise. A good leader like Maudlin knows when to follow his passions and when to bow to necessity in order to secure a good result.

MECHANISMS OF INFLUENCE

Despite their frequent obliviousness to the injustice of their compensation and advantages, platinum leaders understand that they have been blessed with extraordinary resources. And they seek to employ those resources to address problems in the world around them. This generally happens through philanthropy, the wielding of prestige to influence others, and the development of organizations into instruments for the common good.

Philanthropy

The most obvious day-to-day difference between an executive and the average person is income. As the most tangible thing that separates the haves from the have-nots, money, when given philanthropically, can not only do a great deal of good but can communicate concern for the well-being of others.

All 550 of the leaders I interviewed are philanthropists in some form or another. The average amount of annual charitable giving was just under $800,000. The lowest amount given was $1,500, and the largest was $100,000,000, with 12 other leaders giving at least eight figures. Less than half regularly give under six figures, and a quarter gave over $1 million during the 10 years of this study. According to Federal Reserve data, the top 1 percent of earners (a group less exclusive than this leadership set but similar in composition) account for 30 percent of philanthropic giving.

Many leaders also shared stories of spontaneous, small investments. They talked about putting the son of their secretary through college or loaning money to a friend. Several described seeing a television special on homelessness or reading an article about a displaced refugee family and being so inspired as to form a council on homelessness or to sponsor a refugee family. We all feel sympathy when we hear stories of need or tragedy, but because of their tremendous resources, these leaders are able to do something meaningful about it.

The vast majority of leaders' giving is not to individuals but to organizations. Most leaders who give take a strategic approach to their philanthropy, carefully planning their giving, and investigating the organizations they give to, to make as large an impact as possible. For them, giving to a charity is more like venture investing; they want to see a return on their capital—changed lives, measurably improved communities. "I used to be one of these people that did contributions like peanut butter, you know, give everybody a little," said one woman who today gives primarily to her alma mater. "A few years back, I decided, you know, I'd really rather concentrate where I give in order to try to make more of an impact."

The overwhelmingly most popular giving cause was education, with 66 percent of the leaders giving to educational causes, largely colleges and universities. In fact, the more money a leader gave away, the more likely she was to give to education. Colleges and universities have the advantage over aid and charity organizations in that leaders have firsthand experience with them. Sponsoring a child in Africa is unquestionably a good deed, but endowing a medical center at one's alma mater can be a more personally meaningful investment because of the individual connection to the school. And the new center could ultimately impact that child in Africa on a systemic level.

The next most popular giving category was religious causes, which a third of the leaders donated to. (Giving to community, art, or antipoverty causes were each mentioned by less than 15 percent of leaders.) Significantly more conservatives than liberals gave at least seven figures. Business executives, who make much more than do their analogs in other fields, gave the most. In fact, only 4 of the 94 leaders who regularly give over $1 million annually are *not* in business.

Philanthropy is more than just writing a check for these leaders; most have some sort of passion project where they insert time and energy for the greater good. Over half serve on the board of a nonprofit organization, and nearly 10 percent have their own foundations through which they channel their giving. One NBA Hall-of-Famer started a service-based elementary school for disadvantaged kids in the twilight of his career. Kay Krill, the CEO of Ann Taylor, launched "Ann Cares," a corporate charitable initiative focusing on women, children, and the environment. Neil Clark Warren of eHarmony said he and his wife "love giving money away" and primarily give anonymously. Many nonprofit executives give a significant portion of their salaries back to their organizations.

I found an interesting trend among a few other leaders (like David Weekley of Texas-based David Weekley Homes): they found companies, make millions, and then step down. For these leaders, the largest benefit of their financial success is their ability to give back, so they retire from corporate life to focus on strategic philanthropy. eBay founder Pierre Omidyar, for example, is only in his forties, but his primary focus now is philanthropy. Like Bill Gates, he is becoming increasingly known more for his philanthropy than for the technological service he created. His legacy of giving may outlast the company that made it all possible.

Omidyar's largest gift to date was $100 million to Tufts University (his alma mater) to form the Omidyar-Tufts Microfinance Fund. Rather than simply put his name on a dorm or endow a department chair, he wanted to make an investment that would involve the university in his passions, encouraging business initiative among the less fortunate.

Clout

Sometimes the prestige a leader lends to an organization is more valuable than whatever she can give to it financially. Money can go far, but a leader's reputation can have a multiplicative effect of attracting attention and funding from additional sources.

After serving in the White House as the surgeon general, David Satcher received job offers from institutions such as Harvard and Stanford. But Lou Sullivan, a friend of Satcher's and the outgoing president of Morehouse, was looking to start a National Center of Primary Care and wanted the well-known Satcher as its director. It needed Satcher's clout. But Morehouse could offer none of the perks of the other institutions: no endowed chair, not even a contract. On a visit to Stanford, Satcher's wife told him, "You know, David, Stanford's made us a great offer. But I know you, and I know your heart is at Morehouse, where you can make the greatest difference." So Satcher returned to his alma mater in Atlanta.

There were points when Satcher wondered if his decision had been a mistake. When the new Morehouse President Jim Gavin was fired, Satcher was pressured to assume an interim presidency, which he eventually did. This was not the role Satcher had hoped to play, but he was committed to using his influence to do what was best for Morehouse. Most observers believe he did the right thing by going to Morehouse, where he had the highest potential for impact on the new program.

Perhaps the most well-known example of a leader who has translated prestige into political power is U2's Bono. Bono is a world famous rock star, but his musical fame is closely followed by his fame as a human-rights advocate. PEPFAR, mentioned at the beginning of the chapter, was spurred on by Bono's agreement to trade a political endorsement for financial investment in AIDS care on the part of the G. W. Bush administration. When Paul O'Neill was treasury secretary, he initially turned down a meeting with Bono, saying, "I think his music is fine, and I'm sure he's fine, but I just don't have time to do social stuff." Eventually, however, Bono was able to secure an appointment with him. And according to O'Neill, "Bono convinced me in 15 minutes that maybe he wasn't just a rock star." The two wound up taking a highly publicized trip to Africa together in 2002. O'Neill said the trip was good for him in that "it helped me to get some issues on the table about USAID policy that I thought had been neglected forever and needed to be redressed." Bono's prestige got him in the door with O'Neill, and he was able to open O'Neill's eyes both to needs and to opportunities to meet them.

Clout is most effective as currency when it is invested in small organizations like Morehouse or lesser-known causes like AIDS in Africa in the 1990s. The right person's investment can elevate an institution or a movement to the international scene.

Organizations for the Common Good

"We don't like suits around here," said the security guard as I was ushered upstairs at Southwest's headquarters in Dallas. Apparently, I had chosen the wrong outfit to wear to the quirky corporate headquarters. Outside, a group of employees played sand volleyball, and wall hangings made the space feel more like a family home than a company's base of operations. I was on my way to meet the most powerful woman in the high-flying world of U.S. aviation, Colleen Barrett. Barrett is not your typical corporate executive. She did not graduate from an Ivy League school; in fact, she only attended junior college. She does not have a passport, or even a driver's license, and for many years, she was a struggling legal secretary.

Barrett started her career as a single mother working for a lawyer named Herb Kelleher. When one of Kelleher's clients founded Southwest Airlines (a Texas interstate carrier), he was hired as the corporate secretary of the new company. When Southwest's first president literally walked out of the boardroom, the directors held an emergency meeting and asked Kelleher to step in as interim president. "The others [on the board] were politicians and investors," Barrett explained. "They didn't know anything about the business, and of course, the whole business up until that point had pretty much been lawsuits." Kelleher could not serve as both president and corporate secretary, so the board blithely appointed Barrett as the new corporate secretary. Eventually, she worked her way up to company president.

Not only was her path to the top out of the ordinary, but so are her methods. As the airline grew, federal legislation threatened to force Southwest to relocate its base at Dallas's Love Field to the massive Dallas/Fort Worth International Airport. But Southwest didn't want to abandon its community. Considerable conflict arose with the city, the federal government, and other airlines about whether Southwest could expand its business and still remain at Love Field.

Southwest decided to take its fight to the people, believing more in populism than elite cronyism. Using ads in local newspapers, the airline asked patrons to write their members of Congress, and it filled 18-wheelers with petitions in what Barrett described as a "take-it-to-the-streets, take-it-to-the-people" campaign. According to Barrett, this had been the company's only option: "We didn't have any money. We couldn't afford $100,000 campaigns. We had to do it all street-smart, because that's all we had." The plan worked. Newspapers across Texas ran front-page stories about Southwest. Barrett told me: "We didn't have the money, so we had to get the publicity the other way, and we became really the best David-and-Goliath story in the United States of America."

And today the plucky little airline still operates out of Love Field. Its stock is even listed as "LUV" on the New York Stock Exchange, and Southwest has become the most profitable airline since deregulation in the late 1970s.

Thanks to Barrett and her priorities—including something called "the culture committee"—"LUV" has become a catchphrase at Southwest. There is a People Department instead of a Human Resources Department. Frontline employees are trusted with the power to make decisions when customers have problems. This faith in and dedication to employees inspires a great deal of loyalty. One article describes the atmosphere at Southwest as "a startling amount of office hugging and kissing in lieu of handshakes; elaborate practical jokes; and on-the-premises beer drinking at headquarters, as long as it is after 5 P.M. . . . anything to lighten the mood and put a little bounce in the step of nearly 35,000 Southwest employees."[5] In the buttoned-down airline industry where tensions are hot and any provocation could lead to a strike, Southwest's culture of levity and camaraderie may just be the thing that kept it strong as other airlines declined. Thanks to Herb Kelleher and Colleen Barrett, this single airline has democratized air travel for working families, helped small businesses, and proven that a major company can be countercultural.

Positive Corporate Culture Today, if you walk into the Container Store anywhere in the country, Chairman Emeritus Garrett Boone just might be your retailer. Boone, who cofounded the declutterer's paradise in 1978 with business partner Kip Tindell, still likes to keep his hand in sales. When he visits one of the company's 60 stores, he leads employee sales training and will work the sales floor himself. Growing up, Boone never imagined that he would go into retail. He thought it was "the lowest of the low." But today he feels very differently:

> There's nothing more challenging, more fun, than retail selling. . . . Everything is real-time. You don't get to retreat to some ivory tower to think about this customer for days; you've got to form an instant bond with them. . . . You've got to immediately be good at investigating and asking questions and figuring out what connection you can strike between their needs and our products.

The Container Store is noted for its friendly atmosphere and for employee devotion. It has an employee turnover rate of less than 10 percent, compared to the retail average of 100 percent.[6] Employee care is a large part of The Container Store's ethos. The company is pickier than most— hiring only 3 percent of its job applicants. It pays higher than the national average for retail positions and consistently make Fortune's list of 100 Best Companies to Work For.

The Container Store's "Foundational Principles" are evident in the daily running of the company. For example, the principle "An Air of Excitement" is bolstered by daily huddles every morning as employees share birthdays, product tips, and goals for the day. "Man in the Desert Selling" holds that just as a man coming out of the desert would require not only water but also rest and shelter, so customers need more than a simple provision of their immediate needs; they need solutions to their organizational dilemmas. Boone and Tindell's business model demonstrates how platinum leaders transform their values into corporate cultures of opportunity and empowerment.

Boone acknowledged that leading such a successful business has provided him awareness to expand his influence, and he tries to make the most of it.[7] "It's good for me. It's not for my ego, but it obviously allows me to do various things in the nonprofit world and the foundation world . . . that are useful," Boone said. The best leaders are able to leverage their clout, philanthropy, and organizational influence toward their unique passions. Boone Family Foundation has three clear foci: the environment, children, and women. Boone's philanthropic focus on women was inspired in large part by his mother who, he said, had she been born 20 years later, "would have been a corporate executive." "I also just believe that women [should] have an equal partnership in directing the outcome of the world, because if they're not there, I think things won't turn out well." And since the majority of The Container Store's customer base is female, Boone sees further importance in supporting causes that benefit his patrons. He told me specifically about his work encouraging and financing women to run in political campaigns and funding businesses started by women. Boone not only gives his money to support this cause, but he makes sure it is lived out in The Container Store's management. At the time of the interview, he said that 10 of The Container Store's 13 vice presidents were women.

VIEW FROM THE TOP

Like Garrett Boone, the majority of the leaders in this study are people you have likely never heard of, especially when it comes to the business and nonprofit leaders. When we look at the forces that shape the world around us, we see governments and major companies—anonymous behemoths. And even then, we only see the results of their movements diluted through perception, time, and distance. But behind the media blind, behind the corporate identities and the government showmanship, are people. People whose everyday actions can change history. They are the people at the helm of society's most powerful institutions. And each leader has a personal ethic, unique motivations, and a specific journey.

Whatever their abundance or lack, every leader starts out with at least two things: potential and opportunity. The lotteries of genetics and socioeconomics determine how much young leaders will be able to trade on their natural talents or the accumulated advantages of their upbringing, but it is up to the protoleader to make the most out of what he has. This skill—the ability to maximize opportunity—is perhaps the key indicator of true platinum leaders. They take what is given to them—education, connections, experiences—and leverage them toward success. They may not always do it well, but they never stop learning and doing better the next time. This is especially important when it comes to gaining entrée into the matrix of power. All it takes is one key relationship or mentorship, and protoleaders who are able to capitalize on this connection begin the climb to securing access to and position within the top tier of society.

But being a leader is not only about maximizing. Protoleaders must also learn to generalize. Platinum leadership requires more than management skills and specialized knowledge. It requires a broad understanding of the varied aspects of powerful organizations and a capacity to handle the myriad responsibilities of an executive—resolving personnel issues, vision casting, culture building, and financial management, among others. They need to have interest in and comprehension of the many disparate facets of organizations and leadership. In short, a leader needs to embrace a liberal arts approach to life. Perhaps the easiest way to both cement access to the matrix of power and to develop this liberal arts mind-set is through a catalyst (such as the White House Fellowship), a program or experience sponsored by a national institution that gives a protoleader opportunities to develop her generalist mind-set and connections to superior networks while she undertakes meaningful work.

Of course, what is a leader without his bully pulpit? Without the title of CEO, admiral, or senator? A leader's power not only comes from his organization, but it is exercised *through* his organization. A CEO has clout in the larger world, but she has the most influence among her own constituents and in the organizational resources at her direct disposal.

Platinum leadership is more than a job. Depersonalized by their positions, these leaders are subject to public anger and blame for negative consequences of things both within and beyond their control. Often they are forced to endure criticism from people ignorant of all the facts, keep a positive demeanor in the midst of intense pressure, or suffer in silence over a failed venture. And the hours go way beyond nine to five, so the role has a tendency to take over every aspect of a person's life. Leaders must daily weigh their responsibilities to the thousands of people affected by their work and to the few but precious members of their families and inner circles.

This is the fundamental tension of platinum leadership: on one hand, leaders are simply people with unique histories and quirks, likes and dislikes, strengths and failings. But on the other hand, in the eyes of their constituents and the wider world, leaders are synonymous with their institutions, larger-than-life figures with great power, whose personal lives are taken into account only in the face of scandal. With so much expected of them, many leaders buy into their own hype and imagine they merit ludicrously high salaries and perks prevalent among today's executives.

As much as leaders struggle with this tension between their ordinary lives and their extraordinary responsibilities, this juncture of personal passions and professional opportunities is precisely where leaders draw out their opportunities for positive influence. As individuals, they have unique dreams and motivations, and as leaders, they have the resources to act on these things and the scope to do it on a large scale. In order to make the largest impact for the common good, leaders are called to maximize every opportunity. At their best, platinum leaders not only make change, but they lead others in desiring and implementing this change as well.

A Strategic Investment for Global Impact

In 1977, Kien Pham was literally adrift. He was one of 300 Vietnamese refugees on a boat in the middle of the South China Sea. Pham recalled an evening on that boat when he and his father were gazing out over the water and his father shared with him some words of wisdom: "When you become successful in the future, share it with other people. I didn't do enough of it, and that contributed to the root of the problem that led to the revolution in our country. Poor people went to the enemies." There are a thousand different directions that Pham's life could have taken from that point in the South China Sea. Perhaps it was his father's words that set him on a course to achieve success and to share it with others.

Pham's family wound up in Colorado, where he attended the University of Colorado, Boulder. At UC Boulder, Pham attended a lecture by Congressman Tim Wirth, who mentioned the White House Fellowship as a key experience in his development. Six years later, after an MBA from Stanford, Pham was selected as a Fellow at age 27, and he received some media attention for his remarkable rise from Vietnamese refugee to working in the White House in just eight years. After his fellowship, his career took off. Pham worked at Procter & Gamble, at the Pentagon, and as vice president at Tenneco Gas in Houston. "I am a strong believer in making a difference in what I do every day, whether it is in a private-sector job or with my family or in a public project. I'm driven by that," Pham said. But he found that his success in the private sector was not enough. He did not want to just give back through charitable contribution but also through his personal influence.

In 1997, Pham got back in touch with Tim Wirth, the congressman who had introduced him to the White House Fellowship. Wirth had gone on to serve as a U.S. senator and then in the Clinton administration as the undersecretary of state for global affairs in the State Department. Wirth's responsibilities included human rights policy. Pham reminded Wirth that there were still 400 political prisoners held captive in Vietnam 22 years after the war. (The U.S. government had tried to secure their liberty without success.) Pham asked for Wirth's support, and then he asked for and received a corporate sabbatical from Tenneco. Returning to his home country, Pham introduced himself to U.S. Ambassador Pete Peterson, a former prisoner of war. They crafted a plan to use Pham's contacts in the Vietnamese government to win the release of *one* political prisoner. When they did, Pham advised, the ambassador was to "clap very loudly" in praise of the Vietnamese government. Through back channels, Pham put his plan in action, a prisoner was released, and the U.S. embassy applauded the action enthusiastically. Then Pham did it again. And again. He secured the release of one prisoner at a time, and at each occasion, the ambassador would praise the Vietnamese government. Eventually, the Vietnamese leaders grew to like the sound of the diplomatic corps clapping. After several months, Pham returned to his Vietnamese government contact and suggested that they switch "from retail to wholesale," that there be a grand amnesty for the year 2000 in which all remaining political prisoners would be released at once. The Vietnamese government, after being slowly wooed and eased into the idea, eventually agreed. Shortly before the turn of the millennium, Pham achieved his goal; all the prisoners, some who had been held captive for decades, were released.

This was a great political accomplishment. And it was also personal. When Pham started thinking about this initiative, he was motivated by the freedom and joy he could bring to so many people, but he was also motivated by thinking about one person in particular. There was one man on his mind every step of the way—from the boat in the South China Sea, to his classes at UC Boulder, to shaking hands with President Reagan as a White House Fellow, to his final negotiations with the Vietnamese government. This man was Pham's uncle, who was one of those 400 political prisoners. Today his uncle walks as a free man in California as the direct result of Pham's calculated risks in search of a better life for himself and others. Pham shared with me a Vietnamese saying that perfectly captured the risks and rewards of leadership, "If you don't go into the jungle, you cannot catch a tiger."

Platinum leaders live lives of high risk and high reward, maximizing every opportunity to make the biggest impact. Behind every organization is a leader, gifted with authority, influence, and power. And each leader has a personal story, nested in her networks, upbringing, and motivations that reverberates through her actions to influence her organization and the world.

Conclusion

In early 2013, everyone had something to say about JCPenney Company CEO Ron Johnson. The Apple retailing wunderkind, had been hired to transform the dowdy retail giant, but after just 17 months on the job, Penney's board fired Johnson, whose revolutionary plans backfired, costing the company over $2.5 billion in cash. The board then turned to former Penney CEO, Myron "Mike" Ullman, to bring stability to the beleaguered company. This decision was met with some agitation, as Ullman, though certainly competent, had been at the helm during the recession, which hit retailers hard. At the same time, his leadership had produced some measurable results. At the time of his retirement in 2012, one in two families in the United States shopped at JCPenney over the course of a year, customer-satisfaction scores were higher at Penney than at Nordstrom, and the company's employee-engagement scores (a measure of employee satisfaction) matched those of Starbucks. Indeed, he was seen as exceptional among his CEO peers. In 2010, the Yale Chief Executive Institute honored Ullman's work with its Legend in Leadership Award.

I first met Ullman many years earlier in 2004, the first time he was contemplating the invitation to take the helm of JCPenney, which was recovering from the brink of bankruptcy. We met over breakfast at The Pierre, a ritzy hotel bordering Central Park. Ullman's plain-spoken demeanor and no-nonsense vibe revealed his Midwestern upbringing, but he's been an achiever for a long time. Ullman first started making waves when he was appointed the chief business officer at the University of Cincinnati at age 29. Later, coming off a year in Washington as a White House Fellow, Ullman lined up a Cincinnati-based vice presidency with grocery giant Kroger but was lured to Dallas by Federated Department Stores for an interview. His interviewer told him something that made him reassess his goals:

It's not about the title or the money; it's about what you are going to learn, because you're starting over. Yeah, you're bright and all that kind of stuff, and you've been to the White House. But it

*means nothing if you can't contribute to the company. I suspect
that you are going to have trouble at Kroger unless they give you
a job where you can learn something. So how much is it going to
take to have you come here?*

His wife joined him in Dallas for the weekend, and they decided
that Federated was a good fit. He agreed that the learning opportunity
was the most valuable thing he could pursue right now, and he took
a position as the head of their warehouse. He accepted Federated's
lowest salary offer—an unheard-of practice, especially since they had
been willing to negotiate—in order to enter the company at a place
befitting his experience and not his perceived rank. Ullman worked
his way up quickly through seven jobs in four years, receiving a good
business education in the process, which he considered more valuable
than his paycheck.

Ullman eventually left Federated to serve as the group managing
director of Wharf (Holdings), a large business conglomerate in Hong
Kong (at the request of Wharf's chairman, Ullman's college roommate).
After two years, he heard from Macy's—which at that time was facing
serious financial trouble. He was hired as an executive vice president
and was promoted to CEO when Macy's declared bankruptcy. Rather
than simply liquidate the company—as some suggested—he turned it
around. Within two years, he had sold Macy's to Federated for over $4
billion. After the merger, Ullman intended to take a year off, but he was
approached by Duty Free Shoppers (DFS), a privately held firm that sells
high-end goods in international airport terminals and downtown stores.

A couple years after Ullman took the helm of DFS, it was bought by
Bernard Arnault, the wildly successful French businessman and currently
the fourth-richest person in the world. Arnault wanted Ullman to stay on
and eventually asked him to take over leadership of his larger company,
LVMH (Moët Hennessy – Louis Vuitton), the massive luxury-goods
conglomerate. Ullman had to commute from San Francisco—where
his family needed to stay because of health issues for two of his
daughters—to Paris, where LVMH is based. He held this role until
his degenerative muscular and spinal condition made it hard for him to
walk and impossible to commute internationally. At the time he stepped
down, Ullman was the world's leading retail guru, having led successful
enterprises on three continents.

Ullman's post-LVMH "retirement" consisted of both corporate and nonprofit board obligations with companies such as Starbucks, Ralph Lauren, Taubman, Segway, and Global Crossing. Then a desperate JCPenney board approached him, and again, he saw a chance to do something challenging. But he is perhaps most inspired by his work as chairman of Mercy Ships, a faith-based nonprofit that provides free surgery and health care to people in developing nations through a hospital ship that travels the West African coast. More than any other individual among the 550 I interviewed, Ullman not only demonstrated for me how to integrate one's Christian commitments—which are important to me personally—into one's leadership but also how to do this in a competitive, pluralistic world in a way that is not off-putting.

I became so impressed with Ullman that I recruited him to join the board of Gordon College after I assumed the presidency. This was the context in which I went to visit him shortly after he reassumed the top job at Penney in April of 2013. Ron Johnson had been gone less than a month, and the waffling of the board on leadership had the larger business community convinced Penney was on the brink of ruin. I expected the company headquarters to be in disarray; after all, they were still in a financial free fall. But everything seemed relatively calm. While walking back to Ullman's office, I asked his assistant about the mood since Ullman had returned a few days earlier: "How's morale these days?"

Her response was direct. "It's so much better," she said. "We know Mike loves us, and nothing draws out trust like love." Indeed.

INCARNATIONAL LEADERSHIP

We learn leadership most powerfully not from a book but from seeing it modeled. At its root, leadership hinges on the relationship between followers and the leader. And if there is an underlying design to the matrix of power in our society, it is the latticework of relational ties that bind us together to one another and to our institutions. I am convinced that the relational dimension of leadership requires those who seek influence to think carefully about the ways their personal values and faith commitments intersect with their responsibilities. In my own life, I have found this exercise to be tremendously helpful in clarifying the most important ways I can use my influence for the common good. Great leaders exercise influence through relationships—not just by walking a mile in our moccasins but by literally putting ourselves in the other person's place. This is incarnation. It's sacrificial. It's committed. It's all-in. In what follows, I outline a few key principles that I found while looking at the lives of great leaders who sought to integrate their values with their leadership roles.

Act personally, but think institutionally. Leadership is messy and complicated, and we often fall short of the ideals we set for ourselves, but without those ideals, leadership devolves into mere task management. In relationships with followers, leaders must develop what I would call savvy kindness, a deliberate approach to leading softly while fully understanding the hard realities of institutional life.

Hugh Heclo's wonderful book, *On Thinking Institutionally*, rightly reminds us that lasting cultural change occurs through major organizations. If we want to make a significant difference in the world, we have to think institutionally. I encourage my students to embrace, not avoid, big institutions as they look for jobs. When large institutions—such as the federal government or major corporations—implement a new approach or policy, the nation follows suit. But those innovations almost always start at the margins of the organization—and at low levels, where recent college graduates predominate. (One White House official confided to me that nearly all of an administration's policies are drafted by workers in their twenties: "We're led by a confederacy of kids.")

So how do we think institutionally without becoming jaded by the machinations of bureaucratic structures? By acting personally. We need noble, principles that compel us to take a genuine personal interest in the lives of those around us. We do this when we write notes of appreciation to outstanding employees, thanking them for their shared commitment to our cause. We look out for the institution's best interests when we realize that serious illness and death in the lives of employees necessitate our time, interest, and often our presence. And in my years of working at all kinds of institutions, I have never had a colleague take umbrage when I told him I was praying for him. These are all ways we demonstrate savvy kindness as leaders. Now, we must be prudent in how such messages are communicated and be mindful of how they may affect leader-follower relationships, but being sensible about the place of our personal values in the public square does not require being silent.

Maximize opportunities, but leave something behind. I am a big proponent of maximizing the opportunities that we are given. For this reason, I encourage students to meet personally the guest speakers who visit campus and to follow up with handwritten letters afterwards. You only get one chance to make a first impression, and I have seen a number of times how these kinds of actions have helped students secure internships or job interviews. Yet there can be a crassness to these sorts of transactions; self-advancement must be tempered with a wider view of how we should relate to one another. This is especially so for those in positions of power. The maximizing mind-set is what blinds so many executives to the extreme inequity of their salaries relative to their employees. We need regular reminders of those with lesser resources or opportunities, and that is where the ancient Jewish concept of gleaning is instructive.

In the book of Deuteronomy, Hebrew owners of land are told to avoid harvesting the corners of their wheat fields so that the poor are able to gather their own food. Even the animals should be free to eat while they harvest— much more so should workers benefit from the success of their companies. Gleaning contradicts the maximizing impulse, and it's a helpful reminder to all leaders of the need for margin in our own lives. As Dennis Bakke suggests in *Joy at Work*, a leader might push decision-making down to lower levels of the organization as a way of empowering those below. Or a firm can create more "margin" in employees' work schedules to encourage creativity and collaboration. Every day, we need to consider how we can leave enough behind for others to glean.

Great leaders sacrifice. Transformative power (at an institution, in a personal relationship, or in our daily work) almost always comes from great sacrifices. And moral authority—which is the leader's greatest currency for influence—develops not through usurping power, as some might contend, but through self-giving sacrifice. A number of leaders give up time with their families or the opportunity to have a family at all. Others no longer pursue their hobbies. Some companies even encourage this behavior by creating an insular organizational culture that requires workers to give up everything for the job. But I want to advocate for a more fundamental kind of sacrifice: a willingness to trade the privileges that make the leader's lifestyle more bearable in exchange for more substantial, and nobler, influence.

"Why not move into a nicer home?" I asked one Silicon Valley venture capitalist who decided to remain in his modest residence. "Because it frees me up to do more things philanthropically," he responded, "and the decision we've made gives me a chance to talk about my faith. My faith also compels me to pursue a lifestyle significantly beneath my means; it's how I live it out." The counterintuitive finding I encountered time and again in this study is simply that leaders gain influence by giving things up. By eschewing the perks that society has come to associate with powerful positions, we generate earnest questions from observers and followers. Around the world, I found people who made similar decisions to sacrifice what I would regard as their due (given their workloads and grueling schedules). Some sacrificed trivial things like close-in parking spaces or corner offices. Others gave up significantly more—multimillion-dollar executive bonuses, access to private planes, or invitations to special vacations or family retreats. When appropriate, they often passed these perks on to others who could enjoy them; other times, they simply saved their organization the money that would have otherwise been spent. What they gained in each case was tremendous respect and appreciation—not only from those who benefited directly from these sacrifices but also from those who considered such sacrifices excessive.

Power is alluring and addictive, yet it can be a tremendous catalyst for good. The surest antidote to the destructive nature of power in our world is for a leader to relinquish the personal benefits of power and to redirect those benefits to serve and bless those who would not otherwise receive them. In essence, the highest use of power is when it is sacrificed for the benefit of those with less power.

Mike Ullman helped me to see this concept in tangible form. He described it this way:

> *Leadership is a gift, but it's also a skill in the sense you have to not want it for you, you have to want it for them. If you want it for them, a selfless leader approach is, I think, the most effective way to lead.... I think to the extent that you leave behind something better than you inherited it, that's what it's about.*

Ullman's return to the CEO role in 2013 heralded a very public power struggle on the Penney board, one that resulted in the departure of activist investor Bill Ackman. But Ullman, who offered to return for an annual salary of one dollar, remained in the role out of a love for the company and its people. More recently, Ullman showed his solidarity with his stockholders by purchasing over 1 million dollars' worth of Penney's floundering stock himself. At root, leadership is a relationship of mutual power that advances a collective effort. Moral authority earned through sacrifice is the surest way for a leader to exercise that power for the greatest good.

At the beginning of Ron Johnson's tenure, everyone expected him to lead J. C. Penney on to great things. He is—by numerous accounts—a good and kind man, and his success in launching Apple's retail stores is still legendary. But his experience, which should have been his greatest strength, actually became his greatest liability. I learned from multiple sources that Johnson followed closely advice that he received from Steve Jobs before taking the Penney job: "Listen to your heart; listen to yourself, and no others." He applied much of the Apple formula to the Penney brand but without counsel from those who knew the company and its customers better than he. With little or no market research and no gradual rollout of his innovations (such as discontinuing discounts and coupons, redesigning the store layouts, and introducing more boutiques into the brand), Johnson alienated loyal customers and failed to attract new ones. The results were disastrous. They were compounded by the fact that he was out of touch with the core of the Penney business; he was living in another world. Literally. Rather than moving to Texas, Johnson commuted from the Bay Area. He also fired 19 of the top 22 officers at his company. Many saw his actions as revolutionary, but in all the wrong ways.

This is the peril of power. When it becomes solely about the preferences of a leader, empires fall and enterprises fail. Never before has confidence in society's leaders been so low, and the challenges we face so great. While lots of leadership literature today talks about trusting intuition and your heart, the clear message of the Bible is that the heart is, above all things, deceptive. When you *are* the job, you have to have remind yourself constantly of this reality. Simple daily practices can keep a leader from falling into the trap of self-deception. These include demonstrating savvy kindness to others, leaving enough for others to glean, and choosing to sacrifice what is your due. In so doing, we develop a leadership style grounded in love.

Notes

Introduction

1. This methodology, which I refer to as the "leapfrog method" (developed in my earlier work) gave me significantly more access to leaders than the "snowball" method off of which it is based, which was perfected by John Schmalzbauer (*People of Faith: Religious Conviction in American Journalism and Higher Education* [Ithaca, NY: Cornell University Press, 2003]) and Charles Kadushin ("Friendship Among the French Financial Elite," *American Sociological Review* 60 [1995]: 202–221). Asking leaders to recommend me to each other allowed me to avoid a host of secretarial gatekeepers and organizational barriers. (See D. Michael Lindsay, *Faith in the Halls of Power* [New York: Oxford University Press, 2007], 248 and 299 n. 1 for a fuller description of leapfrog methodology.)

2. See the appendix for more information on these variables and analysis.

3. See R. Marie Griffith, *God's Daughters: Evangelical Women and the Power of Submission* (Berkeley: University of California Press, 1997).

4. I conducted all of the interviews myself to avoid the bias of multiple interviewers, and at least 5 percent of the interviews were first coded independently by two research assistants and then tested to ensure intercoder reliability.

5. The initial screening process to determine which of the 550 leaders should be classified as platinum leaders involved traditional positional analysis. For leaders in business, this classification included those who held the roles of chairman, vice chairman, president, CEO, CIO, CFO, CTO, COO, executive vice president, senior vice president, treasurer, corporate secretary, or general counsel for a Fortune 1000 firm or the *Forbes* "Largest Private Companies" list. For leaders in academia, this included those who held the role of dean, provost, or president at a nationally ranked college or university

(as defined by the *U.S. News & World Report* rankings). For leaders in government and law, platinum leaders included those who held the positions of president/vice president of the United States, a commissioned officer of the White House (assistant, deputy assistant, or special assistant to the president), a senior official within the Executive Office of the President, a secretary, deputy secretary, undersecretary, assistant secretary, or general counsel for one of the 15 federal departments, head of one of 42 independent federal agencies, or civilian officer or flag officer of the Army, Navy, or Air Force. It also included members of the U.S. Senate and the House of Representatives, the librarian of Congress, the U.S. solicitor general, justices of the U.S. Supreme Court, ambassadors or ranking diplomats appointed to represent one nation to another, governors of the states and territories of the United States (or analogs in other countries), and chief executive officers of national and global policy and trade organizations. In the nonprofit sector, platinum leaders included the top paid officer and his/her senior executives (who were direct reports), and the organizational founder of any of the charities included in the *Forbes* list of 200 largest charities by annual revenue. For those in media, we included those who were president, vice president, CEO, editor, featured regular columnist, executive producer, news anchor, or television personality at one of the 14 national media outlets in the United States (ABC, CBS, NBC, Fox, MSNBC, CNN, the *New York Times*, the *Washington Post, USA TODAY*, the *Wall Street Journal, Associated Press, TIME, Newsweek*, and *U.S. News & World Report*) or at a nationally available cable television channel or a corresponding institution in another country. In addition to these positional analyses, platinum leaders included those artists, entertainers, and performers whose work was exhibited in an elite venue (such as Carnegie Hall) or who held membership in a highly selective artistic group (such as the Metropolitan Opera) in at least one of the following domains: dance, drama, music (opera, orchestra, vocal performance), visual arts, photography, painting, and sculpture. We included leading models and designers who were members of the *Chambre Syndicale de la Haute Couture* or editor at an associated publication. We also included those who had been executive producer, screenwriter, director, actor, or artist on a widely distributed movie, television show, or music album throughout the entertainment industry, as well as professional athletes, head coaches, and owners in one of the seven top-grossing professional sports leagues (National Football League, National Basketball Association, Major League Baseball, NASCAR, Professional Golfers' Association, Ladies Professional Golfers' Association, and National Hockey League).

6. Michel Foucault, *Discipline and Punish: The Birth of the Prison*, trans. Alan Sheridan, 1977 (New York: Vintage, 1995), 202.

7. One out of every nine significant personal influences mentioned by the leaders in this study was another study participant.

Chapter 1 Act Personally, But Think Institutionally

1. Richard L. Zweigenhaft and G. William Domhoff, *The New CEOs: Women, African American, Latino, and Asian American Leaders of Fortune 500 Companies* (Lanham, MD: Rowman & Littlefield, 2011).

2. The literature on interlocking directorates is extremely robust and has demonstrated how a small group of people exercise disproportionate power in elite circles through multiple board affiliations. See Val Burris, "The Interlock Structure of the Policy-Planning Network and the Right Turn in U.S. State Policy," *Research in Political Sociology* 17 (2008): 3–42; Clifford Kono, Donald Palmer, Roger Friedland, and Matthew Zafonte, "Lost in Space: The Geography of Corporate Interlocking Directorates," *American Journal of Sociology* 103 (1998): 863–911; William G. Roy, "The Unfolding of the Interlocking Directorate Structure of the United States," *American Sociology Review* 48 (1983): 248–257; Mark S. Mizruchi, *The American Corporate Network, 1904–1974* (Beverly Hills: Sage Publications, 1982); Beth Mintz and Michael Schwartz, "Interlocking Directorates and Interest Group Formation," *American Sociological Review* 46 (1981): 851–869; Ronald S. Burt, "A Structural Theory of Interlocking Corporate Directorates," *Social Networks* 1 (1979): 415–435; Michael P. Allen, "The Structure of Interorganizational Elite Cooptation: Interlocking Corporate Directorates," *American Sociological Review* 39 (1974): 393–406; Peter C. Dooley, "The Interlocking Directorate," *American Economic Review* 59 (1969): 314–323; Michael Useem, "Corporations and the Corporate Elite,"

Annual Review of Sociology 6 (1980): 41–77; Michael Useem, "Business Segments and Corporate Relations with U.S. Universities," *Social Problems* 29 (1981): 129–141; Michael Useem, *The Inner Circle: Large Corporations and the Rise of Business Political Activity in the U.S. and U.K.* (New York: Oxford University Press, 1984). The literature demonstrates that in all the networks examined, there is a broad, loosely linked network of powerful people, integrated by a group that Useem refers to as "the inner circle." The people in this inner circle act as network hubs, holding a wide range of formal and informal connections to other people of influence throughout the network.

3. In 1981, 70 percent of Fortune 500 manufacturing firms had at least one board member who also sat on another corporate board. See Mark S. Mizruchi, "What Do Interlocks Do? An Analysis, Critique, and Assessment of Research on Interlocking Directorates," *Annual Review of Sociology* 22 (1996): 271–298; Val Burris, "Interlocking Directorates and Political Cohesion among Corporate Elites," *American Journal of Sociology* 111 (July 2005): 249–283; Michael C. Dreiling, "The Class Embeddedness of Corporate Political Action: Leadership in Defense of the NAFTA," *Social Problems* 47 (February 2000): 21–48; John P. Heinz, Edward O. Laumann, Robert H. Salisbury, and Robert L. Nelson, "Inner Circles or Hollow Cores? Elite Networks in National Policy Systems," *Journal of Politics* 52 (1990): 356–390.

4. Sabra Chartrand, "Head of Peace Corps Named United Way President," *New York Times*, August 27, 1992, www.nytimes.com/1992/08/27/us/head-of-peace-corps-named-united-way-president.html.

5. See Mark S. Granovetter, "The Strength of Weak Ties," *American Journal of Sociology* 78 (May 1973): 1360–1380.

Chapter 2 Leadership Begins at 20

1. Curiously, though doctors are often well compensated and hold high-status positions in society, there are very few among America's top institutional drivers. In fact, only 2 percent of those I interviewed held a medical degree.

2. "Too Many Suits," *Economist*, November 26, 2011, www.economist.com/node/21539924. This was despite my going to considerable

lengths to recruit female participants to the study. Given that other studies (Thomas R. Dye, *Who's Running America? The Bush Restoration*, 7th ed. [Upper Saddle River, NJ: Prentice Hall, 2002]) have estimated that around 10 percent of America's leadership is female, there is no indication that my extra effort significantly affected the data—rather it allowed me to capture a more complete picture of women's experiences in leadership.

3. Ariane Hegewisch, Claudia Williams, and Vanessa Harbin, "The Gender Wage Gap by Occupation," fact sheet, the Institute for Women's Policy Research, April 2012, www.iwpr.org/publications/pubs/the-gender-wage-gap-by-occupation-1.

4 Juan M. Madera, Michelle R. Hebl, and Randi C. Martin, "Gender and Letters of Recommendation for Academia: Agentic and Communal Differences," *Journal of Applied Psychology* (November 2009): 1591–1599.

5. Garance Franke-Ruta, "Robert Putnam: Class Now Trumps Race as the Great Divide in America," *Atlantic*, June 30, 2012, www.theatlantic.com/politics/archive/2012/06/robert-putnam-class-now-trumps-race-as-the-great-divide-in-america/259256/. See also William Julius Wilson, *The Declining Significance of Race* (Chicago: University of Chicago Press, 2012).

6. Nine percent of the leaders who talked about their upbringing mentioned symbols of status or wealth that identified them as coming from privilege—an impressive statistic when we realize that at most, the upper class represents about 1 percent of the American populace. However, when trying to compare these with other statistics on class, one must bear in mind that attempting to identify the class background of elites is more of an art than a science. The lines between classes are always blurry, and as political scientist Thomas Dye reminds us, "America's upper classes avoid using the term class altogether."

7. This is especially notable when compared to Thomas Dye's estimated breakdown of the elite—30 percent upper class, 70 percent middle class. Though conducted with more strict definitions than the present study, Dye's methodology obscured the presence of a significant poor and working-class segment, because he used college attendance as an indicator of a middle-class background. However, our study was replete with Horatio Alger stories of leaders like Tom Johnson,

Bill Greehey, and Patrick Harker, who, despite growing up in the world of pipefitters, grocery clerks, and gypsum-mill workers, found ways to get to college on their way to greatness.

8. For more on single parenthood statistics, see Federal Interagency Forum on Child and Family Statistics, *America's Children: Key National Indicators of Well-Being 2000* (Washington, DC: U.S. Government Printing Office, 2000); "Births to Unmarried Women by Country: 1980 to 2008" (Table 1335), *Statistical Abstract of the United States: 2012* (Washington, DC: U.S. Census Bureau, 2012), 840, www.census.gov/compendia/statab/2012/tables/12s1335.pdf; and Sara McLanahan and Gary Sandefur, *Growing Up with a Single Parent: What Hurts, What Helps* (Cambridge, MA: Harvard University Press, 1994).

    For more on the effects of Family Structure, see Mary Parke, "Are Married Parents Really Better for Children? What Research Says About the Effects of Family Structure on Child Well-Being," annotated version of a Couples and Marriage Research and Policy brief, Center for Law and Social Policy, 2003.

    Those who grow up with a single parent get significantly less time and attention devoted to them than those who grow up in two-parent homes. See Jason DeParle, "Two Classes, Divided by 'I Do,'" *New York Times*, July 14, 2012, www.nytimes.com/2012/07/15/us/two-classes-in-america-divided-by-i-do.html.

    The prominence of first borns is consistent with other findings that have shown that firstborns are overrepresented among heads of state around the world, members of U.S. Congress, state governors in the United States, and numerous other elite leader groups. See, for example, L. H. Stewart, "Birth Order and Political Leadership," in *A Psychological Examination of Political Leaders*, ed. Margaret G. Hermann with Thomas W. Milburn (New York: Free Press, 1977), 205–306; Valerie M. Hudson, "Birth Order of World Leaders: An Exploratory Analysis of Effects on Personality and Behavior," *Political Psychology* 11 (September 1990): 583–601.

9. This provides an important nuance to the theory of accumulated advantage, in that it suggests that for everything, there is a season. Going to college too early or too late made it difficult for leaders to really take advantage of the opportunities on offer. Theoretically, it is not just the type or amount of social and cultural capital that a person accumulates that matters, but the order in which that social

or cultural capital is acquired. Thus, getting a second bachelor's degree from Brown after acquiring one from Harvard is of no use in the rise to the top, but a second bachelor's degree acquired from Oxford through a Rhodes scholarship is a different matter entirely.

10. Mark Silk and Leonard Silk famously claimed that Harvard, in particular, provided the roots of what they referred to as "the Establishment" (Leonard Silk and Mark Silk, *The American Establishment* [New York: Basic Books, 1980]). Ronald Story similarly made the case that starting in the nineteenth century, Harvard provides a site of solidarity for Boston's upper class (Ronald Story, *The Forging of an Aristocracy: Harvard and the Boston Upper Class, 1800–1885* [Middletown, CT: Wesleyan University Press, 1980]). Similarly, Michael Useem and Jerome Karabel have noted that those who obtain a bachelor's degree from an elite institution (as defined by their top 11 schools) are much more likely to become CEOs, multiple directors, and business association leaders, than are those who did not attend a top university or did not graduate from college. They also found that those who attended a lower-tier undergraduate college can increase their chances of becoming a top executive through attending a top law or MBA program, though they will still be less likely to become executives than are their peers who attended top undergraduate schools (Michael Useem and Jerome Karabel, "Pathways to Top Corporate Management," *American Sociological Review* 51 [1986]: 184–200). In my study, an elite undergraduate university was defined as one included in the top 25 research universities or top 25 liberal arts colleges as ranked by *U.S. News & World Report* in 2010, West Point, the U.S. Naval Academy, the U.S. Air Force Academy, or Oxford or Cambridge (in England).

11. Pamela Haag, "Are Elite Colleges Worth It?" *Chronicle Review* (October 30, 2011): B11.

12. The concepts of *social capital* and *cultural capital* are crucial to an understanding of leadership. James S. Coleman defined social capital as "the value of those aspects of social structure to actors, as resources that can be used to realize their interests" (James S. Coleman, *Foundations of Social Theory* [Cambridge, MA: Belknap Press, 1990], 305). Robert Putnam approaches social capital from more of a macro-sociological perspective than Coleman's, saying that "social capital refers to connections among individuals—social networks and the norms of reciprocity and trustworthiness that arise from

them" (Robert D. Putnam, *Bowling Alone: The Collapse and Revival of American Community* [New York: Simon & Schuster, 2000], 18–19). Elsewhere, Putnam points out that the operative ingredients of social capital are the "features of social organization, such as trust, norms, and networks, that can improve the efficiency of society by facilitating coordinated actions," (Robert D. Putnam, *Making Democracy Work: Civic Traditions in Modern Italy* [Princeton, NJ: Princeton University Press, 1993], 167). See Coleman, *Foundations of Social Theory*; Putnam, *Bowling Alone*; Randall Collins, *Interaction Ritual Chains* (Princeton, NJ: Princeton University Press, 2004); Putnam, *Making Democracy Work*.

13. John P. Heinz, Edward O. Laumann, Robert H. Salisbury, and Robert L. Nelson in an innovative study based on modeling the positions of leaders graphically found that among political notables in Washington, D.C., those who exercise leadership in their respective fields of expertise are those who occupy central, mediating positions, with connections to multiple networks and specializations. See John P. Heinz, Edward O. Laumann, Robert H. Salisbury, and Robert L. Nelson, "Inner Circles or Hollow Cores? Elite Networks in National Policy Systems," *The Journal of Politics* 52 (1990): 356–390.

14. See United States Census Bureau, "Number of Inhabitants, United States Summary," *Census of Population: 1950*, Vol. II, Part I, Table 26 (missing data for Las Vegas, Nevada, derived from Table 24).

15. Since I went *to* each of my interviews, I used the location of the interview as a proxy for the interviewee's present location. Fifty-five percent of the interviews were conducted in just six urban areas: Washington, D.C.; New York City; Los Angeles; Houston; Dallas; and the San Francisco Bay area. This tendency of high-powered individuals to have a higher level of mobility and to concentrate in cities is a pattern that has long been noted in investigations of leaders' social origins. See Roy Hinman Holmes, "A Study in the Origins of Distinguished Living Americans," *The American Journal of Sociology* 34: (1929): 670–685; Sanford Winston, "The Mobility of Eminent Americans," *The American Journal of Sociology* 41 (1936): 624–634.

16. Of those who told me where they first went when they left home, 55 percent went to Europe, 21 percent went to Mexico, Central America, or South America; 13 percent went to Asia; and 5 percent went to Canada. There were a significant number whose first travel experiences were before the age of 15 (24 percent of those who told me when they first traveled abroad), with a few traveling abroad even before their first birthdays.

17. Thirty-three percent of those I interviewed were multilingual, as compared to 26 percent of the general population, a statistically significant difference. See Chris McComb, "About One in Four Americans Can Hold a Conversation in a Second Language," Gallup, April 6, 2001.

18. This global awareness is typical of a third-culture kid (TCK), defined by David Pollock as "a person who has spent a significant part of his or her developmental years outside the parents' culture." (David C. Pollock and Ruth E. Van Reken, *Third Culture Kids: Growing Up Among Worlds* [Boston, MA: Nicholas Brealey, 2009], 13). In her introduction to the book's 2009 (revised) edition, Van Reken points out that the Obama White House included a large number of TCKs in senior positions, including Valerie Jarett (assistant to the president for public engagement and intergovernmental affairs), Timothy Geithner (secretary of the Treasury), Major General (Ret.) J. Scott Gration (special envoy to Sudan and later ambassador to Kenya), and the president himself. In a curious twist that mostly eluded public notice, his opponent in the 2008 election, John McCain, was also a TCK.

19. One possible explanation for this pattern comes from the work of Sharon Collins, who points out that in the wake of affirmative action legislation, many blacks were promoted quickly into racialized positions in departments dealing with affirmative action, community relations, or urban affairs. Though this gave them an initial jump in status and a higher salary, often these positions were dead-end jobs with few prospects for advancement. It may be that blacks were recruited from these dead-end jobs as external candidates for leadership positions. See Sharon M. Collins, "Black Mobility in White Corporations: Up the Corporate Ladder but Out on a Limb," *Social Problems* 44 (February 1997): 55–67.

Chapter 3 More Breadth, Less Depth

1. John Gardner, as quoted in Patricia O'Toole's *White House Fellows: A Sense of Involvement, A Vision of Greatness* (Washington, DC: White House Fellows Foundation, 1995), v. For a complete description of the White House Fellows Program, including my survey findings, see Rice University, *Surveying America's Leadership: A Study of the White House Fellows* (Houston, TX: Rice University, 2009).

2. Johnson initially told LBJ that he could not stay on after his Fellowship year because of his debt to Peyton Edison. But LBJ was not a man whose desires could be so easily deterred; he wrote a two-page letter to Edison, the gist of which being, "If your president and the country needs Tom, can you spare him?" LBJ called Johnson "my boy," and Lady Bird referred to him as "the son LBJ never had." Johnson remained with them—working at LBJ's broadcasting station in Austin, Texas—until LBJ's death in 1973.

3. Thomas E. Cronin, "Thinking and Learning about Leadership," in *The Leader's Companion: Insights on Leadership Throughout the Ages*, ed. J. Thomas Wren (New York: Free Press, 1995), 30.

4. Meg Jay, *The Defining Decade* (New York: Hachette Book Group, 2012).

5. There were a few White House Fellows, I must acknowledge, who felt that the fellowship experience was not helpful to their career trajectory. Analyzing these responses, I found that those with this opinion tended to fall into one of two categories. One group were those who already had such high social and cultural capital as to make the infusion of capital that the White House Fellowship provides irrelevant. Typical of this were the heirs of wealthy, prestigious families, and winners of highly prestigious scholarships like the Rhodes, Marshall, or Luce scholarships. The other group was composed of those who went into fields for which they felt the White House Fellowship did not prepare them.

6. In the fall of 2008, I launched a systematic analysis of the program, its participants, and its impact on American democracy. It included a 72-question survey of living Fellows and explored three areas: (1) what Fellows were like before the Fellowship and how they learned about

the program, (2) what the Fellowship experience meant to them (personally and professionally) and how it has affected their life since, and (3) the Fellows' background, attitudes, and experiences and how they compare to those of the general population. The survey achieved a 78 percent response rate among the program's 627 living Fellows ($N = 473$). After gathering additional information on all 627 Fellows, I conducted semistructured interviews with 100 Fellows, principals, commissioners, and directors.

7. John P. Kotter, "What Leaders Really Do," *Harvard Business Review* (December, 2001): 3–12, http://hbr.org/2001/12/what-leaders-really-do/ar/6.

8. We found on closer examination that classes that had representation had higher levels of conflict, though the women and minorities themselves were in general less likely to report conflict than the males and whites. This appears to indicate that where there are more women or minorities, there is a greater consciousness of the unique challenges they face. For a more detailed discussion, see D. Michael Lindsay, Ariela Schachter, Jeremy R. Porter, and David C. Sorge, "Parvenus and Diversity in Elite Cohorts," forthcoming.

9. D. Michael Lindsay, "U.S. Military and the White House Fellowship: Contact in Shaping Elite Attitudes," *Annual Review of Political and Military Sociology* 38 (2010): 53–76.

10. Samuel Andrew Stouffer, *Communism, Conformity, and Civil Liberties: A Cross-section of the Nation Speaks Its Mind* (Garden City, NY: Doubleday, 1955); J. Allen Williams Jr., Clyde Z. Nunn, and Louis St. Peter, "Origins of Tolerance: Findings from a Replication of Stouffer's Communism, Conformity, and Civil Liberties," *Social Forces* 55 (December 1976): 394–408.

11. John W. Gardner, *On Leadership* (New York: Free Press, 1990), xix.

12. Thomas E. Cronin, "Thinking and Learning about Leadership," *Presidential Studies Quarterly* 14 (Winter, 1984): 22–24, 33–34. Cronin says, "While the mission of the college may be to educate 'the educated person' and society's future leaders, in fact the incentive system is geared to training specialists. Society today rewards the expert or the super specialist—the data processors, the pilots, the financial whiz, the heart surgeon, the special team punt returners, and so on. Leaders, however, have to learn to become generalists and

usually have to do so well after they have left our colleges, graduate schools, and professional schools" (23). See Mark Peltz, "Essay on How Liberal Arts Colleges Promote Leadership," *Inside Higher Ed* (May 14, 2012), www.insidehighered.com/views/2012/05/14/essay-how-liberal-arts-colleges-promote-leadership.

13. The Fellowship is the perfect opportunity for those in the military to understand how government works. As these Fellows move into higher positions with greater interaction with civilians (like a posting at the Pentagon or as the head of West Point), they have to learn how to get things done outside of the military. As one three-star general described it, "In these jobs you get later on as a strategic leader, your constituencies broaden, and you've got to understand where they're coming from and how to address them and communicate with them. The Fellowship was sort of a jumping-off point for me on that."

14. This is a point Pierre Bourdieu makes much of in his work, *The Forms of Capital*. He even says that the relationship between time spent acquiring cultural capital and cultural capital gained is so tightly correlated that the former can be used as a proxy for the latter. However, this does not take into account several mediating aspects, including the quality of the program of study and the actual cultural capital of one's instructors. Exposure to senior leaders for such extended periods of time, paired with the other strengths of the White House Fellowship, allows Fellows to gain cultural capital very rapidly. See Pierre Bourdieu, *The Forms of Capital* in *Handbook of Theory and Research for the Sociology of Education*, ed. John G. Richardson (New York: Greenwood Press 1986), 241–258.

15. See Pierre Bourdieu, *Distinction: A Social Critique of the Judgment of Taste* (Cambridge, MA: Harvard University Press, 1984).

Chapter 4 The Essence of Leadership

1. Charles Babington, "Cerebral Sarbanes Aloof to Limelight," *Washington Post*, March 12, 2005, www.washingtonpost.com/wp-dyn/articles/A28241-2005Mar11.html.

2. James MacGregor Burns, *Leadership* (New York: Harper & Row, 1978), 15.

3. Most sociological definitions of power begin with that of Max Weber, who defines power as the probability that one actor will be in a

position to carry out his own will despite resistance (Max Weber, "Class, Status, Party," *Max Weber: Essays in Sociology*, ed. Hans H. Gerth and C. Wright Mills [London: Routledge, 1946, 1991], 180–195). Michel Foucault treats power as a property not of the person who wields it, but as a property of the network of relationships that acts through the people who occupy particular powerful positions (Michel Foucault and James D. Faubion, *Power* [New York: New Press, 2000]).

4. These early-morning routines often include what Randall Collins would describe as rituals of self-entrainment. These put a leader into a physical rhythm through exercise; a conversational rhythm through correspondence or spending time thinking, reflecting, praying; or an information-processing rhythm through reading relevant news or reports. The stock of self-entrained emotional energy gives the leader the emotional resources to sustain energy throughout the day. See Randall Collins, *Interaction Ritual Chains* (Princeton, NJ: Princeton University Press, 2004) and Randall Collins, *Violence: A Micro-sociological Theory* (Princeton, NJ: Princeton University Press, 2008).

5. Daniel Goleman, *Working with Emotional Intelligence* (New York: Bantam Dell, 1998), 317. Alternatively, Matthews, Zeidner, and Roberts define it broadly as "a set of core competencies for identifying, processing, and managing emotion" (Gerald Matthews, Moshe Zeidner, and Richard D. Roberts, *The Science of Emotional Intelligence: Knowns and Unknowns* [New York: Oxford University Press, 2007], 3). For more on the subject, see Peter Salovey and John D. Mayer, "Emotional Intelligence," *Imagination, Cognition, and Personality* 9 (1990): 185–211. The idea underlying Goleman's bestselling book has received significant criticism from the scientific community, however, particularly from psychologists of personality and intelligence. Some go so far as to call Goleman's 1995 definition "a laundry list of virtually every positive quality of character except for cognitive intelligence" (Matthews, Zeidner, and Roberts, *Science of Emotional Intelligence*, 5). There is little scholarly consensus on what emotional intelligence might actually be, whether an ability or a trait, and whether it indeed can be used to predict success. On the other hand, psychologists have studied the correlations between performance and each of the so-called big five personality

variables: neuroticism, extraversion, openness to experience, agreeableness, and conscientiousness. They found that extroversion was the most strongly correlated to leadership, followed by conscientiousness and openness to experience. See Timothy A. Judge, Joyce E. Bono, Remus Illies, and Megan W. Gerhardt, "Personality and Leadership: A Qualitative and Quantitative Review," *Journal of Applied Psychology* 87 (2002): 765–780.

6. As quoted in Charles Duhigg, *The Power of Habit: Why We Do What We Do in Life and Business* (New York: Random House, 2012), 99.

7. See CBS press release, July 28, 2010, *The Futon Critic*, www.the futoncritic.com/news/2010/07/28/cbs-announces-four-companies-participating-in-the-second-season-of-the-emmy-award-nominated-series-undercover-boss/20100728cbs02.

Chapter 5 Strength in the Crucible of Crisis

1. As Erving Goffman famously pointed out, there are sincere performers and cynical performers—those who buy in to the stories they portray, and those who do not. The natural assumption for many people, one enshrined even in Goffman's choice of terminology, is that there is something normatively better about a sincere performance than a cynical one, particularly when it comes to leaders. A cynical performance, if detected, can raise charges that a leader is a hypocrite simply trying to gain public trust or sympathy for his own presumably nefarious purposes. Senior leaders must pull off a Goffmanian performance that corresponds to the public's expectations of their ascribed level of agency. See Erving Goffman, *The Presentation of Self in Everyday Life* (New York: Anchor Books, 1959).

2. Ralph Waldo Emerson, *Self Reliance* (New York: Empire, 2011).

3. Ronald A. Heifetz and Marty Linsky, *Leadership on the Line: Staying Alive through the Dangers of Leading* (Boston: Harvard Business School, 2002).

4. This was the first Pulitzer Prize in Public Service to be won by the *Times* since 1972. See Editors, "About 'A Nation Challenged,'" *New York Times*, editors' note, January 6, 2002, www.nytimes.com/2002/01/06/world/a-nation-challenged-editors-note-about-a-nation-challenged.html; "The 2002 Pulitzer Prize Winners: Public Service,"

The Pulitzer Prizes, www.pulitzer.org/citation/2002-Public-Service; New York University, "NYU's Carter Journalism Institute Names Five Newspaper Series, Four Books, and a Radio Program Decade's Top 10 Works of U.S. Journalism," press release, April 5, 2010, www.nyu.edu/about/news-publications/news/2010/04/05/nyu_s_car ter_journal.html.

5. Ian I. Mitroff, *Why Some Companies Emerge Stronger and Better from a Crisis: 7 Essential Lessons for Surviving Disaster* (New York: American Management Association, 2005).

6. Rubin once shared a *Time* magazine cover with Alan Greenspan and Larry Summers over a title, "The Committee to Save the World" *Time*, February 15, 1999.

Chapter 6 Lead with Your Life

1. In 2007 Jean-Pascal Daloz found that Scandinavian political elites exude "conspicuous modesty" (such as riding public transportation to work) as a way of building rapport with citizens and embodying the political ideal of representativeness. Jean-Pascal Daloz, "Political Elites and Conspicuous Modesty: Norway, Sweden, Finland in Comparative Perspective," *Comparative Social Research* 23 (2007): 173–212.

2. Supplemental work at home—work done on evenings or weekends in addition to a full-time job—has been around throughout industrial history, but it has grown in recent decades with the prevalence of new information technologies. Further, Alladi Venkatesh and Nicholas Vitalari found that people work from home in order to get things done that they are unable to suitably accomplish in the workplace, not out of a desire to spend more time with their families. Alladi Venkatesh and Nicholas P. Vitalari, "An Emerging Distributed Work Arrangement: An Investigation of Computer-Based Supplemental Work at Home," *Management Science* 38, no. 12 (1992): 1687–1706.

3. Sixteen percent of informants mentioned that they stopped eating when making a difficult decision.

4. Data from the General Social Survey reveals that 71 percent of salaried women professionals are married or have been married, which is significantly more than the elite women profiled in this study. Tom W. Smith, Peter Marsden, Michael Hout, and Jibum

Kim, *General Social Surveys, 1972–2010* [machine-readable data file] (Chicago: National Opinion Research Center [producer]; Storrs, CT: The Roper Center for Public Opinion Research, University of Connecticut [distributor], 2011).

5. Arlie Russell Hoschschild, *The Second Shift: Working Families and the Revolution at Home* (New York: Penguin, 2003).

6. Rousseau's work primarily concerns the state, but when John Rawls revived his ideas in the mid-twentieth century, he expanded the idea of the social contract to touching "the way in which the major social institutions fit together into one system, and how they assign fundamental rights and duties and shape the division of advantages that arises through social cooperation" (John Rawls, *Political Liberalism* [New York: Columbia University Press, 1996], 258).

7. Hannah Shaw and Chad Stone, "Tax Data Show Richest 1 Percent Took a Hit in 2008, but Income Remained Highly Concentrated at the Top," *Center on Budget and Policy Priorities*, May 25, 2011, www.cbpp.org; Stephen Miller, "Modest Salary Growth, Tougher Goals for Executives in 2012," *Society for Human Resource Management* (December 1, 2011), www.shrm.org.

8. Jessica Silver-Greenberg and Nelson D. Schwartz, "Citigroup's Chief Rebuffed on Pay by Shareholders," *New York Times DealBook*, April 17, 2012, http://dealbook.nytimes.com/2012/04/17/citigroup-shareholders-reject-executive-pay-plan/.

9. There was no significant difference among beliefs about compensation across other categories. Partisan differences shape attitudes on this issue much more than do differences along lines of gender, region of the country, or sector of the workplace.

10. See Jeffrey M. Jones, "Most Americans Favor Gov't. Action to Limit Executive Pay," *Gallup Economy*, June 16, 2009.

11. Stephanie Strom, "Lawmakers Seeking Cuts Look at Nonprofit Salaries," the *New York Times*, July 27, 2010, A12.

12. Leah Nathans Spiro, "Ticker Tape in the Genes," *BusinessWeek*, October 21, 1996.

13. See Jason Corcoran, "UBS Bets on Private Wealth Ties to Tilt Russian M&A Tables," *BloombergBusinessweek*, November 15, 2011, www.businessweek.com/news/2011-11-15/ubs-bets-on-private-wealth-ties-to-tilt-russian-m-a-tables.html; "Private Pursuits," *The Economist*, May 19, 2012, www.economist.com/node/21554745.

Chapter 7 Lead for Good

1. See Sheryl Gay Stolberg, "In Global Battle on AIDS, Bush Creates Legacy," *New York Times*, January 5, 2008, http://select.nytimes.com/gst/abstract.html?res=FB0B17F83B550C7B8DDDA00894DD404482&pagewanted=2&pagewanted=all; James Traub, "The Statesman," *New York Times*, September 18, 2005, www.nytimes.com/2008/01/05/washington/05aids.html?_r=1&pagewanted=all.
2. Max Weber, *From Max Weber: Essays in Sociology*, ed. and trans. Hans Heinrich Gerth and C. Wright Mills (New York: Oxford University Press, 1946).
3. It is common to see the ethic of conviction play out in the lives of people of faith; as Weber said, "A Christian does what is right and leaves the outcome to God."
4. Max Weber, "The Nations State and Economic Policy (Freiburg Address)" in *Weber: Political Writings*, ed. and trans. P. Lassman and R. Speirs (Cambridge: Cambridge University Press, 1895/1994).
5. Jeff Bailey, "Southwest. Way Southwest," *New York Times*, February 13, 2008, www.nytimes.com/2008/02/13/business/13southwest.html?pagewanted=all.
6. Barbar Than, "The Container Store Cheers Office Romance, Love This Valentine's Day," *DailyFinance*, February 14, 2011, www.dailyfinance.com/2011/02/14/the-container-store-cheers-office-romance-love-this-valentine-s/. Retail stores have such high turnover because many employees start and quit their jobs within one year.
7. In founding The Container Store, Boone launched a whole new retail category—storage and organization. He sees himself as equal parts entrepreneur and retailer, crediting The Container Store's success both to its market niche and to the customer service that results from the firm's commitment to its employees.

Appendix

1. For example, I interviewed Princeton University President Shirley Tilghman about her field of genomics in advance of an interview with Francis Collins, then director of the National Human Genome Research Institute.

2. Demographic variables include race/ethnicity, age, gender, political leaning, places of residence, marital status, number of children, spouse's occupation, education, and religious background. Social variables include private club memberships, civic and community involvements, and charitable contributions. Professional variables include career histories (titles and organizations), military/government service measures, university affiliations, and financial indicators including net assets, home values, and annual income. Network variables include board memberships, involvement in political and policy groups, and membership in college alumni and professional associations.

3. These sources include news outlets such as the *New York Times*, the *Wall Street Journal*, *Fortune*, *Forbes*, *BusinessWeek*, the *Chronicle of Higher Education*, and the *Chronicle of Philanthropy* as well as free electronic resources such as websites of city and county tax-appraisal boards and online sources such as LexisNexis, GuideStar, LinkedIn, MarketWatch, Muckety, Hoover's Online, Salary Survey, Theyrule.net, and ZoomInfo. I have also secured subscriptions to the Corporate Library, the Federal Yellowbook, Foundation Center Online, iWave Prospect Research Online, Marquis Who's Who, and 10K Wizard.

Appendix

The PLATINUM Study (Public Leaders in America Today and the Inquiry into their Networks, Upbringings, and Motivations) is a 10-year comprehensive examination of public leadership at the highest levels of American society. Drawing on social-scientific analyses, the multiyear project explores how leaders influence their organizations, communities, and society as a whole. Five hundred and fifty leaders participated in the study, including two former presidents of the United States, 80 U.S. cabinet secretaries, dozens of senior White House officials across nine administrations, over 200 chief executive officers (including the CEOs of 20 percent of the Fortune 100), dozens of celebrated artists, performers, and writers, and over 100 top leaders from the nonprofit sector. The PLATINUM Study has amassed the largest and most exhaustive set of interview data conducted with leaders in every sector of society.

I learned through my earlier research to value the interviews of *previous* occupants of elite positions, especially when they are suggested multiple times through the reputational method of informant selection. The data are the richer because of this flexibility, because the reputational method—coupled with positional selection—allowed for the inclusion of former presidents Jimmy Carter and George H. W. Bush. Such flexibility allowed for comparisons over time, grouping elites from the same generation to test for similarities of responses and accounts of power among those who held leadership positions during the same decade. Because the focus of this study is on patterns within and across society's elite and not about the variables required to join the elite per se, this study's design is not susceptible to the methodological error of sampling on the dependent variable. I am also interested in the breadth of elite accounts, so a large number of informants is appropriate, as has been the case with other successful qualitative projects.

I recognize that informant accounts may or may not be accurate reflections of their actions. Extensive background research is required to mitigate this potential bias by identifying episodes where an informant's rhetoric did not match his or her behavior and probing informants for inconsistencies and anomalies. A benefit of studying elites is that much has been written by and about them in major media outlets; this information was consulted before each interview. And as was the case in my earlier work, I conducted preliminary interviews with other knowledgeable sources about the informant's field when needed.[1] Finally, collecting and analyzing interview data can introduce a number of biases, especially when it is conducted by a team. I conducted all of the interviews myself to avoid the bias of multiple interviewers, and at least 5 percent of the interviews were first coded by two research assistants and then tested to ensure intercoder reliability. These safeguards not only buttress the conclusions I draw from the study but also strengthen the arguments of scholars who will rely on these data in the future.

All 550 interviews were transcribed and coded by a member of the research team along 100 variables to map the informant's demographic, social, professional, and network profiles.[2] Most of these data were drawn from the interview transcript, and additional data was drawn from electronic and print sources,[3] that allowed us to maximize each interview by avoiding questions that could be answered elsewhere. The combined response rate of interviews requested was 87 percent.

In addition to qualitative analysis, the research team compiled 122 "countable" variables in areas such as demographics, charitable giving, education, family background, career, and personal lifestyle. The research team combed through the transcripts and briefing materials to gather this information for each person in the study.

Throughout the process, analyses followed an iterative approach, whereby new themes were discovered for analysis and recoded on previously analyzed transcripts. While numerical frequencies of calculable data (such as whether the informant mentions having a mentor) were collected, the analytic emphasis was on finding qualitative degrees of commonness across cases and systematically analyzing negative cases. The interviews sought to probe for different kinds of personhood (including vocabularies of motive) and to tap informants' frameworks about power, autonomy, agency, and identity.

The following lists the 550 participants in the PLATINUM Study:

Full Name	Organization or Title	Date	City	State
Joan Abrahamson	President, Jefferson Institute; President, Jonas Salk Foundation; MacArthur Fellow	10-Feb-2010	Pasadena	CA
Peter Ackerman	Managing Director, Rockport Capital; Founding Chair, International Center on Nonviolent Conflict	21-Jun-2011	Washington	DC
John Aden	President, Mac Tools; SVP, Walmart	14-Jun-2005	Farmington	CT
Howard Ahmanson	Founder, Fieldstead and Company	27-Apr-2004	Newport Beach	CA
Roberta Ahmanson	Founder, Fieldstead and Company	27-Apr-2004	Newport Beach	CA
Claude Allen	Assistant to the President for Domestic Policy, Deputy Secretary, Health and Human Services	7-Dec-2004	Washington	DC
Chuck Allen	COO, North American Mission Board	16-Sep-2005	Osprey Point	MD
Thad Allen	Commandant, U.S. Coast Guard	20-Jan-2010	Washington	DC
Joel Allison	President and CEO, Baylor Health Care System	19-Apr-2011	Dallas	TX
Katherine Leary Alsdorf	Executive Director, Redeemer Presbyterian Church	14-Jul-2004	New York	NY
J. Brady Anderson	Administrator, United States Agency for International Development; Director, World Vision International; U.S. Ambassador to Tanzania	27-Mar-2004	Austin	TX
Leith Anderson	President, National Association of Evangelicals	23-Aug-2005	*Telephone interview*	

(continued)

Full Name	Organization or Title	Date	City	State
Robert C. Andringa	President, Council for Christian Colleges and Universities	10-Jul-2003	Washington	DC
Victor Anfuso	Chairman, Christian Copyright Licensing Inc.	19-Aug-2004	Portland	OR
Charles Ansbacher	Conductor, Colorado Springs Symphony Orchestra; Founding Conductor, Boston Landmarks Orchestra	14-Aug-2009	Cambridge	MA
Guy Anthony	CFO, Stentor; Group Controller for Microprocessors and Assistant Treasurer for Intel Capital, Intel	19-May-2004	Brisbane	CA
Michael Armacost	Ambassador to the Philippines; Ambassador to Japan; President, Brookings Institution; Undersecretary of State for Political Affairs	19-Nov-2009	Palo Alto	CA
Dick Armey	Majority Leader, U.S. House of Representatives (R-TX)	2-Feb-2005	Washington	DC
William L. Armstrong	U.S. Senator (R-CO)	30-Sep-2004	Denver	CO
Gerard Arpey	CEO, AMR and American Airlines	7-Apr-2011	Fort Worth	TX
John Ashcroft	U.S. Attorney General; Senator (R-MO); Governor of Missouri	6-May-2011	Arlington	VA
Timothy Atkin	Executive Vice President and COO, SRA International	8-Dec-2009	Arlington	VA
Ronald Austin	Producer, *Mission Impossible, Charlie's Angels, Hawaii Five-O, The Father Dowling Mysteries*	14-May-2005	El Segundo	CA
Jim Awtrey	CEO, Professional Golfers Association of America	13-Aug-2005	Short Hills	NJ

Full Name	Organization or Title	Date	City	State
James A. Baker III	Secretary of State; Secretary of Treasury; White House Chief of Staff	12-Nov-2004	Houston	TX
Dennis Bakke	Co-founder, President, and CEO, AES; Co-founder, President, and CEO, Imagine Schools	5-Aug-2004	Washington	DC
Stephen Baldwin	Actor	1-Oct-2004	Bachelor's Gulch	CO
Colleen Barrett	President, Southwest Airlines	19-Aug-2009	Dallas	TX
Daniel Bartlett	Counselor to the President; Chairman and CEO, Public Strategies; President and CEO, Hill & Knowlton	25-May-2011	Austin	TX
Joe Barton	U.S. Representative (R-TX)	2-Sep-2009	Arlington	TX
Dean Batali	Co-executive Producer, *That 70s Show*	26-Sep-2004	Glendale	CA
Janet Batchler	Writer, *Batman Forever*; Writer, *Smoke and Mirrors*	10-May-2005	Beverly Hills	CA
Lee Batchler	Writer, *Batman Forever*; Writer, *Smoke and Mirrors*	19-May-2005	Beverly Hills	CA
Mariam Bell	Director of Public Policy, The Wilberforce Forum	4-Sep-2004	Osprey Point	MD
Y Marc Belton	Executive Vice President, General Mills	31-May-2005	Minneapolis	MN
George Bennett	CEO, State Street Investment Corporation	29-Aug-2004	Falmouth	MA
Monty J. Bennett	President and CEO, Remington Hotel Corporation	13-Oct-2004	Dallas	TX
Marcy Benson	Director, President's Commission on White House Fellowships	2-Mar-2009	Denver	CO
Fredrick S. Benson III	Vice President, Weyerhaeuser; President, United States – New Zealand Council	17-Aug-2009	Mt. Desert	ME

(continued)

Full Name	Organization or Title	Date	City	State
David Beré	President and Chief Strategy Officer, Dollar General Corporation	7-Oct-2009	Nashville	TN
Brenda Berkman	New York City's first female firefighter	21-Oct-2009	Washington	DC
Mark Berner	Managing Partner, SDG Resources	14-Jul-2004	New York	NY
Jeffrey Bewkes	Chairman and CEO, Time Warner	26-Apr-2011	New York	NY
Veronica Biggins	Assistant to the President of the United States, William J. Clinton, and Director of Presidential Personnel	16-Oct-2010	Atlanta	GA
James Billington	Librarian of the United States Congress	1-Mar-2011	Washington	DC
Michael Birck	Co-founder and Chairman of Tellabs	1-Jun-2010	Chicago	IL
Brian Bird	Writer and Producer, *Step by Step, Touched by an Angel*	8-Nov-2004	Rancho Santa Margarita	CA
Dennis Blair	Director of National Intelligence; United States Navy admiral	21-Jun-2011	Washington	DC
Ronald Blue	President, Christian Financial Professionals Network	28-Feb-2005	Atlanta	GA
Jacqueline Blumenthal	Director, President's Commission on White House Fellowships	19-Jan-2010	Washington	DC
Myrna Blyth	Editor-in-Chief, *Ladies' Home Journal*; Chair, President's Commission on White House Fellowships	10-Nov-2009	New York	NY
Derek Bok	President, Harvard University	30-Jun-2010	Boston	MA
Joshua Bolten	White House Chief of Staff; Director of the Office of Management and Budget; White House Deputy Chief of Staff	19-May-2011	Washington	DC
David Bonderman	Founding Partner, Texas Pacific Group	1-Jun-2011	San Francisco	CA
Pat Boone	Entertainer	23-Apr-2004	Los Angeles	CA

Full Name	Organization or Title	Date	City	State
Garrett Boone	Co-founder and Co-chairman, The Container Store	10-Aug-2010	Dallas	TX
John Borling	Major General, U.S. Air Force	9-Nov-2009	Chicago	IL
James Bostic	Senior Vice President, Georgia-Pacific Corporation	18-Dec-2009	Atlanta	GA
Terry Botwick	Senior Vice President, CBS Entertainment; Founder and CEO, Thunderpoint Studios	3-Oct-2005	Los Angeles	CA
Sandra Bowden	President, Christians in the Visual Arts	20-Aug-2004	Chatham	MA
William Bowen	President, Princeton University	6-Oct-2010	New York	NY
William G. Boykin	Deputy Under Secretary of Defense for Intelligence	21-Jun-2005	Washington	DC
John Brandon	Vice President of the Americas and Asia Pacific, Apple Computers, Inc.	20-May-2004	Cupertino	CA
William K. Brehm	Chairman, SRA International Inc.; Assistant Secretary of Defense	13-Jan-2005	Vienna	VA
Eli Bremer	2008 U.S. Olympian in Pentathlon	22-Dec-2009	Colorado Springs	CO
Paul Brest	President, The William and Flora Hewlett Foundation; Dean, Stanford Law School	1-Jun-2011	Menlo Park	CA
Frank Brock	President, Covenant College	7-May-2003	Chattanooga	TN
Clayton Brown	Founder, President, Chairman, and CEO, Clayton Brown & Associates	8-Oct-2004	Wheaton	IL
Daniel Bryant	Assistant Attorney General	10-Dec-2004	Washington	DC
J. Fred Bucy	Executive Vice President, COO, President, and CEO, Texas Instruments	23-Dec-2009	Dallas	TX

(*continued*)

Full Name	Organization or Title	Date	City	State
Bob Buford	Chairman and CEO, Buford Television; Founder, The Buford Foundation; Co-founder, Leadership Network	12-Apr-2004	Dallas	TX
T. Robert Burke	Chairman, AMB Property Corporation	10-May-2011	San Francisco	CA
Doug Burleigh	President, Young Life	8-Sep-2004	Gig Harbor	WA
George H. W. Bush	President of the United States; Director, CIA; U.S. Ambassador to China; U.S. Representative (R-TX); Ambassador to the United Nations	9-Feb-2005	*Responded via email*	
Howard Butt	President, H. E. Butt Foundation; Vice Chairman, H. E. Butt Grocery Company; Administrator, Leadership Laity Forum	17-Feb-2005	San Antonio	TX
Gaylen Byker	President, Calvin College	17-Jun-2004	*Telephone interview*	
Kurt Campbell	Assistant Secretary of State for East Asian and Pacific Affairs; Co-founder and CEO, Center for New American Security	9-Dec-2009	Washington	DC
Bill Campbell	Chairman and CEO, Intuit Inc; Chairman, Apple; Chairman, Columbia University	10-May-2011	Palo Alto	CA
Tony Campolo	Professor, Eastern University; President, Evangelical Association for the Promotion of Education	3-Mar-2006	Cherry Hill	NJ
Richard G. Capen	U.S. Ambassador to Spain; Publisher and Chairman, the *Miami Herald*	8-Nov-2004	Del Mar	CA
Andrew Card	White House Chief of Staff; Deputy Chief of Staff; Secretary of Transportation	2-Mar-2011	Washington	DC

Full Name	Organization or Title	Date	City	State
R. Byron Carlock Jr.	President and CEO, CNL Lifestyle Companies	12-Apr-2004	Dallas	TX
Joel Carpenter	Provost, Calvin College	26-Mar-2004	Waco	TX
Thomas Carr	Director, President's Commission on White House Fellowships	21-Jan-2010	Sullivan's Island	SC
Philip J. Carroll	CEO, Shell Oil; Chairman & CEO, Fluor Corporation	5-May-2011	Houston	TX
Garrey Carruthers	Governor, New Mexico; Dean, College of Business, New Mexico State University	18-Sep-2009	Las Cruces	NM
Brad Carson	U.S. Representative (D-OK)	1-Mar-2010	Tulsa	OK
Jimmy Carter	President of the United States; Governor, Georgia	16-Nov-2004	Atlanta	GA
Marshall Carter	Chairman, New York Stock Exchange Group; Deputy Chairman, New York Stock Exchange Euronext; Chairman and CEO, State Street Bank	12-Nov-2009	Cambridge	MA
Philip Cassidy	Executive Director, The Business Council	1-Mar-2011	Washington	DC
S. Truett Cathy	Founder, Chairman, and CEO, Chick-fil-A	1-Mar-2005	Atlanta	GA
Clarence P. Cazalot Jr.	President and CEO, Marathon Oil	18-Apr-2011	Houston	TX
Morris Chapman	President and CEO, Southern Baptist Convention	25-Apr-2006	Nashville	TN
Michael Chertoff	Secretary of Homeland Security	28-Oct-2009	Washington	DC
Clayton Christensen	Robert and Jane Cizik Professor of Business Administration, Harvard Business School	13-Nov-2009	Boston	MA
Henry Cisneros	U.S. Secretary of Housing and Urban Development; President, Univision	3-Dec-2009	San Antonio	TX

(*continued*)

Full Name	Organization or Title	Date	City	State
Stephen Clapp	Dean, The Juilliard School	6-Jan-2005	New York	NY
Wesley Clark	General, U.S. Army; Supreme Allied Commander, NATO	20-Jan-2010	Washington	DC
Richard Clarke	Chief Counter-Terrorism Advisor, National Security Council	28-Oct-2010	Washington	DC
Robert L. Clarke	Comptroller of the Currency	22-Feb-2011	Houston	TX
Jerry Colangelo	Owner, Arizona Diamondbacks; Owner, Phoenix Suns	29-Oct-2004	Phoenix	AZ
Michael Coleman	President and CEO, Integrity Media	23-Sep-2004	New York	NY
Rodney Coleman	Assistant Secretary of the U.S. Air Force	29-Sep-2009	Tampa	FL
William Coleman	Senior Partner, O'Melveny & Myers LLP; Secretary of Transportation	6-May-2011	Washington	DC
Timothy C. Collins	Founder, Senior Managing Director, and CEO, Ripplewood Holdings LLC	20-Sep-2004	New York	NY
Francis S. Collins	Director, National Institutes of Health; Director, National Human Genome Research Institute	18-Sep-2005	Washington	DC
Charles Colson	Founder, Prison Fellowship; Founder and Chairman, The Wilberforce Forum; Special Counsel to the President	17-Jul-2004	Washington	DC
Kent Colton	Executive Vice President and CEO, National Association of Home Builders	30-Sep-2009	Tampa	FL
Jeffrey Comment	President, Chairman, and CEO, Helzberg Diamonds	23-Oct-2004	Kansas City	MO
Kevin Compton	Partner, Kleiner Perkins Caufield & Byers	11-Aug-2005	Palo Alto	CA
Gary Cook	President, Dallas Baptist University	2-Apr-2005	Dallas	TX

Full Name	Organization or Title	Date	City	State
Kyle Cooper	Title designer for 52 films	26-Sep-2004	Malibu	CA
William R. Cotter	President, Colby College; President, African-American Institute	13-Nov-2009	Concord	MA
Michael Cromartie	Vice President, Ethics and Public Policy Center	16-Jul-2003	Washington	DC
Thomas Cronin	President, Whitman College; Acting President, Colorado College	21-Dec-2009	Colorado Springs	CO
Les T. Csorba	Special Assistant to the President for Presidential Personnel	22-Feb-2005	Houston	TX
Phillip Cullom	Rear Admiral, U.S. Navy	7-Dec-2009	Crystal City	VA
Howard Dahl	Founder, President and CEO, Amity Technology	5-Mar-2011	Naples	FL
Gary Daichendt	Executive Vice President of Worldwide Operations, Cisco Systems	23-Apr-2004	Crystal Cove	CA
John H. Dalton	Secretary of the Navy	16-Jul-2004	Washington	DC
John Danforth	U.S. Senator (R-MO)	7-Sep-2010	St. Louis	MO
Thomas Daschle	Senate Majority Leader; U.S. Senator (D-SD)	1-Mar-2011	Washington	DC
David Davenport	President, Pepperdine University	19-May-2005	Malibu	CA
Peter Dawkins	Vice Chairman, Citigroup Private Bank; Executive Vice President and Vice Chairman, Travelers Insurance; Chairman and CEO, Primerica Financial Services; Brigadier General, U.S. Army; Heisman Trophy winner	15-Feb-2010	Rumson	NJ
John De Luca	President and CEO, Wine Institute; Deputy Mayor, San Francisco	12-Aug-2009	San Francisco	CA
Max De Pree	CEO, Herman Miller	9-Jul-2004	Holland	MI
Rudy deLeon	Deputy Secretary of Defense; Senior Vice President, Boeing Company	13-Jan-2005	Washington	DC

(*continued*)

Full Name	Organization or Title	Date	City	State
Scott Derrickson	Director, *The Exorcism of Emily Rose*	31-Jul-2004	Glendale	CA
Dick DeVos	President and CEO, Alticor; President and Chairman, Amway; Founder and President, Windquest Group	9-Jul-2004	Grand Rapids	MI
Gene Dewey	Director, President's Commission on White House Fellowships	17-Feb-2010	Washington	DC
Bob Diamond	President and CEO, Barclays PLC	4-Oct-2010	New York	NY
Dave Dias	Vice President, InterWest Insurance Services	20-May-2004	Menlo Park	CA
John J. DiIulio Jr.	Director, Office of Faith-Based & Community Initiatives	2-Nov-2004	Philadelphia	PA
Jamie Dimon	Chairman and CEO, JPMorgan Chase	3-Feb-2011	New York	NY
Edward Djerejian	Founding Director, James A. Baker III Institute for Public Policy; Managing Partner, Djerejian Global Consultancies; Ambassador to Syria and Israel	24-May-2011	Houston	TX
David Dockery	President, Union University	26-Mar-2004	Waco	TX
Bob Doll	Chief Equity Strategist, BlackRock Inc.	27-Apr-2011	Plainsboro	NJ
John Donahoe	President and CEO, eBay	9-Dec-2010	San Francisco	CA
Byron Dorgan	Co-chair of the Government Relations Practice, Arent Fox; Senator (D-ND)	21-Jun-2011	Washington	DC
Marjorie Dorr	President and CEO, Anthem Blue Cross and Blue Shield Northeast Region	12-Apr-2005	North Haven	CT
Cheryl Dorsey	President, Echoing Green; Vice-Chair, President's Commission on White House Fellowships	10-Nov-2009	New York	NY

Full Name	Organization or Title	Date	City	State
Stephen Douglass	President and Chairman, Campus Crusade for Christ	22-Nov-2004	Orlando	FL
Hudson Drake	Director, President's Commission on White House Fellowships; Partner, Carlisle Enterprises LLC	5-Mar-2010	La Jolla	CA
Michael T. Duke	President and CEO, Walmart	31-Mar-2005	Bentonville	AR
Tony Dungy	Head Coach, Indianapolis Colts	6-Jun-2006	Indianapolis	IN
Archie W Dunham	President and CEO, ConocoPhillips	21-Feb-2005	Houston	TX
Bruce Dunlevie	General Partner, Benchmark Capital	7-Jun-2011	*Telephone interview*	
David Eaton	General Partner, Arizona Diamondbacks and Phoenix Suns	29-Oct-2004	Phoenix	AZ
Don Eberly	Director of Private Assistance for Iraq, State Department; Deputy Director, Office of Faith-Based & Community Initiatives	15-Jul-2004	McLean	VA
Bob Edmonds	Brigadier General, U.S. Air Force	12-Jun-2008	Washington	DC
Leon Edney	Admiral, U.S. Navy; Vice Chair of Naval Operations; Supreme Allied Commander Atlantic, NATO; Commander-in-Chief, U.S. Atlantic Command; Commandant of Midshipmen, U.S. Naval Academy	16-Nov-2009	Coronado	CA
Janet Eissenstat	Director, President's Commission on White House Fellowships	13-Jun-2008	Washington	DC
Steve Ellis	Managing Director, Bain and Company	1-Jun-2011	San Francisco	CA
Lynn Elsenhans	President, Shell Oil Company; CEO, Shell Oil Products; Chair and CEO, Sunoco	24-Feb-2011	Houston	TX

(continued)

Full Name	Organization or Title	Date	City	State
Allan C. Emery Jr.	Founder and President, ServiceMaster Hospital Corporation	28-Aug-2004	Weymouth	MA
Peter Engel	Executive Producer, *Saved by the Bell, Last Comic Standing, Hang Time*	15-Nov-2005	Santa Monica	CA
Gordon England	United States Deputy Secretary of Defense and United States Secretary of the Navy	19-Apr-2011	Fort Worth	TX
Ted W. Engstrom	President and CEO, World Vision; President, Youth for Christ International	13-Oct-2005	Seattle	WA
Sheldon Erikson	President, Chairman, and CEO, Cameron	8-Feb-2011	Houston	TX
Dave Evans	Co-founder and Vice President, Electronic Arts	20-May-2004	Menlo Park	CA
Donald L. Evans	Secretary of Commerce	11-Feb-2005	Washington	DC
Marsha Evans	Rear Admiral, U.S. Navy; Chief of Staff, U.S. Naval Academy; President and CEO, American Red Cross; National Executive Director, Girl Scouts of the USA; Acting Commissioner, Ladies Professional Golf Association; Deputy Director, President's Commission on White House Fellowships	21-Nov-2009	Houston	TX
Bill Ewing	Senior Vice President of Production Administration, Columbia Pictures	3-Oct-2005	Studio City	CA
John Faraci	Chairman and CEO, International Paper	21-Jun-2011	*Telephone interview*	
David Farr	Chairman and CEO, Emerson Electric	15-Mar-2011	St. Louis	MO
Larry Faulkner	President, Houston Endowment; President, University of Texas at Austin; Provost, University of Illinois at Urbana-Champaign	21-Oct-2010	Houston	TX
Drew Faust	President, Harvard University	15-Jul-2011	Cambridge	MA

Full Name	Organization or Title	Date	City	State
Steve Feldman	Director, *Sesame Street, Barney and Friends, Politically Incorrect with Bill Maher*	17-May-2005	Pasadena	CA
Mike Fenzel	Director for Transnational Threats, National Security Council	18-Nov-2009	Carmel	CA
Micheal Flaherty	Co-founder and President, Walden Media	3-Feb-2005	Washington	DC
Leighton Ford	President, Leighton Ford Ministries; Vice President, Billy Graham Evangelistic Association; Chairman, Lausanne Committee for World Evangelization	19-Sep-2005	Seattle	WA
Dick Foth	Associate, The Fellowship	7-Dec-2004	Arlington	VA
Peter Fox	Chief Commercial Officer, Air Transport Services Group	28-Jul-2010	Orlando	FL
Randy Frazee	Pastor, Willow Creek Community Church	7-Nov-2005	Chicago	IL
Thomas Frist Jr.	Co-founder, Chairman and CEO, Hospital Corporation of America	2-Dec-2010	Nashville	TN
Robert Fryling	Publisher, InterVarsity Press; Vice President, InterVarsity Christian Fellowship	12-Nov-2006	Chicago	IL
Susan Fuhrman	President of Teachers College, Columbia University; President, National Academy of Education	17-Feb-2011	New York	NY
Makoto Fujimura	Visual Artist; Founder, International Arts Movement	23-Aug-2004	New York	NY
Ellen Futter	President, American Museum of Natural History; President, Barnard College	3-Feb-2011	New York	NY

(*continued*)

Full Name	Organization or Title	Date	City	State
George Gallup Jr.	Chairman, The Gallup Institute	24-Jun-2005	Princeton	NJ
Pat Gelsinger	Chief Technology Officer, Intel; President and COO, EMC Information Infrastructure Products, EMC Corporation	2-Oct-2004	Bachelor's Gulch	CO
Michael Gerson	Assistant to the President for Speechwriting; Assistant to the President for Policy and Strategic Planning	17-Mar-2005	Washington	DC
Elliot Gerson	American Secretary of Rhodes Trust; Executive Vice President of Policy and Public Programs, International Partnerships, Aspen Institute	28-Oct-2010	Washington	DC
Kathie Lee Gifford	Entertainer; Former Co-host, *Live with Regis & Kathie Lee*	23-May-2005	New York	NY
Louis Giuliano	President, Chairman, and CEO, ITT Industries	18-Nov-2004	White Plains	NY
Jeffrey Glueck	CEO, Skyfire; Chief Marketing Officer, Travelocity	10-Dec-2009	New York	NY
Brian Godawa	Screenplay writer, *To End All Wars; The Visitation*	17-May-2005	Los Angeles	CA
Timothy Goeglein	Special Assistant to U. S. President George W. Bush; Deputy Director of the White House Office of Public Liaison	20-May-2011	Washington	DC
Bill Greehey	President, Valero Energy; Chairman and CEO, Valero Energy Corp.; Chairman of the Board and Director, NuStar Energy LP; Chairman of the Board and Director, NuStar GP Holdings	13-Dec-2010	San Antonio	TX
Hank Greenberg	Chairman and CEO, American International Group, Inc.; Chairman and CEO, C.V. Starr & Co., Inc.	3-Feb-2011	New York	NY

Full Name	Organization or Title	Date	City	State
Vartan Gregorian	President, Carnegie Corporation	6-Dec-2010	New York	NY
Barry Griswell	CEO, Principal Financial Group	15-Nov-2010	Des Moines	IA
David Grizzle	Senior Vice President– Customer Experience, Continental Airlines; Chief Counsel, Acting COO, Air Traffic Organization, FAA	31-Dec-2004	Charleston	SC
Will A. Gunn	General Counsel, U.S. Department of Veterans Affairs	28-Aug-2009	Washington	DC
Sanjay Gupta	CNN Chief Medical Correspondent; Associate Chief at Grady Hospital	12-Aug-2010	Atlanta	GA
Robert D. Haas	President, COO, Chairman and CEO, Chairman Emeritus, Levi Strauss & Co.	18-Nov-2009	San Francisco	CA
Richard N. Haass	President, Council on Foreign Relations; Director of Policy Planning for the Department of State; Vice President, Director of Foreign Policy Programs, Brooking Institution; Senior Associate, Carnegie Endowment for International Peace; Special Assistant to President George H.W. Bush	25-Apr-2011	New York	NY
William F. Hagerty IV	Co-founder and Managing Director, Hagerty, Peterson & Co., LLC; COO and CFO Ultra Stores; Co-CEO of Powerway, Inc.; CEO and founder of Lehman Brothers' Asian Asset Management Stage 3form (ALAM)	2-Dec-2010	Nashville	TN

(continued)

Full Name	Organization or Title	Date	City	State
Ted Haggard	Founder and Pastor, New Life Church; President, National Association of Evangelicals	4-Oct-2004	Colorado Springs	CO
Tony P. Hall	U.S. Ambassador to the United Nations Agencies for Food and Agriculture; Chief, the United States Mission to the UN Agencies; Executive Director, UNICEF; Member of the U.S. House of Representatives (D-OH), Member, Ohio House of Representatives, Member, Ohio Senate; Executive Director, The Alliance to End Hunger	4-Feb-2005	Washington	DC
John Hamre	Deputy Secretary of Defense; President and CEO, Center for Strategic and International Studies	4-Feb-2005	Washington	DC
John Hanford	U.S. Ambassador-at-Large for International Religious Freedom; Director, Congressional Fellows Program	14-Jan-2005	Washington	DC
Dave Hannah	Chairman and CEO, Impact XXI; Founder, Athletes in Action	8-Nov-2004	San Diego	CA
Patrick Harker	President, University of Delaware; Dean, The Wharton School, University of Pennsylvania	16-Feb-2010	Newark	DE
James Harmon	Founder, Chief Investment Officer and Chairman, Caravel Fund International; President and Chairman, Export-Import Bank of the United States	6-Oct-2010	New York	NY
Sam Haskell III	Worldwide Head of Television, the William Morris Agency	15-Nov-2005	Los Angeles	CA
Jody Hassett Sanchez	News and Documentary Producer, ABC World News Tonight	20-Mar-2005	Arlington	VA

Full Name	Organization or Title	Date	City	State
Nathan Hatch	President, Wake Forest University	23-Feb-2011	Houston	TX
Gary Haugen	President and CEO, International Justice Mission	22-Nov-2005	Washington	DC
Wallace Hawley	Co-founder, InterWest Partners	10-Aug-2005	Menlo Park	CA
Michael Hayes	Director, National Security Council Defense Policy and Strategy	27-Aug-2009	Washington	DC
Daryl Heald	President, Generous Giving	28-Jul-2005	Chattanooga	TN
Margaret Heckler	Secretary of Health and Human Services	6-Feb-2005	Washington	DC
George Heilmeier	Senior Vice President and Chief Technical Officer, Texas Instruments; Special Assistant, Secretary of Defense; Director, Defense Advanced Research Projects Agency	12-Sep-2009	Dallas	TX
Tami Heim	Executive Vice President, Thomas Nelson; President, Borders Inc.	21-Aug-2004	Detroit	MI
Jay F. Hein	Director, Office of Faith-Based & Community Initiatives; Sagamore Institute	7-Nov-2003	Indianapolis	IN
John Hennessy	President, Stanford University	9-Dec-2010	Stanford	CA
Adam Herbert	President, University of North Florida; President, Indiana University Systems	29-Sep-2009	Jacksonville	FL
Frances Hesselbein	CEO, Girl Scouts of the U.S.A.; President and CEO, Leader to Leader Institute	4-Oct-2010	New York	NY
Alec Hill	President and CEO, InterVarsity Christian Fellowship	11-Feb-2005	*Telephone interview*	
Carla Hills	U.S. Trade Representative; Secretary of Housing and Urban Development; Chairman and CEO, Hills & Company	1-Mar-2011	Washington	DC

(continued)

Full Name	Organization or Title	Date	City	State
Roderick M. Hills Jr.	Chairman, Securities and Exchange Commission	1-Mar-2011	Washington	DC
Donald P. Hodel	President and CEO, Focus on the Family, Secretary of the Interior; Secretary of Energy	4-Oct-2004	Colorado Springs	CO
Kirk Hoiberg	Senior Managing Director, CB Richards Ellis' Global Corporate Services; Principal, Trinitas Partners	20-May-2004	San Francisco	CA
J. Douglas Holladay	Founder and Partner, Park Avenue Equity Partners; Senior Officer, Goldman Sachs & Co.	9-Dec-2004	Washington	DC
Donald D. Holt	Editor, *Fortune*; Editor, *Newsweek*	25-Oct-2004	Wheaton	IL
Samuel Howard	Chairman and CEO, Xantus Corporation	9-Oct-2009	Nashville	TN
R. Glenn Hubbard	Chairman, White House Council of Economic Advisors; Dean, Columbia Business School	23-Aug-2004	New York	NY
Philip G. Hubbard	COO, Chicago Research and Trade	26-Oct-2004	Northfield	IL
Mike Huckabee	Governor, Arkansas	29-Jul-2004	Little Rock	AR
Karen Hughes	Counselor to the President; Senior Advisor to the President	21-Jan-2005	Washington	DC
Wayne Huizenga	Owner, Miami Dolphins; Owner, Florida Marlins; Founder and Chairman, Huizenga Holdings, Inc.; Executive, Blockbuster, AutoNation, and Waste Management	19-Oct-2004	Fort Lauderdale	FL
Walter Humann	Executive Vice President and Chairman, Hunt Consolidated	13-Oct-2009	Dallas	TX
Asa Hutchinson	Under Secretary of Homeland Security	10-Dec-2004	Washington	DC
David Iglesias	U.S. Attorney, District of New Mexico	28-Aug-2009	Washington	DC
Jeff Immelt	Chairman and CEO, General Electric	30-Mar-2011	Houston	TX

Full Name	Organization or Title	Date	City	State
William Inboden	Senior Director for Strategic Planning, National Security Council	4-Feb-2005	Washington	DC
Stuart M. Irby	President and CEO, Stuart C. Irby Company	21-Jul-2004	Jackson	MS
Maryana Iskander	COO, Planned Parenthood	3-Oct-2010	New York	NY
Ann Iverson	CEO, Laura Ashley; President and CEO, Kay-Bee Toys	15-Jun-2005	New York	NY
Susan Ivey	President, Chair, and CEO, Reynolds American	17-May-2011	Fort Lauderdale	FL
Peb Jackson	Vice President of Public Affairs, Saddleback Church and Purpose Driven Ministries; Founding Director and Senior Vice President, Focus on the Family	16-Sep-2004	Osprey Point	MD
Kay Coles James	Director, Office of Personnel Management	17-Sep-2004	Washington	DC
David Jeffrey	Provost, Baylor University	26-Mar-2004	Waco	TX
Jon Jennings	Assistant Coach, Boston Celtics; Co-owner, President and General Manager, Maine Red Claws, Acting Assistant Attorney General, U.S. Department of Justice	17-Aug-2009	Portland	ME
Martin Jischke	President, Purdue University; President, Iowa State University; Interim President, University of Oklahoma	28-Sep-2009	West Lafayette	IN
Ronald P. Joelson	Senior Vice President and Chief Investment Officer, Prudential Financial Services; Senior Vice President and Chief Investment Officer, Genworth Financial	3-Dec-2004	Newark	NJ
Paul Johnson	CEO, Paul Johnson & Company	8-Jul-2004	Birmingham	MI
Stephen L. Johnson	Administrator, Environmental Protection Agency	25-Oct-2005	Washington	DC

(continued)

Full Name	Organization or Title	Date	City	State
Tom Johnson	Special Assistant to the President; President, Chairman, and CEO, CNN; Publisher, President, and CEO, Los Angeles Times	18-Dec-2009	Atlanta	GA
Clay Johnson III	Assistant to the President and Director of Presidential Personnel; Deputy Director, Office of Management and Budget	23-Oct-2008	Washington	DC
Douglas Johnston	Founder and President, International Center for Religion and Diplomacy	11-Feb-2005	Washington	DC
Dale P. Jones	President, Halliburton	12-Apr-2004	Dallas	TX
W. Landis Jones	Director, President's Commission on White House Fellowships	20-Oct-2009	Washington	DC
James Jones	National Security Advisor	31-May-2011	*Telephone interview*	
Reginald L. Jones III	Managing Partner, Greenbriar Equity Group	18-May-2011	Rye	NY
Vernon Jordan Jr.	Senior Managing Director, Lazard Frères & Co.; Chairman of the Clinton Presidential Transition Team	6-Oct-2010	New York	NY
Robert Joss	Dean, Stanford Graduate School of Business; CEO, Westpac Banking Corporation	11-Aug-2009	Palo Alto	CA
David Karnes	U.S. Senator (R-NE); President and CEO, The Fairmont Group	7-Dec-2009	Washington	DC
Howard Kazanjian	Producer, *JAG, Raiders of the Lost Ark, Star Wars: Return of the Jedi*	8-Nov-2004	Pasadena	CA
Frank Keating	Governor, Oklahoma; President and CEO, American Bankers Association	7-Mar-2011	Houston	TX
Kurt Keilhacker	Chairman, The Veritas Forum; Managing Partner, TechFund Capital	15-Oct-2004	*Telephone interview*	
Timothy Keller	Senior Pastor, Redeemer Presbyterian Church	12-May-2005	New York	NY

Full Name	Organization or Title	Date	City	State
Larry Kellner	Chairman and CEO, Continental Airlines	18-Feb-2011	Houston	TX
Jeff Kemp	President, Stronger Families; NFL player	16-Jul-2004	Washington	DC
Bruce Kennedy	CEO, Alaska Air Group	8-Sep-2004	Seattle	WA
Donald Kennedy	President, Stanford University	8-Dec-2010	Palo Alto	CA
Nannerl Keohane	President, Duke University; President, Wellesley College	5-Oct-2010	Princeton	NJ
William Kilberg	Solicitor for the U.S. Department of Labor; Partner, Gibson, Dunn & Crutcher	28-Aug-2009	Washington	DC
Robert Kimmitt	Under Secretary of State; Ambassador to Germany; Deputy Secretary of Treasury	6-May-2011	Washington	DC
Richard Kinder	Chairman and CEO, Kinder Morgan; President, Enron	3-Dec-2010	Houston	TX
Betsy King	Ladies Professional Golf Association professional golfer	29-Oct-2004	Scottsdale	AZ
Greg King	COO and President, Valero Energy Corporation	12-Oct-2010	San Antonio	TX
John Kingston III	Vice Chairman and General Counsel, Affiliated Managers Group	27-May-2011	Beverly	MA
Paul Klaassen	Co-founder, Chairman, and CEO, Sunrise Assisted Living; Chairman, The Trinity Forum	15-Jul-2004	McLean	VA
Todd Komarnicki	Producer, *Elf*; Writer, *Perfect Stranger*; Producer, *Meet Dave*	29-Apr-2004	New York	NY
C. Everett Koop	U.S. Surgeon General	27-Aug-2004	Dartmouth	NH
Richard Kovacevich	Chairman and CEO, Wells Fargo & Co.	3-Mar-2010	San Francisco	CA
Keith Krach	CEO, 3Points, Inc.; Chairman, Purdue University	8-Dec-2010	Menlo Park	CA
Kay Krill	Director, President, and CEO, Ann Taylor Stores Corporation	8-Jun-2011	New York	NY

(*continued*)

Full Name	Organization or Title	Date	City	State
Peter Krogh	Dean, Edmund A. Walsh School of Foreign Service, Georgetown University; Dean, Fletcher School of Law and Diplomacy, Georgetown University; Special Assistant to the Secretary of State	27-Aug-2009	Washington	DC
Mark Kuyper	President and CEO, Evangelicals Christian Publishers Association	6-Nov-2005	Chicago	IL
Linda Lader	President, Renaissance Institute	12-Apr-2005	New Haven	CT
Drew Ladner	Chief Information Officer, U.S. Treasury Department; President and CEO, Pascal Metrics	5-Aug-2004	Washington	DC
Jim Lane	Founder and President, New Canaan Society; Chairman and CEO, SG Capital Partners; Founding member of the Global Private Equity Business and General Partner, Goldman Sachs & Co.	22-Apr-2005	Princeton	NJ
Neal Lane	Director, National Science Foundation; Assistant to the President for Science and Technology and Director of the White House Office of Science and Technology Policy	27-Jan-2011	Houston	TX
Kenneth Langone	Founder, Home Depot	25-Apr-2011	New York	NY
Mark Laret	CEO, UCSF Medical Center	10-May-2011	San Francisco	CA
Steve Largent	President and CEO, CTIA-The Wireless Association; U.S. Congressman (R-OK); NFL player	4-Aug-2004	Washington	DC
Ralph S. Larsen	Chairman and CEO, Johnson & Johnson	23-Jun-2004	Wyckoff	NJ
Kenneth R. Larson	Owner and CEO, Slumberland	1-Jun-2005	St. Paul	MN
William Lauder	Chairman and CEO, Estée Lauder Companies	8-Jun-2011	New York	NY

Full Name	Organization or Title	Date	City	State
Steven Law	Deputy Secretary of Labor; President and CEO, American Crossroads; President, CrossroadsGPS; Chief Legal Officer and General Counsel, U.S. Chamber of Commerce	14-Jan-2005	Washington	DC
David Le Shana	President, Seattle Pacific University; President, George Fox University; Chairman, Azusa Pacific University	19-Aug-2004	Lake Oswego	OR
Jerry Leamon	Global Managing Partner, Deloitte Touche Tohmatsu	4-Oct-2010	New York	NY
Jack LeCuyer	Executive Director, White House Fellows Foundation and Association	13-Jun-2008	Washington	DC
Ronald Lee	Assistant Postmaster General	19-Jan-2010	Washington	DC
David Leebron	President, Rice University	22-Feb-2011	Houston	TX
David Leitch	General Counsel and Group Vice President, Ford Motor Company; Deputy Counsel to the President	6-Dec-2004	Washington	DC
William Lennox Jr.	Lieutenant General, U.S. Army; Superintendent, U.S. Military Academy	8-Dec-2009	Arlington	VA
Nicholas Leone III	President and CEO, Global Fund Group, LLC	17-Feb-2011	New York	NY
Thomas C. Leppert	Chairman and CEO, The Turner Corporation	9-Dec-2009	Dallas	TX
Arthur Levinson	Chairman and CEO, Genentech	10-Jun-2011	*Telephone interview*	
Lauren Libby	Vice President and Chief Operating Officer, The Navigators; President, Trans World Radio	4-Apr-2005	Colorado Springs	CO
Keith Lindner	Co-president, American Financial Group; President and COO, Chiquita Brands International	9-Jun-2004	Cincinnati	OH
Art Linkletter	Television host, *People Are Funny, House Party, Kids Say the Darndest Things*	19-May-2005	Beverly Hills	CA

(continued)

Full Name	Organization or Title	Date	City	State
A. Duane Litfin	President, Wheaton College	8-Oct-2004	Wheaton	IL
Bernard Loeffke	Major General, U.S. Army; Commanding General, U.S. Army Southern Command	1-Oct-2009	Fort Lauderdale	FL
Erik Lokkesmoe	Chairman, The Voice Behind; Vice President, Walden Media; Director of Communications, National Endowment for the Humanities	5-Sep-2004	Osprey Point	MD
Terry Looper	President and CEO, Texon	17-Feb-2005	Houston	TX
Nancy Lopez	LPGA professional golfer	25-Aug-2004	Kutztown	PA
James Loy	Deputy Secretary of Homeland Security; Coast Guard Commandant; Senior Counselor, Cohen Group	2-Mar-2011	Washington	DC
Tom Luce	Assistant Secretary of Planning, Evaluation, and Policy Development, U.S. Department of Education; CEO of National Math and Science Initiative	19-Apr-2011	Dallas	TX
Luis Lugo	Director, Pew Forum on Religion and Public Life	13-Jan-2005	Washington	DC
Gabe Lyons	Co-founder, Relevate	16-Sep-2005	Osprey Point	MD
Hugh O. Maclellan Jr.	President, Maclellan Foundation	1-Oct-2004	Bachelor's Gulch	CO
Nicole Malachowski	First female pilot in the U.S. Air Force Thunderbirds	8-Dec-2009	Arlington	VA
Theodore Roosevelt Malloch	Chairman and CEO, The Global Fiduciary Governance LLC	3-Feb-2005	Washington	DC
Richard Malloch	President, Hearst Business Media; Senior Vice President, The Hearst Corporation	26-Apr-2011	New York	NY
Joel Manby	CEO, Saab USA; Chairman, President and CEO, Herschend Family Entertainment	28-Feb-2005	Norcross	GA
Julissa Marenco	President, ZSG Station Group	8-Dec-2009	Arlington	VA
Bill Marriott	Chairman and CEO, Marriott International	19-May-2011	Bethesda	MD

Full Name	Organization or Title	Date	City	State
Anthony Marx	President, Amherst College	22-Feb-2011	*Telephone interview*	
Walter Massey	President, Morehouse College; Chairman, Bank of America	5-Mar-2011	Naples	FL
Karen Mathis	President, American Bar Association; President and CEO, Big Brothers Big Sisters of America	27-Apr-2011	Philadelphia	PA
Mickey Maudlin	Editorial Director and Vice President, HarperOne	7-Dec-2010	San Francisco	CA
Mark Mays	President and CEO, Clear Channel Communications	12-Oct-2010	San Antonio	TX
Robert J. Mazzuca	Chief Scout Executive, Boy Scouts of America	23-Dec-2010	Irving	TX
John McCarter	President and CEO, The Field Museum; Senior Vice President and Partner, Booz Allen Hamilton	14-Sep-2009	Chicago	IL
Rich McClure	President, UniGroup; CEO, United Van Lines and Mayflower Transit	15-Mar-2011	Fenton	MO
Alonzo McDonald	Deputy White House Chief of Staff; Managing Director, McKinsey & Company; Founding Chairman, The Trinity Forum; Co-founder, Chairman, and CEO, Avenir Group	8-Jul-2004	Birmingham	MI
Stephen McEveety	*Producer, The Passion of the Christ*, Icon Productions	5-Sep-2004	New York	NY
David McFadzean	Executive Producer, *Home Improvement; staff writer, Roseanne*	27-Sep-2004	Pasadena	CA
Robert McFarlane	National Security Advisor	27-Aug-2009	Arlington	VA
Gail McGovern	President and CEO, American Red Cross	2-Mar-2011	Washington	DC
Harold McGraw III	President, Chairman, and CEO, McGraw-Hill Companies; Chairman, Business Roundtable	18-May-2011	New York	NY
Joel McHale	Television host, *The Soup;* actor, *Community*	8-Nov-2004	Los Angeles	CA

(continued)

Full Name	Organization or Title	Date	City	State
Margaret McKeown	Judge, U.S. Court of Appeals (9th Circuit); Partner, Perkins Coie	21-Oct-2009	Washington	DC
Drayton McLane	Chairman, McLane Group; Chairman, McLane Corporation; Chairman and CEO, Houston Astros; Vice Chairman, Walmart	5-May-2011	Houston	TX
Burton McMurtry	Founding General Partner, Technology Venture Investments	9-Dec-2010	Palo Alto	CA
Robert C. McNair	Owner, Chairman and CEO, Houston Texans	15-Apr-2011	Houston	TX
Mac McQuiston	President and CEO, CEO Forum	4-Apr-2005	Colorado Springs	CO
Curtis McWilliams	President and CEO, CNL Restaurant Properties	23-Nov-2004	Orlando	FL
Dana Mead	Chairman and CEO, Tenneco; Chairman, MIT Corporation	15-Oct-2009	Houston	TX
Edwin Meese III	U.S. Attorney General and Counselor to the President	14-Sep-2004	Washington	DC
Doris Meissner	Commissioner, U.S. Immigration and Naturalization Service	20-Oct-2009	Washington	DC
Jim Mellado	President, Willow Creek Association	18-Jun-2004	*Telephone interview*	
Ken Melrose	Chairman and CEO, Toro Company	4-Jun-2011	Orono	MN
John Mendelsohn	President, University of Texas M.D. Anderson Cancer Center	16-Mar-2011	Houston	TX
Morton Meyerson	Chairman and CEO, Perot Systems; President, Electronic Data Systems	29-Dec-2010	Dallas	TX
Gayle Miller	President, Anne Klein II	31-Jul-2004	Hollywood	CA
Norman Miller	Chairman and CEO, Interstate Batteries	14-Oct-2004	Dallas	TX
Jody Miller	Founder and CEO, Business Talent Group; Executive Vice President and COO, Americast	9-Feb-2010	Pacific Palisades	CA
Billy Mitchell	Chairman and CEO, Carter & Associates	15-Apr-2004	Atlanta	GA

Full Name	Organization or Title	Date	City	State
Cindy Moelis	Director, President's Commission on White House Fellowships	7-Dec-2009	Washington	DC
Wes Moore	Investment Banker, Citigroup	10-Nov-2009	New York	NY
Thomas Morgan	CEO, Hughes Supply Company	22-Nov-2004	Orlando	FL
James C. Morgan	President, Chairman, and CEO, Applied Materials	8-Dec-2010	San Francisco	CA
John Morgridge	Chairman and CEO, Cisco Systems	9-May-2011	Menlo Park	CA
Allen Morris	President, Chairman, and CEO, The Allen Morris Company	19-Oct-2004	Coral Gables	FL
Malcolm S. Morris	Chairman and CEO, Stewart Information Services Corporation and Stewart Title Guaranty Company; Chairman, Stewart Title Company	12-Nov-2004	Houston	TX
William Mounger	CEO, Tritel Communications	4-Apr-2009	Jackson	MS
Richard Mouw	President, Fuller Theological Seminary	27-May-2003	Pasadena	CA
Ed Moy	Director, U.S. Mint; Special Assistant to the President, Office of Presidential Personnel	16-Jul-2004	Washington	DC
Anne Mulcahy	Chair and CEO, Xerox Corporation	4-Oct-2010	New York	NY
Ken Myers	Host and Producer, Mars Hill Audio Journal	23-Sep-2005	*Telephone interview*	
John Naber	President, U.S. Olympic Alumni Association; Olympic swimmer	18-May-2004	Pasadena	CA
Paul D. Nelson	President, Evangelical Council for Financial Accountability	1-Aug-2003	Washington	DC
Larry Nelson	Champions Tour professional golfer	8-Jul-2004	Dearborn	MI
Steven R. Nelson	Executive Director, MBA Program Harvard Business School	27-Aug-2004	Cambridge	MA
Howard Nemerovski	Founding Partner, Howard Rice Nemerovski Cannady Falk & Rabin	11-Aug-2009	Novato	CA

(*continued*)

Full Name	Organization or Title	Date	City	State
David Neuman	President, Walt Disney Network Television; President, Touchstone Television; Chief Production Officer, CNN; President and CEO, Digital Entertainment Network; President of Programming, Current TV; Programming President, NBC; President of Programming, Channel One	3-Nov-2009	Hollywood	CA
Greg Newman	Co-founder and Senior Vice President of Marketing and Sales, C2B Technology; Founding Partner, Macromedia; Senior Director of Internet Technologies, Oracle	19-May-2004	Burlingame	CA
Armand Nicholi	Author; faculty member, Harvard Medical School	27-Aug-2004	Concord	MA
Jack Nicklaus	Professional golfer	6-Jan-2010	North Palm Beach	FL
Neil Nicoll	President and CEO, YMCA	7-Apr-2011	Dallas	TX
David Novak	CEO, Yum! Brands	22-Dec-2010	Louisville	KY
Peter Ochs	Founder and Chairman, Fieldstone Communities; Co-Founder and Chairman, First Fruit, Inc.	26-Apr-2004	Newport Beach	CA
Steve Odland	Chairman and CEO, Office Depot; President, Chairman, and CEO, AutoZone, Inc.	7-Jan-2010	Boca Raton	FL
Richard Ohman	President and CEO, Colonial Penn Life Insurance; President, The Trinity Forum	26-Aug-2004	Hancock	NH
Daniel Oliver	Vice Admiral, U.S. Navy; President, Naval Postgraduate School	11-Aug-2009	Monterey	CA
Gilbert Omenn	Executive Vice President for Medical Affairs and CEO, University of Michigan Health System; President and Chairman, American Association for the Advancement of Science	19-Oct-2009	Washington	DC

Full Name	Organization or Title	Date	City	State
Pierre Omidyar	Founder and Chairman, eBay	14-Dec-2009	Honolulu	HI
Paul O'Neill	Secretary of the Treasury; Chairman and CEO, Alcoa; Deputy Director of the Office of Budget and Management	16-Mar-2011	Houston	TX
John Ortberg	Senior Pastor, Menlo Park Presbyterian Church; Teaching Pastor, Willow Creek Community Church	16-May-2005	Pasadena	CA
M. Kenneth Oshman	Chairman and CEO, Echelon Corporation	11-May-2011	Atherton	CA
James Owens	Chairman and CEO, Caterpillar	15-Mar-2011	Peoria	IL
Jim Padilla	President and COO, Ford Motors	20-Oct-2009	Leesburg	VA
Greg Page	President and CEO, Cargill	4-Jun-2011	Wayzata	MN
Cary Paine	Executive Director, The Stewardship Foundation	10-Sep-2004	Seattle	WA
Kevin Palau	President, Luis Palau Association	2-Oct-2004	Bachelor's Gulch	CO
Luis Palau	Founder, Luis Palau Association	6-Oct-2006	Houston	TX
Earl Palmer	Senior Pastor, University Presbyterian Church	14-Oct-2003	Princeton	NJ
Mark Palmer	Ambassador to Hungary; State Department	20-May-2011	Washington	DC
Richard Parsons	Chairman, Citigroup; Chairman and CEO, Time Warner; Associate Director of the Domestic Council and Senior White House Aide to the President	3-Feb-2011	New York	NY
Jon Passavant	Celebrity fashion model	20-Feb-2006	New York	NY
Rena Pederson	Vice President and Editorial Page Editor, *The Dallas Morning News*	13-Nov-2004	Dallas	TX
Michelle Peluso	Executive Vice President, Sabre Holdings; President and CEO, Travelocity	11-Nov-2009	New York	NY
Gordon Pennington	Director of Marketing, Tommy Hilfiger	7-Sep-2004	New York	NY
John Pepper	Chairman, Walt Disney; Chairman and CEO, Procter & Gamble	23-May-2011	*Telephone interview*	

(continued)

Full Name	Organization or Title	Date	City	State
Ken Perez	Senior Vice President of Marketing, Omnicell; Vice President of Marketing, Jacent Technologies	20-May-2004	Mountain View	CA
Jane Cahill Pfeiffer	Chairwoman, NBC	1-Oct-2009	Vero Beach	FL
Kien Pham	CEO, VietNamNet Media Group	23-Oct-2009	Washington	DC
Thomas L. Phillips	Chairman and CEO, Raytheon	30-Aug-2004	Boston	MA
John Phillips	Founding Partner, Phillips & Cohen LLP; Chairman, President's Commission on White House Fellowships	16-Feb-2010	Washington	DC
Percy Pierre	Vice President for Research and Graduate Studies, Michigan State University; President, Prairie View A&M University; Dean, School of Engineering, Howard University	17-Dec-2009	New Orleans	LA
Eric Pillmore	Senior Vice President of Corporate Governance, Tyco	10-May-2005	Princeton	NJ
William M. Pinson	Executive Director, Baptist General Convention of Texas	2-Jan-2005	Dallas	TX
Kevin Plank	Founder and CEO, Under Armour	29-Oct-2010	Baltimore	MD
Steve Poizner	State Insurance Commissioner of California; Founder and CEO, SnapTrack, Inc.; Founder and CEO, Strategic Mapping, Inc.	19-Nov-2009	Los Gatos	CA
C. William Pollard	CEO, ServiceMaster	24-May-2004	Wheaton	IL
Roger Porter	IBM Professor of Business and Government, Kennedy School of Government, Harvard University; Assistant to the President for Economic and Domestic Policy; Director of the White House Office of Policy Development; Executive Secretary of the President's Economic Policy Board	14-Aug-2009	Cambridge	MA

Full Name	Organization or Title	Date	City	State
Donald E. Powell	Chairman, Federal Deposit Insurance Corporation	19-Feb-2006	Washington	DC
Colin Powell	Secretary of State; National Security Advisor; Chairman of Joint Chiefs of Staff; General, U.S. Army	26-Aug-2009	Alexandria	VA
Larry Pugh	President, Chairman, and CEO, V. F. Corporation	6-Jan-2010	Naples	FL
James Purcell Jr.	Assistant Secretary of State; Director, Bureau of Refugee Programs	19-May-2011	Washington	DC
John Pustay	Lieutenant General, U.S. Air Force	8-Dec-2009	Sterling	VA
Merrit Quarum	CEO, Qmedtrix Systems, Inc.	31-Jul-2004	Calabasas	CA
David Radcliffe	President, Chairman, and CEO, The Southern Company	15-Apr-2004	Atlanta	GA
Michael Regan	CEO, Transzact Technologies	7-Oct-2004	Chicago	IL
Steven Reinemund	Chairman and CEO, PepsiCo	13-Nov-2004	Dallas	TX
Brad Rex	Vice President of EPCOT, The Walt Disney Company	23-Nov-2004	Orlando	FL
Herbert Reynolds	President, Baylor University	26-Mar-2004	Waco	TX
Mercer Reynolds	U.S. Ambassador to Switzerland and Lichtenstein	9-Jun-2004	Cincinnati	OH
Condoleezza Rice	Secretary of State	8-Dec-2010	Palo Alto	CA
James Richardson	President, Alexandria Real Estate Services	19-May-2004	Palo Alto	CA
Rozanne Ridgway	Ambassador to Finland and to East Germany; Assistant Secretary of State, European and Canadian Affairs	1-Mar-2011	Alexandria	VA
Paul Robbins	President and Publisher, Christianity Today International	6-May-2004	Wheaton	IL
Pat Robertson	Founder and Chairman, The Christian Broadcasting Network; Founder and Chancellor, Regent University	24-Oct-2003	Virginia Beach	VA

(*continued*)

Full Name	Organization or Title	Date	City	State
David Robinson	Hall of Fame NBA player, San Antonio Spurs	1-Oct-2004	Bachelor's Gulch	CO
Joyce Robinson	Vice President and Executive Director, Marie Walsh Sharpe Foundation	4-Oct-2004	Colorado Springs	CO
Josue Robles Jr.	President and CEO, USAA; Major General, U.S. Army	12-Oct-2010	San Antonio	TX
Gerard R. Roche	Senior Chairman, Heidrick & Struggles International	16-May-2011	West Palm Beach	FL
Mark Rodgers	Principal and Co-founder of Clapham Group; Leader, Faith & Law; Staff Director, Senate Republican Conference; Chief of Staff to Senator Rick Santorum	5-Sep-2004	Osprey Point	MD
Gary Rogers	Chairman, Federal Reserve Bank of San Francisco; Chairman, Levi Strauss & Co.; Founder, Chairman and CEO, Dreyer's	3-Mar-2010	Oakland	CA
William L. Roper	Dean, School of Medicine, University of North Carolina at Chapel Hill (UNC); Vice Chancellor for Medical Affairs and CEO, UNC Health Care System; Dean, School of Public Health, UNC	2-Jan-2010	Chapel Hill	NC
Matthew K. Rose	President, Chairman, and CEO, Burlington Northern Santa Fe	3-Jan-2005	Dallas	TX
Andrew Rosenthal	Editorial Page Editor, the *New York Times*	17-Feb-2011	New York	NY
Barry Rowan	Executive Vice President, CFO and Chief Administrative Officer, Vonage	27-Apr-2011	Holmdel	NJ
Robert Rubin	Chairman, Council on Foreign Relations; Secretary of the Treasury; Director, National Economic Council; Chairman, Citigroup	17-May-2011	New York	NY

Full Name	Organization or Title	Date	City	State
George Rupp	President, Rice University; President, Columbia University; President, International Rescue Committee	10-May-2008	Houston	TX
Skip Ryan	Founding Pastor, Park Cities Presbyterian Church; Moderator of the General Assembly of the Presbyterian Church in America; Chancellor and Professor of Practical Theology at Redeemer Seminary	5-Apr-2004	Dallas	TX
Denny Rydberg	President, Young Life	4-Apr-2005	Colorado Springs	CO
John Sage	Co-founder and CEO, Pura Vida Coffee	10-Sep-2004	Seattle	WA
David Sampson	Deputy Secretary of Commerce	6-Dec-2004	Washington	DC
Thomas Saponas	Vice President, Hewlett-Packard	21-Dec-2009	Colorado Springs	CO
Paul Sarbanes	U.S. Senator (D-MD)	18-Feb-2010	Washington	DC
David Satcher	Surgeon General; Assistant Secretary for Health, U.S. Department of Health & Human Services	16-Aug-2010	Atlanta	GA
John Saxon	Founding partner, Saxon Attorneys	26-Feb-2010	Birmingham	AL
Lynn Schenk	U.S. Representative (D-CA)	16-Nov-2009	San Diego	CA
Horst Schulze	President, Ritz-Carlton	1-Mar-2005	Atlanta	GA
Brent Scowcroft	National Security Advisor	21-Jun-2011	Washington	DC
John Seffrin	CEO, American Cancer Society	1-Nov-2010	Atlanta	GA
Robert Seiple	President, World Vision; Founder, Institute for Global Engagement, U.S. Ambassador-at-Large for Religious Freedom	2-Nov-2004	St. David's	PA
George Selden	Director, Christian Embassy	20-Mar-2005	Arlington	VA
Donna Shalala	President, University of Miami; Secretary of Health and Human Services; Chancellor, University of Wisconsin-Madison	5-Jan-2010	Coral Gables	FL

(*continued*)

Full Name	Organization or Title	Date	City	State
Harold Shapiro	President, Princeton University; Chair, National Bioethics Advisory Commission	5-Oct-2010	Princeton	NJ
Dal Shealy	President and CEO, Fellowship of Christian Athletes	1-Dec-2004	*Telephone interview*	
John Shepherd	Actor; producer, *Bobby Jones: Stroke of Genius;* President, Mpower Pictures	19-May-2004	Los Angeles	CA
George Shultz	U.S. Secretary of State; U.S. Secretary of the Treasury; Secretary of Labor; Director of the Office of Management and Budget	7-Dec-2010	San Francisco	CA
William Sick	Chairman and CEO, Business Resources International	3-Jun-2011	Winnetka	IL
Fred Sievert	President, New York Life	21-Sep-2004	New York	NY
Alfred C. Sikes	Chairman, Federal Communications Commission	14-Jul-2004	New York	NY
Karl Singer	AON Insurance; President, Ryan Insurance Group	12-Apr-2004	Dallas	TX
Paul Singer	Senior Vice President and Chief Information Officer, Target	31-May-2005	Minneapolis	MN
Frank Skinner	Chairman and CEO, BellSouth Telecommunications	25-Feb-2005	Atlanta	GA
Robert Sloan	President and Chancellor, Baylor University	18-Apr-2005	Waco	TX
Jeff Smisek	President and CEO, United Airlines; Chairman, President and CEO, Continental Airlines	18-Feb-2011	Houston	TX
Raymond Smith	Principal, Kirell Energy Systems	22-May-2004	El Camino Real	CA
Stan Smith	Professional tennis player	7-Sep-2004	New York	NY
Frederick Smith	President, Chairman, and CEO, FedEX Corporation	9-Jun-2011	Memphis	TN
Fred Smith, Jr.	President, The Gathering	5-Apr-2004	Dallas	TX
Don Soderquist	Senior Vice Chairman and COO, Walmart	28-Jul-2004	Rogers	AR

Full Name	Organization or Title	Date	City	State
Everett Spain	Aide-de-Camp to General David Petraeus; Lieutenant Colonel, U.S. Army	8-Sep-2009	*Telephone interview*	
Roxanne Spillett	CEO, Boys & Girls Club of America	16-Aug-2010	Atlanta	GA
Nancy Stafford	Actress, *Matlock, St. Elsewhere*	9-Nov-2004	Marina del Ray	CA
Ken Starr	Solicitor General; Independent Counsel on Whitewater investigation; Dean, Pepperdine Law School; President, Baylor University	19-May-2005	Malibu	CA
Richard Stearns	President and CEO, World Vision; President and CEO, Lenox; President, Parker Brothers	9-Sep-2004	Bellevue	WA
Isaac Stein	President, Waverly Associates; Chairman, Maxygen; Lead Director, Alexza	9-May-2011	Menlo Park	CA
Thomas Steipp	President and CEO, Symmetricom	11-Aug-2005	San Jose	CA
Randall Stephenson	President, Chairman, and CEO, AT&T	23-Dec-2010	Dallas	TX
Stephen Strickland	Associate Director, President's Commission on White House Fellowships	9-Dec-2010	Washington	DC
William Strong	Vice Chair of Investment Banking, Morgan Stanley	6-Oct-2009	Kansas City	MO
John Surma, Jr.	Chairman and CEO, U.S. Steel	18-May-2011	New York	NY
Deanell Tacha	Federal Judge, U.S. Court of Appeals, 10th Circuit	16-Dec-2009	Kansas City	KS
Shane Tedjarati	CEO, Honeywell China and India	15-Feb-2011	*Telephone interview*	
John Templeton, Jr.	President, John Templeton Foundation	15-Apr-2005	Philadelphia	PA
George Tenet	Director of the CIA	18-May-2011	New York	NY
Cal Thomas	Syndicated columnist, *After Hours with Cal Thomas*	23-Jun-2005	Washington	DC
Frank Thomas	President, Ford Foundation	25-Apr-2011	New York	NY

(continued)

Full Name	Organization or Title	Date	City	State
Thomas J. Tierney	Co-founder and Chairman, The Bridgespan Group; CEO, Bain & Company	30-Jun-2010	Boston	MA
Shirley Tilghman	President, Princeton University	7-Oct-2010	Princeton	NJ
Kimberly Till	President and CEO, Harris Interactive; CEO, TNS North America; Vice President, Microsoft Worldwide Media and Entertainment Group	10-Dec-2009	New York	NY
Glenn Tilton	Chairman of United Continental Holdings; President, Chairman, and CEO, United Continental Holdings	10-Jun-2011	*Telephone interview*	
Michael Timmis	Vice Chairman, Talon LLC	20-Aug-2004	Grosse Pointe Farms	MI
Richard Tompane	President and CEO, Gemfire	31-Oct-2003	Los Altos	CA
Ron Tschetter	Director, Peace Corps	3-Jun-2011	White Bear Township	MN
James S. Turley	Chairman and CEO, Ernst & Young	15-Dec-2010	New York	NY
Ted Turner	Chairman, Turner Enterprises, Inc.; Chairman, United Nations Foundation; Vice Chairman, Time Warner, Inc.; President and Chairman, Turner Broadcasting Systems, Inc.	25-Feb-2010	Atlanta	GA
Hatim Tyabji	CEO, Verifone; Chairman, Bytemobile	9-May-2011	Santa Clara	CA
John Tyson	Chairman, Tyson Foods	27-Jul-2004	Springdale	AR
Myron Ullman	Chairman and CEO, JCPenney, Macy's, Inc., Moët Hennessy Louis Vuitton	19-Aug-2009	Dallas	TX
James Unruh	President, Chairman, and CEO, Unisys	28-Oct-2004	Scottsdale	AZ
Chase Untermeyer	Ambassador to Qatar; Director of Presidential Personnel and Assistant to the President	15-Feb-2011	Houston	TX

Full Name	Organization or Title	Date	City	State
Rollin van Broekhoven	Judge; Attorney for Department of Defense	7-Dec-2004	Washington	DC
Daniel Vasella	CEO, Novartis Pharmaceuticals	3-Feb-2011	New York	NY
Charles Vest	President, MIT; President, National Academy of Engineering	19-May-2011	Washington	DC
Daniel Vestal	Executive Coordinator, Cooperative Baptist Fellowship	19-Apr-2005	Waco	TX
Phil Vischer	Creator, *Veggie Tales*	12-Nov-2005	Wheaton	IL
Paul Volcker	Chairman, Federal Reserve; Chairman, Economic Recovery Advisory Board	25-Apr-2011	New York	NY
Michael Volkema	President, Chairman, and CEO, Herman Miller	17-Nov-2004	New York	NY
Roderick von Lipsey	Director, National Security Council	13-Jun-2010	Washington	DC
Ken Wales	Producer, *Amazing Grace*, *Christy*	23-Nov-2003	Santa Monica	CA
Debra Waller	Jockey	22-Mar-2005	New York	NY
Jim Wallis	President and Chief of Sojourners; Founder Call to Renewal	31-Dec-2005	Charleston	SC
Patrick Walsh	Admiral, U.S. Navy; Commander, U.S. Pacific Fleet	14-Dec-2009	Pearl Harbor	III
Diana Chapman Walsh	President, Wellesley College	12-Feb-2011	Boston	MA
Joseph C. Walter III	CEO, Walter Oil	17-Feb-2005	Houston	TX
Kurt Warner	NFL player	2-Jun-2005	Phoenix	AZ
Michael Warren	Producer, *Happy Days, Family Matters, Step by Step*	26-Apr-2004	Westlake Village	CA
Neil Clark Warren	Chairman and Co-founder, eHarmony	1-Jul-2010	Kennebunkport	ME
Sherron Watkins	Vice President of Corporate Development, Enron	21-Feb-2005	Houston	TX
James Watt	Secretary of the Interior	28-Oct-2004	Wickenburg	AZ
David Weekley	Founder and Chairman, David Weekley Homes	12-Nov-2004	Houston	TX
Peter Wehner	Deputy Assistant to the President and Director of Strategic Initiatives	4-Aug-2004	Washington	DC

(*continued*)

Full Name	Organization or Title	Date	City	State
Clifton Wharton	Chairman and CEO, TIAA/CREF; President, Michigan State; Deputy Secretary of State	17-Feb-2011	New York	NY
Edward E. Whitacre Jr.	Chairman and CEO, General Motors; CEO, AT&T	31-Mar-2011	San Antonio	TX
Jocelyn White	Director, President's Commission on White House Fellowships	9-Dec-2009	Washington	DC
John Whitehead	Chairman of World Trade Center Memorial Foundation; Co-Chairman and Senior Partner, Goldman Sachs; Director, NY Stock Exchange; Deputy Secretary of State	4-Oct-2010	New York	NY
Luder Whitlock	Founder, Excelsis; Executive Director, The Trinity Forum	22-Nov-2004	Orlando	FL
Bill Wichterman	Founder, Faith & Law	28-Oct-2003	Washington	DC
Don R. Willett	Justice, Supreme Court of Texas	25-May-2011	Austin	TX
Don Williams	Chairman and CEO, Trammell Crow	25-Jul-2005	Dallas	TX
Martha Williamson	Executive Producer, *Touched by an Angel*	23-Apr-2004	San Marino	CA
Kathy Wills	Deputy Director, USA Freedom Corps; Special Assistant to the President	16-Jul-2004	Washington	DC
David Wills	President, National Christian Foundation	11-Feb-2005	Washington	DC
John Wilson	Editor, *Books & Culture*	27-Oct-2004	Phoenix	AZ
Ralph Winter	Producer, *X Men, Planet of the Apes, The Fantastic Four*	25-Apr-2004	Glendale	CA
Timothy E. Wirth	U.S. Senator (D-CO); U.S. Congressman (D-CO); Undersecretary for Global Affairs; President, United Nations Foundation	7-Dec-2009	Washington	DC
Robert Wolf	Chairman and CEO, UBS Group Americas; President, UBS Investment Bank	6-Dec-2010	New York	NY

Full Name	Organization or Title	Date	City	State
Gregory Wolfe	Publisher and Editor, *Image: A Journal of the Arts & Religion*	9-Sep-2004	Seattle	WA
Robert Woody	Founder and Chairman, Elgin Energy LLC	5-Mar-2011	Naples	FL
Mark Wrighton	Chancellor, Washington University	7-Sep-2010	St. Louis	MO
Bonnie Wurzbacher	Senior Vice President, Coca-Cola	16-Nov-2004	Atlanta	GA
Paul Wylie	Olympic and professional ice skater	30-Aug-2004	Hyannis	MA
Michael Yang	Founder, Chairman and CEO, mySimon.com; Founder, President and CEO, become.com	11-Oct-2004	Monterey	CA
David Young	Founder, Oxford Analytica	22-Apr-2005	Princeton	NJ
Diane Yu	Chief of Staff and Deputy to the President, New York University; Associate General Counsel, Monsanto; General Counsel, State Bar of California	10-Dec-2009	New York	NY
John Zachry	CEO, Zachry Holdings, Inc.	12-Oct-2010	San Antonio	TX
Jose Zeilstra	VP of Global Finance, JPMorgan Chase	9-Sep-2004	New York	NY

Acknowledgments

This book is the product of hundreds of interview hours, hundreds of thousands of miles spent traveling, countless conversations, and an extraordinary amount of work. Numerous individuals have contributed their wisdom and insight for which we are grateful. First and foremost, *View From the Top* would not have been possible without the many men and women interviewed for this book. I am very thankful for the honesty, referrals, and time of all the study participants. In particular, Craig Calhoun, Makoto Fujimura, George Gallup Jr., Frances Hesselbein, Clay Johnson III, Stanley Katz, Linda Lader, Doris Meissner, Steve Murdock, Jack Nicklaus, Steve Reinemund, George Rupp, John Siniff, Mike Ullman, Michael Useem, John Whitehead, and Michael Yang offered their names and their expertise as members of the study's national advisory council. Additionally, I am grateful to Jack LeCuyer, Bob Edmonds, Janet Eissenstat, and Diane Yu for their help through the President's Commission on White House Fellowships and the White House Fellows Foundation and Association in securing the required access to survey current and former Fellows.

This book would not have been possible without the excellent work of my research assistants: Paul Abraham, Vivian Ban, Matthew Bonem, Myles Bugbee, Matthew Carey, Danny Cohen, Amanda Dworak, Alexandra Espinoza, Lu Frazier, Molly Goldstein, Patrick Kelly, Mary Mikell Lampton, Noemie Levy, Omar Metwalli, Thomas Mitchell, Michelle Nguyen, Payton Odom, Andrew Patterson, Michelle Phillips, Julia Retta, Melissa Sheng, Ariela Schachter, Matthew Wasserman, Graham West, and Catherine Yuh. You've all moved on to do great things, and I am so thankful for the time and energy you devoted to this project. This team functioned under the talented leadership of Pat Hastings and William McMillan, with special thanks to Jon Endean and David Sorge for continuing the work on the manuscript even after I moved to Gordon.

I especially thank colleagues Jennifer Bratter, Marie Cornwall, Justin Denney, Paul DiMaggio, Frank Dobbin, William Domhoff, Kevin Dougherty, Elaine Howard Ecklund, Michael Emerson, Robin Ely,

Christy Gardner, Bridget Gorman, R. Marie Griffith, Wendy Griswold, Conrad Hackett, Suzanne Keller, Rachel Kimbro, Brayden King, Peter Kivisto, Bruce Kogut, Donald Light, Elizabeth Long, Scott Lynch, Rebekah Massengill, Joya Misra, Mark Mizruchi, Monica Najar, François Nielsen, David Nino, Jeremy Porter, Robert Putnam, Mark Regnerus, Sam Reimer, Amy Reynolds, Gabriel Rossman, Martin Ruef, Kristen Schilt, Brad Smith, Christian Smith, Steve Warner, Brad Wilcox, Jay Williams, Robert Wuthnow, Viviana Zelizer, and Ezra Zuckerman for their additional input and feedback while I was developing many of the ideas in this book.

Administrative and logistical support for the project were generously provided by Meagan Alley, Lisa Birenbaum, Carlos Garcia, Ipek Martinez, Kelly Quin, Heather Stern, Shirley Tapscott, and Chris Zalesky.

Support for this study was provided in part through grants from Rice University's Faculty Initiatives Fund, the Spencer Foundation, the James A. Baker III Institute for Public Policy, the Carnegie Corporation of New York, the National Science Foundation, the Andrew W. Mellon Foundation, the Earhart Foundation, the Society for the Scientific Study of Religion, the Religious Research Association, the Aspen Institute, and the Department of Sociology and Center for Study of Religion at Princeton University. I especially thank Ambassador Edward P. Djerejian and Professor Allen Matusow at the Baker Institute, and at the Carnegie Corporation, Geraldine P. Mannion. The H.E. Butt Foundation generously supported this study, and I am deeply grateful to Howard Butt, David Rogers, Mark Roberts, Terry Tigner, and especially Laura Sorrell. The study also could not have occurred without the generous support of Vester T. Hughes, Jack and Sherlie Rowe, and Joanne and Malcolm Turner. Although these funding sponsors provided invaluable support and assistance for this study, the analyses and views expressed in this publication are solely the responsibility of the authors. I gratefully acknowledge the support of Rice University President David Leebron as well as colleagues Lyn Ragsdale, Darrow Zeidenstein, and Jeanette Zey—all of whom supported this study at Rice University. And the Gordon College Board of Trustees, chaired by the incomparable Kurt Keilhacker, embraced and championed my vision for this book, and I am enormously grateful for their partnership in the venture.

This would not have been possible without the enthusiastic support of the Gordon College community. Marge Dwyer, Ted Wieber, Kate

Arnold, Jackie Zagami, India Boland, Hilary Sherratt, Henry Hagen, Dave Hicks, and Sam Stockwell provided essential assistance throughout the writing process. Additionally, Gordon's college communications team was helpful in brainstorming creative ways to communicate the book's big ideas. I thank my Cabinet colleagues—Michael Ahearn, Janel Curry, Jennifer Jukanovich, Barry Loy, Paul Maurer, Rick Sweeney, and Dan Tymann—for their help and encouragement along the way. I also thank friends whose leadership has influenced me in significant ways during this process—Andy Crouch, Brad Eubank, Arty Howard, David Jenkins, Kurt Keilhacker, Walter Kim, Steve Nelson, and John Rodgers. Finally, thanks to the students of Gordon College who inspire me every day.

We thank Richard Narramore, Peter Knox, Linda Indig, and Tiffany Colon of John Wiley & Sons and Bill Leigh of the Leigh Bureau for their enthusiastic support of this book, and we are deeply indebted to Betsy Stokes, our intrepid editor, who consistently improved our thinking through her wise and careful feedback.

Finally, I, Mary Grace, owe my part to the encouragement of Bill, Jan, and Will Hager, Hannah and Hobie Wood, Ann and Wally Ford, Rebeckah Orsatti, Grady Powell, Daniel and Lauren Goans, and the saints at Highrock, among many others. Thank you, David Ragsdale, for setting the stage, Pat Hastings for getting me the job, and Jon Endean for staying through to the end. Most of all, thanks to Rebecca Hager for her enduring patience, for praying with me, and for washing the dishes. Lastly, Michael, thank you for expecting much and also giving much. Your faith in me has given me faith in myself.

And I, Michael, will forever remember the season of life during which this story was completed. Not only did it include some significant professional accomplishments, but, more important, it overlapped with the births of Elizabeth, Caroline, and Emily, whose arrival put this project in proper perspective. I am grateful for the members of my extended family who helped in countless ways with the girls as I traveled the country conducting interviews—Anne Elizabeth, Ronnie, and Ron Ward, Margaret and Bill Duff, my grandmother Lucille Lindsay, and my stepmom Janet Lindsay. It is with deep gratitude for them and for my parents, Susan and Ken Lindsay, and especially my wife, Rebecca, that I dedicate this book to my family, who teach me every day how to lead with love.

Index

HD 57.7 .L556 2014
Lindsay, D. Michael
View from the top